Adirondack Mountain Club
Eastern Trails

Fourth Edition
Forest Preserve Series (4th ed.), Volume 2

Editor, David Thomas-Train

Adirondack Mountain Club, Inc.
Lake George, New York

Copyright © 2012 by Adirondack Mountain Club, Inc.
Cover: Sleeping Beauty Mt. by Carl Heilman II
Other photographs by James Appleyard, Carl Heilman II, John Kettlewell, Richard Nowicki, David Hough, and Jeffrey Trubisz
Maps by Therese S. Brosseau
Hiking boots illustration by Colette Piasecki-Masters
Design by Ann Hough
First edition 1987. Second edition 1994. Third edition 2008. Fourth edition 2012.

 Published by the Adirondack Mountain Club, Inc.
814 Goggins Road, Lake George, NY 12845-4117
www.adk.org

The Adirondack Mountain Club is dedicated to the protection and responsible recreational use of the New York State Forest Preserve and other parks, wild lands, and waters, vital to our members and chapters. The Club, founded in 1922, is a member-directed organization committed to public service and stewardship. ADK employs a balanced approach to outdoor recreation, advocacy, environmental education, and natural resource conservation.

ADK encourages the involvement of all people in its mission and activities; its goal is to be a community that is comfortable, inviting, and accessible.

Library of Congress Control Number: 2012026886

ISBN 978-1-931951-15-9

Printed in the United States of America
20 19 18 17 16 15 14 13 12   1 2 3 4 5 6 7 8 9 10

*To nature's dwindling wilderness:
the places and creatures
on which so much depends,
and those who protect them.*

—David Thomas-Train

WE WELCOME YOUR COMMENTS

Use of information in this book is at the sole discretion and risk of the hiker. ADK, and its authors and editors, makes every effort to keep our guidebooks up-to-date; however, trail conditions are always changing.

In addition to reviewing the material in this book, hikers should assess their ability, physical condition, and preparation, as well as likely weather conditions, before a trip. For more information on preparation, equipment, and how to address emergencies, see the introduction.

If you note a discrepancy in this book or wish to forward a suggestion, we welcome your comments. Please cite book title, year of most recent copyright and printing (see copyright page), trail, page number, and date of your observation. Thanks for your help!

Please address your comments to:
Publications
Adirondack Mountain Club
814 Goggins Road
Lake George, NY 12845-4117
518-668-4447
pubs@adk.org

24-HOUR EMERGENCY CONTACTS

In-town and roadside: **911**

Wilderness emergencies in the Adirondacks: DEC dispatch, **518-891-0235**

Wilderness emergencies elsewhere: **518-408-5850**, or toll-free **877-457-5680**

(See page 23 for more information)

Contents

Overview Maps 6

Preface 7

Introduction 9

Hammond Pond Wild Forest, Crown Point, Moriah Section 25

Pharaoh Lake Wilderness, Schroon Lake, Ticonderoga Section 39

Northwestern Lake George Wild Forest Section 65

Southeastern Lake George Wild Forest Section 85

Hoffman Notch Wilderness, Wilcox Lake Wild Forest,

and Other Areas West of the Northway 85

Glossary of Terms 186

Acknowledgments 187

About the Editor 188

Adirondack Mountain Club 189

Index 192

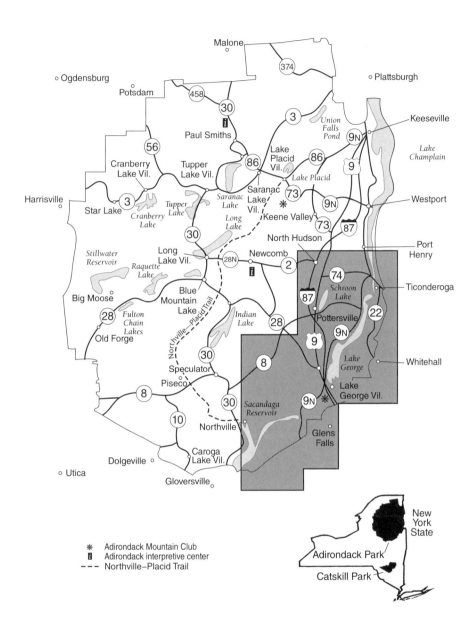

Preface

Each region of the Adirondacks has its own distinct appeal and the East Region is no exception. Bordered by Lake Champlain on the east, the High Peaks, Hoffman Notch Wilderness, and Schroon Lake on the west, and containing the Lake George area in the south, this region is characterized by rolling mountains and foothills, numerous isolated ponds, and some beautiful lakes. Scenery varies from subtle and serene shoreline views to spectacular vistas from lookouts and mountaintops. Many of the trails in the region lead to or connect bodies of water. So, while walking the trails is enjoyable in itself, hiking the trails with a small ultralight canoe adds a whole new dimension to exploring the eastern Adirondacks.

This fourth edition of *Adirondack Mountain Club Eastern Trails* is a substantial revision of the third. Not only have there been a number of changes on the trails themselves, but there are also a number of entirely new trails, particularly as parts of new Nature Conservancy preserves.

The format includes the numbering of all trails with corresponding numbers on the National Geographic Trails Illustrated map. The map, titled *#743 Lake George/Great Sacandaga*, is marked with grid coordinates that correspond to each trail description. In addition, there are now descriptions of potential winter uses of each trail for both ski touring and snowshoeing where appropriate. The list of trails includes only those trails either on public lands or those with public right-of-way, to help avoid problems with private land being closed in the future and potential conflicts with private landowners.

The following is slightly adapted from Carl Heilman's Preface to the second edition, since I endorse his views. In rewriting this guide, I have not included most of the many fine bushwhacks in the region. There are no towering high peaks in the eastern region, but there are many fine lookouts and open rock knobs with spectacular views of the High Peaks, Lake Champlain and Vermont, and the rolling hills of the eastern Adirondacks. One of the appeals of these isolated unmarked lookouts is the challenge of exploring the region and finding them on your own. The purpose of this guidebook is to help people safely traverse the marked and maintained trails throughout the region and to introduce people to its beauty, not to stake out every unknown lookout and untracked pond. As pressures continue to mount on the wild regions of the Earth, my hope is that there will always be some uncharted wilderness for the backcountry adventurer.

The Pharaoh Lake Wilderness, the only wilderness area within the scope of this guidebook, sees a lot of use throughout the summer season. Some parts of this region suffer from considerable overuse, while trails a short distance away are seldom used. To help maintain the character of wilderness, consider seeking out the lesser-used trails, or visit some of the other areas in the region. Although

Pharaoh is the only designated Wilderness Area in the eastern section, some of the trails in the Wild Forest regions are just as isolated, wild, and beautiful as any found in the Adirondack Park. Our use of these sensitive areas determines the quality of every other person's wilderness experience. It is only through our own proper actions (or inactions) that the character of these regions will be maintained for the future.

—*DAVID THOMAS-TRAIN*
Keene Valley, New York
February 2012

Pharaoh Wilderness from Treadway Mt. Carl Heilman II

Introduction

The Adirondack Mountain Club Forest Preserve Series

The Forest Preserve Series of guides to Adirondack and Catskill trails covers hiking opportunities on the approximately 2.5 million acres of Forest Preserve (public) land within the Adirondack Park and close to 300,000 acres in the Catskill Park. The Adirondack Mountain Club (ADK) published its first guidebook, covering the High Peaks and parts of the Northville–Placid Trail, in 1934. In the early 1980s, coinciding with the decade-long centennial celebration of the enactment of the Forest Preserve legislation in 1885, ADK set out to achieve its goal of completing a series of guides that would cover the two parks. This series now includes the following guidebooks:

1 Adirondack Mountain Club High Peaks Trails
2 Adirondack Mountain Club Eastern Trails
3 Adirondack Mountain Club Centrals Trails
4 Adirondack Mountain Club Western Trails
5 Adirondack Mountain Club Northville–Placid Trail
6 Adirondack Mountain Club Catskill Trails

The public lands that constitute the Forest Preserve are unique among all other wild public lands in the United States because they enjoy constitutional protection against sale or development. The story of this unique protection begins in the 1800s and continues today as groups such as ADK strive to guard it. This responsibility also rests with the public, who are expected not to degrade the Forest Preserve in any way while enjoying its wonders. The Forest Preserve Series of trail guides seeks not only to show hikers, skiers, and snowshoers where to enjoy their activities, but also to offer guidelines whereby users can minimize their impact on the land.

THE ADIRONDACKS

The Adirondack region of northern New York is unique in many ways. It contains the only mountains in the eastern United States that are not geologically Appalachian. In the late 1800s it was the first forested area in the nation to benefit from enlightened conservation measures. At roughly the same time it was also the most prestigious resort area in the country. In the twentieth century, the Adirondacks became the only place in the Western Hemisphere to host two winter Olympiads. In the 1970s the region was the first of significant size in the nation to be subjected to comprehensive land use controls.

Geologically, the Adirondacks are a southern appendage of the Canadian

Shield. In the United States the Shield bedrock, which is over one billion years old, mostly lies concealed under younger rock, but it is well exposed in a few regions. Upward doming of the Adirondack mass in the past few million years—a process that is still going on, resulting in the mountains rising a few millimeters every century—is responsible for erosional stripping of the younger rock cover. The stream-carved topography has been extensively modified by the sculpting of glaciers, which, on at least four widely separated occasions during the Ice Age, completely covered the mountains.

Ecologically, the Adirondacks are part of a vegetation transition zone, with the northern, largely coniferous boreal forest (from the Greek god Boreas, owner of the north wind, whose name can be found on a mountain peak and series of ponds in the High Peaks region) and the southern deciduous forest, exemplified by beech-maple stands, intermingling to present a pleasing array of forest tree species. Different vegetation zones are also encountered as one ascends the higher mountains in the Adirondacks; the tops of the highest peaks are truly arctic, with mosses and lichens that are common hundreds of miles to the north.

A rugged and heavily forested region, the Adirondacks were generally not hospitable to Native Americans, who used the region principally for hunting. Remnants of ancient campgrounds have been found in some locations. The native legacy survives principally in place names.

The first European to see the Adirondacks was likely the French explorer Jacques Cartier, who on his first trip up the St. Lawrence River in 1535 stood on top of Mont Royal (now within the city of Montreal) and discerned high ground to the south. Closer looks were had by Samuel de Champlain and Henry Hudson, who came from the north and south, respectively, within a few weeks of each other in 1609.

For the next two centuries the Champlain Valley to the east of the Adirondacks was a battleground. Iroquois, Algonquin, French, British, and eventually American fighters struggled for control over the valley and with it supremacy over the continent. Settlers slowly filled the St. Lawrence Valley to the north, the Mohawk Valley to the south, and somewhat later, the Black River Valley to the west. Meanwhile the vast, rolling forests of the interior slumbered in virtual isolation, disturbed only by an occasional hunter, timber cruiser, or wanderer.

With the coming of the nineteenth century, people discovered the Adirondacks. Virtually unknown as late as the 1830s (the source of the Nile River was located before the source of the Hudson), by 1850 the Adirondacks made New York the leading timber-producing state in the nation. This distinction did not last for long, though, as the supply of timber was quickly brought close to extinction. Meanwhile, mineral resources, particularly iron, were being exploited. After the Civil War, people began to look toward the Adirondacks for recreation. At the same time, resource conservation and wilderness preservation ideas began to take hold, sometimes conflicting with the newfound recreational interests. Conservation and preservation concepts were given legal standing in 1885, when the New York State legislature created the Adirondack Forest Preserve and directed that "the lands now or hereafter constituting the Forest Preserve shall be forever kept as wild forest lands." This action marked the first time a state government had set aside a significant piece of wilderness for reasons other than its scenic uniqueness.

In 1892, the legislature created the Adirondack State Park, consisting of Adirondack Forest Preserve land plus all privately owned land within a somewhat arbitrary boundary surrounding the Adirondacks, known as the "blue line" because it was drawn in blue on a large state map when it was first established. In 1894, in response to continuing abuses of the Forest Preserve law, the state's voters approved the inclusion of the "forever wild" portion of that law in the constitution of New York State, thus creating the only preserve in the nation that has constitutional protection. Today the Forest Preserve (the lands owned by the people of the State of New York) includes 2.5 million acres within the 6-million-acre Adirondack Park, the largest park in the nation outside of Alaska.

After World War I, tourism gradually took over as the primary industry in the Adirondacks. The growth of the second-home industry spurred implementation of land use plans and an Adirondack Park Agency to manage them. While the plans and the Agency have remained controversial, they indicate the need to address the issues facing the Adirondacks boldly and innovatively.

STATE LAND UNITS AND CLASSIFICATIONS
Since 1972, most Forest Preserve lands in the Adirondacks have been classified as either Wilderness, Primitive, or Wild Forest, depending on the size of the unit and the types of use thought to be desirable for it. The largest and most remote units are generally Wilderness, with only foot travel permitted and minimum facilities, such as lean-tos.

Primitive areas are similar, but with a nonconforming "structure" such as a fire tower, road, or private inholding. Wild Forest areas are generally smaller but potentially more intensively used, with snowmobiles and mountain bikes permitted on designated trails. Management of each unit is prescribed in a unit management plan (UMP), which determines what facilities, such as trails or shelters, will be built and maintained as well as any special regulations needed to manage each unit effectively.

USING THIS GUIDEBOOK
Like all the volumes in the Adirondack Mountain Club Forest Preserve Series of guides to Adirondack and Catskill trails, this book is intended to be both a reference tool for planning trips and a field guide to carry on the trail. All introductory material should be read carefully; it contains important information regarding current camping and hiking regulations as well as numerous suggestions for safe and proper travel.

The guide is divided into geographic sections. The introduction to each of these sections gives hikers an idea of the opportunities available in that area as well as information on facilities and regulations common to that section. Each section's introduction also provides recommended hikes in the "short," "moderate," and "harder" categories. Many of these recommended hikes incorporate lesser-used trails in an attempt to make hikers aware of the many beautiful and seldom-visited places aside from the most popular hiking, climbing, and camping areas.

ABBREVIATIONS AND CONVENTIONS
In each of the books in the Forest Preserve Series, R and L, with periods omitted, are used for right and left. The R and L banks of a stream are determined by looking downstream. Likewise, the R fork of a stream is on the R when one faces downstream. N, S, E, and W, again without periods, are used for north, south, east, and west. Compass bearings are given in degrees. N is 0 degrees, E is 90 degrees, S is 180 degrees, and W is 270 degrees.

The following abbreviations are used in the text:

ADK	Adirondack Mountain Club
AMR	Adirondack Mountain Reserve
APA	Adirondack Park Agency
ATIS	Adirondack Trail Improvement Society
ATV	All-terrain vehicle
DEC	New York State Department of Environmental Conservation
GPS	Global Positioning System
PBM	Permanent Bench Mark
USGS	United States Geological Survey
4WD	Four-wheel-drive vehicle
ft	foot or feet
jct.	junction
km	kilometer or kilometers
m	meter or meters
mi	mile or miles
yd	yard or yards

MAPS
Every guidebook is this series matches trail information provided on National Geographic Trails Illustrated maps covering the Adirondack and Catskill Parks. These large-format, two-sided, folding, waterproof maps were created in partnership with ADK. Together the guides and maps are vital hiking tools, the latter also serving as road maps within the Adirondack and Catskill Parks. The following list identifies each map and the Forest Preserve Series guide to which it corresponds. All are available from ADK.

742   Lake Placid/High Peaks (for *High Peaks Trails*)
743   Lake George/Great Sacandaga (for *Eastern Trails*)

744 Northville/Raquette Lake
(for *Central Trails*)
745 Old Forge/Oswegatchie
(for *Western Trails*)
746 Saranac/Paul Smiths (western half corresponds to northwestern portion *Western Trails*; eastern half to the northern *High Peaks Trails*)
755 Catskill Park
744 Northville/Raquette Lake & 742 (west side) Lake Placid/High Peaks (for *Northville–Placid Trail*)

These maps are letter-number coded, with letters running up and down the right and left borders, and numbers running horizontally along the top and bottom. Each trail's coordinate appears with the corresponding description in this book (sample coordinate: A4), and each trail is numbered on the map and in the book. These numbers are not used on any signs on the trails.

Hike descriptions may be supported by page maps located nearby within the text.

All of the maps discussed in the preceding are available from ADK. Other maps, guidebooks, and information also can be obtained from ADK's Members Services Center in Lake George and the High Peaks Information Center on ADK's Heart Lake Property near Lake Placid.

MORE ON N-P TRAIL AND HIGH PEAKS MAPS

ADK also offers two folded pocket-sized maps, one sold in the back of the Northville-Placid Trail guidebook and another sold separately for the High Peaks. Both are based on USGS quadrangles with updated overlays of trails, shelters, campsites, and private land boundaries.

The High Peaks pocket-sized map also shows the boundary between the Eastern and Western zones of the High Peaks Wilderness Area, an important distinction because there are different regulations for each zone. Additional important symbols indicate junctions with private trails and roads that serve as landmarks with which to locate one's position and a reminder that hikers are not to use these roads or trails.was substantially complete by 2006.

TRAIL SIGNS AND MARKERS

Marked and maintained DEC trails for hikers, cross-country skiers, snowshoers, and snowmobilers tend to have signs posted at trailheads and major trail junctions. Trail signs give the distance to named locations on the trail.

Trail markers are plastic disks placed on trees or posts along the trails themselves and on the signs at trailheads and junctions.

The color and type of marker used on a trail is included in the descriptions in this book. (Painted blazes on trees generally indicate property boundaries and should not be confused with marked trails.)

With normal alertness to one's surroundings and exceptions made for lightly traveled trails, most marked trails are easy to follow. Although this guidebook

> **SO WHAT IF IT'S NOT MAINTAINED?**
>
> A formal, DEC-marked trail and a bushwhack form the bookends of hiking possibilities—with lots more range in between than most hikers expect. Unmaintained trails, unmarked trails, "trailless" routes, or herd paths have two things in common: they are unmarked paths, lacking official DEC signs and markers, and they may necessitate advanced orientation skills.
>
> Unmarked paths can range from reasonably well-trodden, well-defined routes with cairns to a whisper of a track with no discernible tread. A hiker's experience with one kind of unmarked path doesn't necessarily assist him or her on another. Hikers should carry a map and compass and know how to use them. They shouldn't let past experience inspire false confidence or tempt them to forego packing a map and compass.

does mention particularly tricky turns or trails that might pose special difficulties, each hiker must remain alert at all times for changes of direction. Group leaders have a particular responsibility not to let inexperienced members of their party travel by themselves. A trail that seems obvious to a more experienced person may not be that way at all to an inexperienced member of the group.

It should go without saying that one should never remove any sign or marker. Hikers noticing damaged or missing signs should report this to the DEC.

All trails described in this guide are on public land or public rights of way that cross private land. The continued goodwill of public-spirited landowners is directly dependent upon the manner in which the public uses this land. The "posted" signs occasionally found on rights of way are usually intended to remind hikers that they are on private land over which the owner has granted permission for hikers to pass. In most cases, leaving the trail, camping, fishing, and hunting are not permitted on these lands. Hikers should respect the owner's wishes.

DISTANCE AND TIME

Trails in this guidebook have been measured with a professional surveyor's wheel and in some cases using GPS devices. Distances are expressed to the nearest tenth of a mile. Shorter distances are expressed as yards, and the number of yards has usually been derived from a wheel measurement in the field.

NOTE: In cases where there is disagreement between a sign and the guide's stated distance, the latter can be assumed to be correct. DEC is informed of discrepancies.

At the start of each section of this guide, there is a list of trails in the region, the mileage unique to the trail, and the page on which the trail description begins. All mileages given in the trail description are cumulative, the beginning of the trail being the 0.0-mile point. A distance summary is given at the end of each description, with a total distance expressed in kilometers as well as in miles. If a trail has climbed significantly over its course, its total ascent in both feet and meters is provided.

To the inexperienced hiker, distances are likely to seem longer on the trail, depending on the weight of the pack, the time of day, and the frequency and degree of ascents and descents. He or she will quickly learn that there is a significant difference between "sidewalk miles" and "trail miles."

No attempt has been made to estimate travel time for these trails. A conservative rule to follow in estimating time is to allow an hour for every one and one-half miles, plus one half hour for each one thousand feet of ascent, letting experience indicate how close the individual hiker is to this standard. Most day hikers will probably go a little faster than this, but backpackers will probably find they go somewhat slower. Some quickening of pace usually occurs when descending, though this may not be true on steep descents.

CELL PHONES

Mobile phones can't always be relied upon in case of an emergency in the backcountry. Despite many highly publicized stories, their use is limited by terrain, distance from communication towers, battery life, and other factors. Those who carry them should, out of consideration for their fellow hikers, use them only when necessary—and should have alternative plans for handling emergencies in case they do not operate.

If you must use your mobile phone in an emergency it is sometimes possible to obtain better range and reception by moving to a higher elevation and/or an area where you are not blocked by steep cliffs or other obstructions.

DAY HIKING AND WILDERNESS CAMPING

It is not the purpose of this series to teach one how to hike or camp. The information below should, however, serve to make hikers aware of the differences and peculiarities of New York's backcountry while giving strong emphasis to currently recommended procedures for reducing environmental damage—particularly in heavily used areas. Users who intend to hike or camp for the first time are urged to consult a current book on the subject, attend one of the many workshops or training sessions available, or at least join a group led by someone with experience.

Except for Johns Brook Lodge, 3.5 miles up the Marcy Trail from Keene Valley (see *Adirondack Mountain Club High Peaks Trails*), there are no huts in the Adirondacks or Catskills for public use, such as are common in the White Mountains of New Hampshire. There are many lean-tos at convenient locations along trails and also many possibilities for tenting. The regulations regarding tenting and the use of lean-tos are simple and unrestrictive. It is important that every backpacker know and obey the restrictions that do exist because they are designed to promote the long-term enjoyment and protection of the resource.

Listed below are some of the most important Forest preserve regulations, many of which pertain to day-hikers as well. The latest versions of the complete rules can be found online at the DEC website (www.dec.ny.gov).

- Except where marked by a "Camp Here" disk, camping is prohibited within 150 feet of roads, trails, lakes, ponds, streams, or other bodies of water.
- Groups of ten or more persons (nine in the High Peaks Region) or stays of more than three days in one place require a permit from the New York State Forest Ranger responsible for the area.
- Lean-tos are available in many areas on a first-come, first-served basis. Lean-tos cannot be used exclusively and must be shared with other campers.
- Use pit privies provided near popular camping areas and trailheads. If none are available, dispose of human waste by digging a hole six to eight inches deep at least 150 feet from water or campsites. Cover with leaves and soil.
- Do not use soap to wash yourself, clothing, or dishes within 150 feet of water.
- Fires should be built in existing fire pits or fireplaces if provided. Use only dead and down wood for fires. Cutting standing trees is prohibited. Extinguish all fires with water and stir ashes until they are cold to the touch. Do not build fires in areas marked by a "No Fires" disk. Camp stoves are safer, more efficient, and cleaner.
- Carry out what you carry in. Use Leave No Trace practices.
- Keep your pet under control. Restrain it on a leash when others approach. Collect and bury droppings away from water, trails, and campsites. Keep your pet away from drinking water sources.

Typical Adirondack lean-to. ADK *Archives*

- Observe and enjoy wildlife and plants but leave them undisturbed.
- Removing plants, rocks, fossils, or artifacts from state land without a permit is illegal.
- Do not feed any wild animals.
- Store food properly to keep it away from animals—particularly bears. No camping is permitted above 4000 feet (1220 meters) at any time of the year in the Adirondacks.
- Except in an emergency or between December 21 and March 21, camping is prohibited above an elevation of 3500 feet in the Catskills.
- At all times, only emergency fires are permitted above 4000 feet in the Adirondacks and 3500 feet in the Catskills.

LEAN-TOS

Lean-tos are available on a first-come, first-served basis up to the capacity of the shelter—usually about eight persons. Thus a small party cannot claim exclusive use of a shelter and must allow late arrivals equal use. Most lean-tos have a fireplace in front (sometimes with a primitive grill) and sanitary facilities. Most are located near some source of water, but each camper must use his or her own judgment as to whether or not the water supply needs purification before drinking. It is in very poor taste to carve or write one's initials in a shelter. Please try to keep these rustic shelters in good condition and appearance.

Because reservations cannot be made for any of these shelters, it is best to carry a tent or other alternate shelter. Many shelters away from the standard routes, however, are seldom used, and a small party can often find a shelter open in the more remote areas.

The following regulations apply specifically to lean-tos, in addition to the general camping regulations listed above:
- No plastic may be used to close off the front of a shelter.
- No nails or other permanent fastener may be used to affix a tarp in a lean-to, but it is permissible to use rope to tie canvas or nylon tarps across the front.
- No tent may be pitched inside a lean-to.

GPS

Many hikers use GPS navigation devices and mobile phones equipped with GPS to find trailheads and navigate the backcountry. Be sure to practice these skills before needing them in a remote area. Keep in mind that GPS reception in some areas may be limited due to surrounding steep terrain and heavy forest cover. And, like all electronic devices, an unintended dip in an icy stream or a lack of fresh batteries can put your equipment out of commission for the rest of your trip.

Prudent hikers will not rely solely on electronic gear. Always carry a map, a guidebook, and a compass, and know how to use them.

National Geographic Trails Illustrated maps are designed to be compatible with GPS. The maps include latitude and longitude markings, as well as UTM grids.

GROUPS

Any group of ten or more persons or smaller groups intending to camp at one location three nights or longer must obtain a permit before camping on state land. This system is designed to prevent overuse of certain critical sites and also to encourage groups to split into smaller parties.

Permits can be obtained from the DEC forest ranger closest to the actual starting point of one's proposed trip. The local forest ranger can be contacted directly; if in doubt about whom to contact, call the DEC's general information line in Ray Brook at 518-897-1200. They will be able to direct you to the proper ranger.

Note that forest rangers' schedules during the busy summer season are often unpredictable. Bear in mind when calling that most rangers operate out of their private homes; observe the normal courtesy used when calling a private residence. Contact by letter is much preferred. Camping with a large group requires careful planning with a lead time of several weeks to ensure a happy, safe outing.

FOREST SAFETY

The routes described in this guidebook vary from wide, well-marked DEC trails to narrow, unmarked footpaths that have become established through long use. With normal alertness and careful preparation the hiker should have few problems in land navigation. Nevertheless, careful map study and route planning are fundamental necessities. Hikers should never expect immediate help should an emergency occur. This is particularly true in winter, when fewer people are on the trails and weather is a more significant factor.

In addition to a map, all hikers should carry a compass and know at least the basics of its use. In some descriptions, the Forest Preserve Series uses compass bearings to differentiate trails at a junction or to indicate the direction of travel above timberline. More important, a compass can be an indispensable aid in the event that you lose your way.

Winter trips, especially, must be carefully planned. Travel over ice on ski and snowshoe trips must be done with caution. The possibility of freezing rain, snow, and cold temperatures should be considered from early September until late May. True winter conditions can commence as early as November and last well into April, particularly at higher altitudes. It is highly recommended that hikers travel in parties of at least four people, be outfitted properly, rest when the need

LEAVE NO TRACE

ADK supports the seven principles of the Leave No Trace program:

1. *Plan Ahead and Prepare*
   Know the regulations and special considerations for the area you'll visit.
   Prepare for extreme weather, hazards, and emergencies.
   Travel in groups of less than ten people to minimize impacts.

2. *Travel and Camp on Durable Surfaces*
   Hike in the middle of the trail; stay off of vegetation.
   Camp in designated sites where possible.
   In other areas, don't camp within 150 feet of water or a trail.

3. *Dispose of Waste Properly*
   Pack out all trash (including toilet paper), leftover food, and litter.
   Use existing privies, or dig a cat hole five to six inches deep, then cover hole.
   Wash yourself and dishes at least 150 feet from water.

4. *Leave What You Find*
   Leave rocks, plants, and other natural objects as you find them.
   Let photos, drawings, or journals help to capture your memories.
   Do not build structures or furniture or dig trenches.

5. *Minimize Campfire Impacts*
   Use a portable stove to avoid the lasting impact of a campfire.
   Where fires are permitted, use existing fire rings and only collect downed wood.
   Burn all fires to ash, put out campfires completely, then hide traces of fire.

6. *Respect Wildlife*
   Observe wildlife from a distance.
   Avoid wildlife during mating, nesting, and other sensitive times.
   Control pets at all times, and clean up after them.

7. *Be Considerate of Other Visitors*
   Respect other visitors and protect the quality of their experience.
   Let natural sounds prevail; avoid loud sounds and voices.
   Be courteous and yield to other users on the trail.

*For further information on Leave No Trace principles,
log on to www.lnt.org.*

arises, and drink plenty of water. Leave trip plans with someone at home and then keep to your itinerary.

DRINKING WATER

For many years, hikers could trust almost any water source in the backcountry to be pure and safe to drink. Unfortunately, as in many other mountain areas, some water sources have become contaminated with a parasite known as Giardia lamblia.

This intestinal parasite causes a disease known as giardiasis—often called "beaver fever." It can be spread by any warm-blooded mammal when infected feces wash into the water; beavers are prime agents in transferring this parasite because they spend so much of their time in and near water. Hikers themselves have also become primary agents in spreading this disease because some individuals appear to be unaffected carriers of the disease, and other recently infected individuals may inadvertently spread the parasite before their symptoms become apparent.

Prevention: Follow the guidelines for the disposal of human excrement as stated above. Equally important, make sure that every member of your group is aware of the problem and follows the guidelines as well. In addition, practicing good hygiene on the trail can help prevent the spread of this and other diseases. The health of a fellow hiker may depend on your consideration.

Water Treatment: No water source can be guaranteed to be safe. Boil all water for 2–3 minutes, utilize an iodine-based chemical purifier (available at camping supply stores and some drug and department stores), or use a commercial filter designed specifically for giardiasis prevention. If after returning from a trip you experience recurrent intestinal problems, consult your physician and explain your potential problem.

HUNTING SEASON

Unlike the national park system, public lands within the Adirondack and Catskill state parks are open to sport hunting. There are separate rules and seasons for each type of hunting (small game, waterfowl, and big game), but it is the big-game season, i.e., deer and bear, that is most likely to concern hikers. Confrontations can occur when hikers and hunters are inconsiderate of the needs and rights of each other. Problems can be greatly reduced by careful planning.

It is advisable to avoid heavily hunted areas during big-game seasons. Consult the DEC website (www.dec.ny.gov) for the latest season schedules. Because it is difficult to carry a deer or bear carcass long distances or over steep terrain, hikers will find few hunters more than a mile from a roadway or in rugged mountain country. Lower slopes of beech, maple, and hemlock have much more hunting pressure than cripplebush, spruce, and balsam fir on upper slopes. Motorized vehicles are not allowed in areas designated as Wilderness, so hike there; most areas designated as Wild Forest have woods roads where vehicles can be used, so avoid these areas, which are likely to be favored by hunters. Try to avoid the opening and closing day of regular deer season. For safety, wear a bright-colored outer garment; orange is recommended.

ADK does not promote hunting as one of its organized activities, but it does recognize that sport hunting, when carried out in compliance with the game laws administered by the DEC, is a legitimate sporting activity.

BEAR CANISTERS

Bears in many parts of the Adirondacks have figured out the long-popular campers' technique of hanging food from a rope strung between two trees. Thus the DEC is now recommending—in some cases requiring—the use of bear-resistant, food-storage canisters.

- Bear canisters required in the Eastern High Peaks Wilderness Area April 1 through November 30.
- These can be obtained from many outdoor retailers, borrowed from many ADK chapters, or rented or purchased at ADK's Heart Lake or Lake George facilities. The canisters also protect food from many smaller forest creatures.
- The DEC's current management goal with respect to bears is to educate campers about proper food storage. Bears unable to get food from campers will, it is hoped, return to their natural diet. Thus campers play an important role in helping to restore the natural balance between bears and humans. Losing one's food to a bear should be recognized as a critical failure in achieving this goal.

BEAR SAFETY

Most wildlife in the Adirondacks and Catskills are little more than a minor nuisance around the campsite. Generally, the larger the animal the more timid it is in the presence of humans. Some animals are emboldened by the aroma of food, however, and bears, the most intimidating of these, quickly habituate to human food sources.

The following tips will reduce the likelihood of an encounter with a bear.
- Never keep food in your tent or lean-to.
- Bear-resistant canisters are now required in the Eastern High Peaks Wilderness Area April 1 through November 30.
- In other areas, use a canister or hang food at least fifteen feet off the ground from a rope strung betwen two trees that are at least fifteen feet apart and one hundred feet from the campsite. (Hangs using a branch have a high failure rate.) Using dark-colored rope tied off five or more feet above the ground makes it less likely that a foraging bear will see the line or find it while sniffing along the ground.

- Wrap aromatic foods well.
- Plan carefully to keep trash and leftovers to a minimum. Wrap in sealed containers such as large Ziploc bags and hang or place in canister.
- Hang your pack, along with clothing worn during cooking.
- Keep a garbage-free fire pit away from your camping area.
- Should a bear appear, do not provoke it by throwing objects or approaching it. Bang pots, blow a whistle, shout, or otherwise try to drive it off with sharp noises. Should this fail, leave the scene.
- Report bear encounters to a forest ranger.

RABIES ALERT
Rabies infestation has been moving north through New York State. Although it is most often associated with raccoons, any warm-blooded mammal can be a carrier.

Although direct contact with a rabid animal in the forest is not likely, some precautions are advisable:
- Do not feed or pet any wild animals, under any circumstances.
- Particularly avoid any wild animals that seem to be behaving strangely.
- If bitten by a wild animal, seek medical attention immediately.

INSECT-BORN DISEASES
Although not unique to the Adirondacks and Catskills, two insects found in these areas carry potentially lethal diseases. Deer ticks can spread Lyme disease, and mosquitos can transmit West Nile virus. These are issues of particular concern in the Catskills.

In both instances, protection is advisable. Wear long pants and long-sleeved shirts and apply an insect repellent with the recommended percentage of N, N-diethyl-meta-toluamide (commonly known as DEET). On returning home, thoroughly inspect yourself and wash yourself and your clothing immediately. Seek immediate attention if any early symptoms (rash, long-term fatigue, headache, fever) arise.

EMERGENCY PROCEDURES

All emergency assistance, including help from the local ranger, is dispatched from the following numbers. Make sure the person going for help has these telephone numbers as well as a complete written description of the type and exact location of the accident. A location marked on the map can be very helpful. If possible, leave a call-back number in the event those responding to the incident require additional information.

- For all emergencies in the Adirondacks, call the DEC 24-hour hotline: 518-891-0235.

- For emergencies elsewhere call 518-408-5850 or 911.

Calling one of the DEC numbers is preferable to calling 911. At the DEC emergency number, the caller is usually able to speak directly with someone who is knowledgeable about the area where the accident has occurred. Mobile phone callers are especially prone to problems because the call may be picked up by a distant tower in a neighboring jurisdiction (or even a different state) with the message then having to be relayed through several agencies.

Crown Point ruins. Carl Heilman II

Hammond Pond Wild Forest, Crown Point, Moriah Section

This section is located in northern part of the eastern Adirondack region, and on the northern portion of the eastern half of Trails Illustrated Map 743. It extends south to NY 74, which runs from Exit 28 on I-87 in the E to Ticonderoga in the W. The E side is a pretty landscape of farmlands along Lake Champlain, while the W side is the extensive Hammond Pond Wild Forest area that is bounded by US 9 on the W. This region underwent extensive review in the late 1980s and most of the suggested improvements have taken place. At present the area sees little use, especially when compared to the Pharaoh Lake Wilderness just to the S. While a trail system connects some of the most popular destinations, several trailless mountains and isolated ponds wait to be explored. The Hammond Pond Wild Forest area is perfect for an ultralight "Lost Pond" boat.

❉ Trails in winter: Most of the marked trails in this region are over low rolling terrain and are perfect for skiing and snowshoeing. Other recommendations for specific trails are listed with the trail descriptions.

Suggested hikes in the region include:

SHORT HIKE:
Arnold Pond—0.3 mi (0.5 km). A short but steep hike to a pretty pond tucked in at the base of a rock slide on Skiff Mt.

MODERATE HIKE:
Peaked Hill—2.2 mi (3.5 km) plus canoe. This is a fun summer route, canoeing across Paradox Lake and then hiking a moderate route to Peaked Hill Pond followed by the steeper climb up Peaked Hill.

	Trail Described	Total Miles (one way)	Page
1	Walker Brook Access	0.7 (1.1 km)	26
2	Bass Lake Trail	3.2 (5.2 km)	26
3	Challis Pond	0.6 (1.0 km)	27
4	Berrymill Flow and Moose Mt. Pond	3.2 (5.2 km)	28
5	Hammond and Bloody Ponds	3.0 (4.8 km)	29
6	North Hudson Trail System	various	30
6A	Fish Dam Trail	1.6 (2.6 km)	31
7	Peaked Hill and Peaked Hill Pond	2.2 (3.5 km)	33
8	Crown Point State Historic Site	2.7 (4.3 km)	33
9	Putts Creek Wildlife Management Area	0.6 (1.0 km)	35

| 10 | Old Ironville Rd. | 2.3 (3.7 km) | 36 |
| 11 | Arnold Pond | 0.3 (0.5 km) | 37 |

1 Walker Brook Access

Trails Illustrated Map 743: V27

With the construction of the Adirondack Northway (I-87) through this area in the mid-1960s came a need to provide access to the W side of the highway, since parking is of course prohibited on the highway itself. There are four points where one can easily cross under the Northway along the 10-mile stretch from North Hudson to Exit 30 near Underwood. Three of these access routes connect with the valleys of West Mill Brook, Walker Brook, plus Shingletree Pond. Access to all is from US 9. All are suitable for snowshoeing; the West Mill Brook Access is the best suited for skiing. All are described in *High Peaks Trails*.

Note that parking for the purpose of hiking or camping is also prohibited at all I-87 rest areas.

▶ Trailhead: This access is 3.7 mi S of Sharp Bridge Campground or 3.4 mi N of North Hudson. Just S of two houses, there is an old green metal signpost at the end of a dirt road. Go down this road for 0.3 mi and park where a poorer road bears R. Bear in mind that this is private land and that the driveway beyond 0.3 mi is not a public road. ◀

Go R and down this poorer road, to the L bank of the Schroon River, which must be forded (difficult in high water) because a bridge has not been replaced (2012). On the far side there is a good road that is followed uphill to a flat area 0.5 mi from US 9. Bear R just beyond and cross under the Northway through a concrete culvert at 0.7 mi (1.1 km). Walker Brook is approximately 0.2 mi beyond, with an old road leading up its R (S) bank giving access to Camels Hump, Niagara, and Nipple Top mts. (the latter is not the 4620-ft High Peak, which is W of the Dix Range from here).

2 Bass Lake Trail

Trails Illustrated Map 743: V27

This is the first body of water among the family of ponds along the Moriah Rd. These ponds all feed the Schroon River to the S.

▶ Trailhead: Drive 2.4 mi N from North Hudson on US 9 to a R (NE) on Rt. 4, known locally as the Moriah Rd. A sign here indicates the way to Port Henry. After this turn, go only 0.2 mi to an old paved road to the R (E). At the end of this is the trailhead with yellow markers. ◀

Leaving the Moriah Rd. (0.0 mi), the old paved road turns to dirt in several hundred yards at an old bridge abutment on both sides of the stream on the L. A fisherman's path goes down the steep bank to the stream. The trail passes a wide place in the stream below at 0.2 mi. Now it cuts along the bank and at 0.3 mi passes shelving falls through the trees on the L. The trail now bends R uphill and away from the stream.

At 0.4 mi, the trail levels off. Crossing a stream, it heads up steeply through birch and hemlock woods. At 0.8 mi, it crosses a small brook. At 1 mi, the trail, still climbing, becomes muddy, eroded and rocky. It soon levels off in a beech woods and then descends along a ridge.

At 1.4 mi, the trail turns L to avoid a blowdown, goes through a sunny area and then enters some tall hemlocks. At 1.6 mi, Bass Lake is visible through the trees, and a side trail L leads 0.2 mi to the W end of the lake by a huge boulder.

The trail continues on to the R parallel to the S shore of Bass Lake. It soon crosses a stream and then at 1.8 mi comes to another side trail that leads a short distance to an informal campsite on Bass Lake. The trail continues on along the shoreline, reaching the outlet at 2.2 mi, where there are signs of beaver activity. At 2.3 mi, it comes to the E end of the lake with nice views back across the water. After passing through a wet area, the trail levels off in open hemlocks at 2.5 mi.

The trail soon descends gradually, with Berrymill Flow visible through the trees at 2.9 mi. The trail roughly parallels the shoreline of the flow, and reaches the jct. with the Berrymill Flow and Moose Mt. Pond Trail (trail 27) at 3.2 mi. From this point it is 1.4 mi to the Hammond Pond trailhead on the Moriah Rd., following the Berrymill Flow and Moose Mt. Pond Trail.

❃ Trail in winter: Suitable for skiing and snowshoeing.

🐾 Distances: To first side trail to Bass Lake, 1.6 mi; to E end of lake, 2.3 mi; to Berrymill Flow and Moose Mt. Pond trail (27), 3.2 mi (5.1 km).

3 Challis Pond

Trails Illustrated Map 743: V28

This is another of the lovely ponds near the Moriah Rd. These are lightly traveled trails which are used mostly by trout fishermen. It would be pleasant to hike in with an inflatable raft or ultralight canoe for further exploring.

▶Trailhead: Drive 2.4 mi N from North Hudson on US 9 to a R (NE) on Rt. 4, known locally as the Moriah Rd. A sign here indicates the way to Port Henry. At 2.6 mi (0.2 mi from US 9) is the trailhead R for Bass Lake (trail 2). At 2.7 mi, turn R again at signs for Moriah and Champlain Bridge. This is a beautiful, winding road. At 5.3 mi, park at a small turnout R at the trailhead for Challis Pond. There might not be a sign, but someone has built a cedar railing on both sides of the trail about 50 ft up from the road.◀

From the road (0.0 mi), the clearly defined trail leads up through hemlock and cedar woods. At 0.3 mi, a stream can be heard on the R but is unseen. There are orange paint blazes on trees.

At 0.4 mi, the pond's outlet stream is on the R. The trail crosses dry ground above a small seep. At 0.5 mi it enters deciduous woods; at 0.6 mi, the pond comes into view through the trees.

A campsite with a blackened boulder is near the edge of the pond. The pond seems to be almost a perfect circle. Bullfrogs call a welcome, as well as chickadees, warblers, thrushes, and nuthatches. Bog laurel, pickerel weed, and pond lilies bloom along the shoreline. There are no beavers here.

To the R, an informal path crosses the outlet stream and then continues through hemlocks around the shoreline, but peters out after 0.2 mi. This is probably used by hunters and anglers.

🚶 Distance: Moriah Rd. to Challis Pond, 0.6 mi (1.0 km).

4 Berrymill Flow and Moose Mt. Pond

Trails Illustrated Map 743: V28

This is an easy trail into some nice wild lands. There's a good opportunity to see some wildlife on the way past the flow. There's a lot of beaver activity near Moose Mt. Pond, giving a close-up look at what they can do with some fairly level drainages. Maps, including the one used as the base map for this book, identify the flow as Berrymill Pond, but trail signs, and consequently this book, refer to it as Berrymill Flow.

▶Trailhead: Drive 2.4 mi N from North Hudson on US 9 to a R (NE) on Rt. 4, known locally as the Moriah Rd. A sign here indicates the way to Port Henry. Proceed 3 mi from US 9 (5.4 mi from North Hudson) to a parking area on the R (S) side of the Moriah Rd. This is just 0.1 mi past the Challis Pond trailhead (trail 3).◀

The trail begins at a rustic set of steps at the S end of the parking lot (0.0 mi) and follows blue markers. It soon joins an old tote road and parallels a stream on a very gradual incline. At 0.4 mi, just before entering an open area with some substantial beaver activity, the trail cuts off to the R (W) and begins climbing a hill. It continues up and down along the hillside until descending to the old tote road again at 0.7 mi.

The trail continues S along the stream through a pretty woods, reaching a fivefoot waterfall on the L (E) at 0.9 mi. It continues on at a gradual grade, reaching the jct. with the Bass Lake Trail (2) at 1.4 mi. This jct. is marked with a DEC signpost.

Just beyond this jct. there is an informal campsite on a small knoll. From here is a nice view S across Berrymill Flow. After passing through the campsite, the trail crosses a bridge across the outlet of the flow, climbs a few stairs, and then begins to follow S along the shoreline of the flow. At 1.7 mi, about halfway down the flow, the trail swings L away from the flow and gradually ascends a couple of small sets of stairs. It soon meets and follows the L bank of a small stream.

At 2.1 mi, still heading E, the trail begins following an old tote road above the stream. The forest is relaxing here, with a lot of tall pines, hemlocks, poplars, and cedars. The trail soon rejoins the stream, but at 2.3 mi veers L away from the stream again. At 2.4 mi, an opening in the trees far to the L gives hope that the pond isn't too far away, but this is just an isolated wet area.

The trail soon ascends a short steep section and at 2.8 mi reaches the first of a couple of recent beaver ponds that flood the trail. It is possible to skirt the flooding through the woods on the L for a short distance.

Following along the beaver ponds, the trail is again flooded at 3.1 mi. Moose Mt. Pond isn't far away, and at 3.2 mi a spur trail to the R leads to an informal campsite with a nice view on the W shore of the pond.

The trail continues E within sight of the shoreline through a pretty woods, reaching the lean-to at 3.5 mi. This is a great site with views from the shore looking across the pond to Moose Mt. and Owl Pate.

❉ Trail in winter: Suitable for skiing and snowshoeing.

🥾 Distances: Parking lot to Bass Lake Trail (2), 1.4 mi; to swing away from Berrymill Flow, 1.7 mi; to Moose Mt. Pond, 3.2 mi; to lean-to, 3.5 mi (5.8 km).

5 Hammond and Bloody Ponds

Trails Illustrated Map 743: V28

▶Trailhead: See above, Berrymill Flow and Moose Mt. Pond (trail 4). The Hammond Pond Trail heads L (SE) from the parking lot. This is a woods road that gradually diminishes to a trail that ends at a beaver flow.◀

From the parking lot (0.0 mi), the woods road crosses a sandy rise in white pines, following red markers, to a bridge at 0.1 mi on solid stone abutments. Now the route is level along the bank above the stream on the R. At 0.2 mi, the trail leaves the stream. At 0.4 mi, a swamp is visible through trees on the L. The trail, strewn with pine needles through woods of white pine, hemlock, birch, and maple, dips gently. After a stand of red pines, it continues on the level through a stand of hemlocks.

At 0.6 mi, there is a stream on the L. There is a culvert for a small feeder stream at 0.7 mi, after which the trail divides. (Uphill to the L on a 0.3-mi spur trail to a wide plank spillway at a dam, there is a good view of Blood Mt.

Robert E. Burnett

across Hammond Pond; total distance to the pond from the trailhead is 1 mi. In July the deer flies are pesky, but in winter this would be a good cross-country ski destination.)

The main trail continues uphill. At 0.8 mi, Hammond Pond comes into view again, and at 0.9 mi another opening gives a view of a weedy edge of the pond. Wildlife is prolific here. On the R is a spring with a black plastic pipe as a faucet.

At 1.2 mi, there is a cement culvert over a dry brook. The trail goes along a small weed-filled pond at 1.4 mi, descending L to a broken bridge at 1.5 mi. The trail is growing in considerably. There is a stream on the R.

At 1.7 mi, another rotting bridge crosses the outlet from Bloody Pond. (To hike the 0.2 mi to Bloody Pond, turn L at a yellow paint blaze on a tree after crossing the bridge. Follow the old yellow paint blazes carefully since the trail is faint and there are some blowdowns. This is a steep, rocky trail with a wonderful chimney to climb through. The pond is a tiny jewel surrounded by thick woods.) The road is interrupted at 1.9 mi by beavers at work. Since it goes onto private land soon, it is time to turn back.

❄ Trail in winter: Suitable for snowshoeing and skiing.

🐾 Distances: To Hammond Pond spur, 0.7 mi (to Hammond Pond via spur, 1 mi); to Bloody Pond spur, 1.7 mi (to Bloody Pond via spur, 1.9 mi); to beaver swamp, 1.9 mi. Cumulative distance to Hammond Pond, Bloody Pond, and beaver swamp, 3 mi (4.8 km).

6 North Hudson Trail System

Trails Illustrated Map 743: T27

This is a very nice new (2009) layout of trails on almost 300 acres of town land, just south of the hamlet of North Hudson, between the Schroon River and Hammond Pond Wild Forest. The trails are mostly on old logging and woods roads in three parcels on both sides of US 9. They are generally flat, with a few steep dips and rises for variety. Their western extensions border the Schroon River at several pretty spots that are great for wading and dipping in the summer. The woods are mostly evergreen with an inviting mossy ground cover. Northway traffic is sometimes within earshot and sometimes silenced by intervening hills. Two maps are available at the trailhead kiosk, or at the Town Hall on the N side of the hamlet along US 9, or on the Town website at http://northhudsonny.com/; one is a small scale overlay on a topographic map; the other is an un-scaled schematic map which does show the names of each trail and its trail marker color. The small town of North Hudson is justifiably proud of this project; it is wonderful to support this effort and those of other towns diversifying their attractions to include trail systems.

The trails are designated for multiple uses—hiking, running, skiing, snowshoeing, horseback riding and mountain biking—but it is quite unlikely that you will encounter other users during your visit. The entire network totals 8.6 mi (14.3 km), and you will need a leisurely four hours to explore it all. All the trails, except one, congregate and loop in an area about half a mile square. The outlier trail, called the Fish Dam Trail, goes 1.6 mi S from the South East Trail on the E side of US 9, through state land, and then W across US 9 to a fish weir on the Schroon River.

With this exception, all the trails are cut and marked (2009) with red, blue, or orange markers, and many intersections are labeled with laminated paper signs on wood backing; the signs have directional arrows and trail names, but are not placed at every junction. Nevertheless, distances between junctions are never more than a quarter-mile, and the sounds of the Northway easily keep hikers oriented. The Fish Dam Trail was somewhat brushy and scantily marked only with orange ribbons in 2009, but better attention to this is promised.

Because the trail network is so tight with short segments, it makes little sense to describe each trail. Consult the map closely.

▶Trailhead: The trail kiosk is located on the Frontiertown Road. Drive E 0.4 mi from Exit 29 of I-87. Turn S and R on US 9 and follow the highway for 0.5 mi. Turn R at the sadly deserted Frontiertown restaurant and parking lot where there is a brown and yellow sign for the North Hudson Trail System. Drive 0.3 mi past the old buildings and parking lots to the trailhead kiosk on the R.◀

❋ Trails in winter: Excellent for snowshoeing and generally fine for skiing, with a couple of short steep chutes that may need to be walked.

6A Fish Dam Trail

Trails Illustrated Map 743: T27

This outlying route can be hiked as an offshoot of the whole North Hudson Trail System (trail 6), or separately. To explore it separately, drive 1.5 mi S of the Blue Ridge Road intersection on US 9 and pull off into a small, unmarked gravel parking area on the E side of the highway. The path is just behind the parking lot and it runs N to the left and S to the right.

The left hand choice leads N 0.4 mi to the Southeast Trail of the town system and is only sporadically marked (12/09) with orange surveyor's tape. It is flat and generally easy to follow, crossing a small stream almost immediately, then a woods road, and finally a wet area before it bears L and meets the rest of the network.

The right-hand choice goes S through mossy woods past a large, fern-covered boulder and reaches a four-way intersection in 0.2 mi. There is a cement highway post and a State Land sign here between the trail and US 9. The L branch soon leads onto private land, while the route straight ahead is the one to follow. This seems to be an abandoned section of the highway, as it is wide, banked, and ditched, and easy to follow with surveying tape markers.

As this old road merges with the new one, cross the highway into a clearing. A well-traveled woods road leads W out of the clearing into dark pine woods toward an informal campsite and salmon weir on the Schroon River. As of late 2009, there are no trail signs, except one part way along the route designating it as access for the disabled.

The road is generally flat and splits several times, but returns to itself as it descends slightly to the river. At 1.3 mi an ATV track heads L and uphill onto private property. The main route continues straight ahead and then curves R downhill to parallel the river. There is a small clearing here, a fire pit, and a plaque on a small boulder. This commemorates the efforts of those who restored the fish dam in 1989. Further along is an outhouse and a pretty path along the river bank. Swimming, wading, and fishing are good here!

❄ Trail in winter: This would be a great near-the-highway route for both skiing and snowshoeing.

Distances: Trail N or L to intersection with Southeast Trail, 0.4 mi (0.6 km). Trail S or R to four-way intersection, 0.2 mi; to crossing of US 9, 0.4 mi; to L fork to private land, 1.3 mi; to campsite at fish dam, 1.6 mi (2.6 km).

7 Peaked Hill and Peaked Hill Pond

Trails Illustrated Map 743: S28

One of the charms of this trail is being able to combine some canoeing and hiking, and then being able to finish up with a swim at the end of a hike on a hot summer day. The trail is not heavily used, so once away from the lake you'll probably have it to yourself.

▶Trailhead: The only public access to the lake and the trail is from the Paradox Lake State Campground boat launch. From the intersection of NY 74 and US 9, N of the hamlet of Schroon Lake, head E on NY 74, passing a canoe and fishing access site on the Schroon River on the S side of the road at 0.6 mi from US 9. A trailhead for the Pharaoh region is on the R at 4.1 mi, with the Paradox Lake State Campground on the L (N) side at 4.3 mi. The boat access site is 0.3 mi on the R along the campground road, just past the entrance gate. There is no sign for the campground once it's closed for the winter. A day-use fee is charged during the summer when the campground is operating. From the boat launch it's approximately a 0.5-mi canoe to the N across the lake, following along the point the campground is on, to the trailhead in a small bay on the N side of the lake.◀

On the lakeside there is a DEC trail sign for the pond and the mountain and a No Camping sign. Here (0.0 mi) the well-marked, blue-marked trail heads N away from the lake. Avoid going R on a side trail that leads to a private road in about 0.2 mi.

The trail climbs on a moderate grade, crossing under a major power line at 0.1 mi. It continues climbing and soon swings L up and across some boulders and through evergreens and hardwoods. At 0.3 mi, the grade levels off as the trail crosses a small mossy stream that cascades down the hillside on the L. The trail soon swings R and gently uphill through the hardwoods, roughly following the brook on the R.

At 0.4 mi, the trail levels again and meanders through the evergreens. A small rock ledge is traversed at 0.7 mi, then, after crossing a small stream, the trail heads up a small hill and through a beautiful mature evergreen forest. Peaked Hill Pond is visible through the trees at 0.9 mi as the trail soon drops to near the level of the pond. A small opening on the shoreline at 1 mi is identifiable with a DEC sign marked "Peaked Hill 1.1 miles." Here there is a view out across the pond, ringed with cedars, hemlock, and birch.

The trail continues around the shoreline of Peaked Hill Pond until at 1.3 mi it turns L (N) away from the pond on a very gradual climb through hardwood forest. After descending slightly, the trail winds along the side of a hemlock-covered hill and drops to cross a stream at 1.6 mi. Climbing along the L branch of the stream, the trail crosses a wet area on some rocks. Very shortly, more climbing begins through the hardwoods, first gradually, then rather steeply in a few spots. The trail turns R just below a boulder, a large glacial erratic, then turns up along a rocky streambed. It veers slightly L around the W side of a small hill at 2 mi. Avoid heading straight ahead toward the boulders and bottom of the cliff.

At the top of the hill, the trail levels for a short distance but soon turns R and climbs fairly steeply again up toward the mountain top. After crossing a small level area near the top, the trail leads up over a ridge of rock to the wooded summit ridge. It is a short distance R to a rocky outcrop at 2.2 mi, with views to the S. Peaked Hill Pond and then Paradox Lake are in the foreground, with Pharaoh Mt. on the L horizon, and on a clear day, Crane Mt. in the distance beyond Schroon Lake.

❋ Trail in winter: This route would be an excellent ski-shoe. Start out skiing on the campground road off NY 74, and ski across the lake to the lakeside trailhead. Good skiers might ski some of the first climb, but snowshoes would be easiest for the ascent. Once on top of the first hill it's a great ski in to the start of the serious climb up Peaked Hill. This is best on snowshoes since the trail ascends almost 700 ft in its last 0.5 mi.

❦ Distances: Lakeside trail sign to top of first hill, 0.4 mi; to sign on Peaked Mt. Pond, 1 mi; to summit ascent, 1.6 mi; to summit lookout, 2.2 mi (3.5 km). Ascent from Paradox Lake to Peaked Hill Pond, 342 ft (104 m); from Peaked Hill Pond to top of Peaked Hill, 750 ft (229 m). Ascent from Paradox Lake, approx. 1100 ft (335 m). Elevation of Peaked Hill, approx. 1900 ft (579 m).

8 Crown Point State Historic Site

Trails Illustrated Map 743: V31–32, and 742: W31–32

Crown Point, with two forts, held major strategic control of Lake Champlain during the Colonial era and is now a protected area of over 350 acres managed by the State of New York. In addition to a self-guided tour of the fascinating ruins of the French and British forts, a lime kiln, and a small but comprehensive museum, the area is laced with walking trails that double in winter for cross-country skiing or snowshoeing. The entire network can be explored easily in two hours. The area is a mix of fields, overgrown meadow, and woods. It is a haven for birds;

High Peaks Audubon conducts an annual bird-banding station here each spring.

The grounds are open 9 AM to 6 PM from May through Columbus Day, and the Museum is open from May 15 through October 31, Thursday through Monday, 9:30 AM to 5 PM. There is a $4 admission fee to the museum.

The trails are also open for use in the off-season, as is the picnic pavilion.

▶Trailhead: The historic site is located on Bridge Rd. (NY 185), just SW of the bridge to Vermont. The entrance is on the W side of the highway 0.4 mi S of the bridge. In season, the road is open, bearing R past the admission booth to the parking lot adjacent to the museum. Off-season, there is parking at the start of the entrance road. Drive S 3.7 mi from the center of town at Broad St. in Port Henry on NY 9N/22 to the intersection with Bridge Rd. (NY 185). Turn L and drive 3.8 mi E and N to the Historic Site entrance on the L.◀

Trails: The trails make up a fairly small but intricate network, with no single trail stretching for more than a half-mile between intersections. See the site map to clarify directions, which follow a counter-clockwise course, starting on the outermost loop. All the trails are well-mowed and as much as 25 ft wide in places. They are inconsistently marked with metal posts, graphics, and arrows, but are easy to follow.

Two hundred yards N of the entrance booth, on the L, is a trail post with a cross-country skiing icon and an arrow pointing L at the edge of the woods. Enter the woods (0.0 mi), and turn R at the first intersection on level ground. This trail reaches a large clearing at 0.2 mi with the ruins of the large fort visible beyond. It then heads downhill across the field, passing an intersection L, toward some picnic tables at 0.3 mi.

The route continues straight N, with two barns coming into view and another intersection toward the tables L at 0.4 mi. Joining a gravel road at 0.5 mi, the route proceeds toward the shore and a rock breakwater, but bear L until a private camp comes into view at 0.6 mi. Turn L uphill on the grassy trail before reaching the camp lawn and wind through an overgrown field to a three-way intersection near a clearing and a small beach at 0.8 mi. The trail L returns uphill to the main clearing near the barns, in another 0.1 mi. All of the cross-trails and intersections in this large clearing are visible from its height of land, so the network is not nearly as confusing as it sounds!

The trail R enters woods on a wide, level path, which gradually bears L and ascends to the picnic tables at the edge of the large clearing at 1.2 mi. Turn R at a trail post along the edge of the field, winding to the ruins of a nineteenth-century lime kiln at 1.3 mi. After the kiln, the trail climbs R out of the field. Sumac bushes and hickory, butternut, and oak trees are all about. At 1.5 mi, the trail, which now has a blue sign with an arrow R, reaches a gravel road at the edge of a field. Turn R and almost immediately L along the gravel, passing a short grassy trail that descends to a dead end at the water. The road is a level straightaway that ends, at 1.9 mi, at a R turn in a clearing near the shore, with a brush pile. Do not follow the dirt woods road straight ahead because it enters private land.

Retrace your steps to an arrow R in 100 yd into a field that you can cross N to a large, lone tree, or follow the gravel lane, bearing R back to the same tree at 2.4 mi. At this point, turn L (N) along the wide mowed trail in the overgrown meadow. As the path reaches the start of a wood, there is a cross-country ski post. Proceed into the woods to an intersection at 2.6 mi. The way straight ahead leads into the main clearing of the fort in another 0.1 mi. The trail R leads back to the start at 2.7 mi.

✤ Trails in winter: Suitable for snowshoeing and cross-country skiing. See opening paragraph of this description. Winter parking is on the access road outside the gate.

🐾 Distances: From start of trail to clearing, 0.2 mi; to intersection with gravel road by barns, 0.5 mi; to L turn before private camp, 0.6 mi; to intersection near small beach, 0.8 mi; to picnic tables, 1.2 mi. To lime kiln, 1.3 mi; to gravel road, 1.5 mi; to end of gravel road in clearing near shore, 1.9 mi; back to intersection opposite large tree at edge of field, 2.4 mi; to start of trail, 2.7 mi (4.4 km).

9 Putts Creek Wildlife Management Area

Trails Illustrated Map 743: U32

This area comprises 113 acres overlooking a marsh on Putnam Creek just N of Crown Point village. As of February 2009, there was no sign of recent attention or maintenance to these lands. It would be an attractive area for bird watching and easy walking if the trails were easier to follow. This WMA is adjacent to Lake Champlain, and the Canadian Pacific train tracks run along its eastern shore.

▶Trailhead: From the S, drive 1.8 mi W and N on NY 9N/22 from Crown Point Central School. (From the N, drive 2.6 mi S on NY 9N/22 from its intersection with Bridge Rd., the turnoff for Crown Point State Historic Site.) At Goodrich Rd., turn E and proceed 0.5 mi to an intersection with Lake Rd. Head straight across the intersection to Wolcott Rd., 0.3 mi, to an asphalt parking space just before the railroad tracks. There is no sign at the entrance, and only sporadic yellow blazes and "Public Hunting Ground" signs along the trail.◀

Leave the parking area (0.0 mi) and navigate across a wet area heading straight S, following yellow paint blazes and contradictory signs. Some say, "No discharge of firearms allowed;"some say, "Public hunting grounds." Hunting is permitted

500 ft inside the boundary of the Wildlife Management Area, a regulation intended to protect the area along the tracks and the houses beyond them. The "Public hunting grounds" signs mark most of the path S and then SW along the top of a bank, where the trail reaches a nice lookout over the marsh in 0.3 mi.

A faint herd path bears L here for 0.1 mi to another good lookout over the water and the train tracks. The R fork winds 0.3 mi mostly W along the edge of the bank. The path reaches a third lookout area and then veers R into the woods and back L through scrub to a posted sign at the property boundary at 0.6 mi. Path-finding skills are necessary here, and a few cut logs are often the only sign that there once was a footpath to follow.

❋ Trail in winter: Short and flat for easy snowshoeing and skiing.

🐾 Distances: To first lookout over marsh, 0.3 mi; to end of trail at "Posted" sign, 0.6 mi (1 km).

10 Old Ironville Rd.

Trails Illustrated Map 743: S29

There is not a more pleasant walk in the woods than this one. Although this road is still passable for 4WD vehicles and is sometimes used by snowmobiles, it is usually empty and quiet, perfect for walking or cross-country skiing. An abandoned town road, it starts in the Town of Crown Point and ends in the Town of Ticonderoga. The Penfield Museum, consisting of several old white frame buildings, is in the center of Ironville; detailed collections regarding early local mining and power generation make it a wonderful half-day destination to combine with this hike. It is open in the summer months and in the fall for a superb Apple Festival.

▶Trailhead: From Chilson on NY 74, drive N 4.5 mi on Corduroy Rd. to the Penfield Museum in Ironville.◀

From the Penfield Museum (0.0 mi) the route proceeds E along the road and then turns R downhill onto Peasley Rd. At 0.1 mi there is a bridge over a series of cascades on Putnam Creek, the outlet of Penfield Pond.

At 0.2 mi, the road splits. Park here on the shoulder. Go R past a house, after which the road narrows and goes into deep woods. There are stone walls on both sides. At 0.4 mi, the road splits again; stay straight, not R. The road comes to the top of a hill, then begins to go downhill. It crosses a culvert at 0.6 mi with a large corner of a stone wall on the L. There is another side road R at 0.7 mi, followed soon by an ascent.

After an old farm clearing, there is a small stream on the R at 0.9 mi, which the route crosses shortly after. The going gets steeper, then levels out at 1 mi. At 1.1 mi, the road enters a stand of large hemlocks and white pine. It goes uphill again at 1.2 mi, through a clearing at 1.3 mi, and continues uphill past old stone walls. At 1.4 mi, another old road enters on the R.

At 1.5 mi there is a five-foot-high iron post on the L (probably marking the

town line between Crown Point and Ticonderoga). The road passes another old farm clearing at a height of land, and then another clearing with an old apple tree at 1.6 mi, just before another old road on the R.
Now the road goes uphill again. At 1.9 mi, there is a beautiful rocky cliff L. Past the top of the hill at 2 mi, the road passes through another clearing. In summer, milkweed blooms and butterflies gather nectar from the fragrant flowers. The road continues nearly level, then goes uphill slightly to meet the Warner Hill Rd. at 2.3 mi. The Warner Hill Rd. is called Towner Hill Rd. in the Town of Crown Point.

❊ Trail in winter: Excellent for skiing or snowshoeing. On skis, the return trip would be mostly downhill; the elevation changes from 894 ft in Ironville to 1256 ft at Warner Hill Rd.

❀ Distances: Penfield Museum to bridge over Putnam Creek, 0.1 mi; to clearing, 1.3 mi; to iron post, 1.5 mi; to rocky cliff, 1.9 mi; to Warner Hill Rd., 2.3 mi (3.7 km).

11 Arnold Pond

Trails Illustrated Map 743: S29

▶Trailhead: This short, very steep trail on the side of Skiff Mt. starts on the N side of NY 74, just W of Eagle Lake and only 0.1 mi E of the trailhead for Tubmill Marsh (trail 15) in the Pharaoh Lake area trail network. The trailhead for Arnold Pond is 7.9 mi E of I-87 Exit 28 (Ticonderoga–Paradox). Park in a lot just E of the trailhead on the S side of the road. The trail is marked with blue DEC disks.◀

The trail starts up the hill by a trail sign for Arnold Pond on the N side of the road (0.0 mi). This steep hillside has loose rock. The trail goes up through rocky woods where wild sweet peas bloom in July. At 0.1 mi there is a view to the S of Bear and Ragged mts. At 0.2 mi, the trail reaches a small col after a very steep climb with loose rock, and soon reaches the top of a ridge. At 0.3 mi, it reaches the edge of Arnold Pond.

A cairn-marked, unmaintained trail continues to the L up toward Skiff Mt. on private land. A short trail leads R down a solid rock walkway to the pond. Many dead trees ring the pond, attesting to the work of ambitious beavers. From the rocky cliffs on the N side of the pond, it is possible to hear or see a raven circling.

❊ Trail in winter: Suitable for snowshoes with crampons, but too steep and rocky for skiing.

❀ Distance: NY 74 to Arnold Pond, 0.3 mi (0.5 km). Ascent from road, 347 ft (105.8 m). Elevation of Arnold Pond, 1300 ft (396.3 m).

Aerial view of Pharaoh Lake and the southern Pharaoh Lake Wilderness
Carl Heilman II

Pharaoh Lake Wilderness, Schroon Lake, Ticonderoga Section

This section contains one of the best known regions in the eastern Adirondacks, the Pharaoh Lake Wilderness. This wilderness area has many lakes and ponds, hills and mountains, and a network of interconnecting trails for trips of varied duration. There are access points to the wilderness from all sides, including the Crane Pond Rd. from the NW corner and the Pharaoh Lake access road on the S central side. These roads are both in a designated wilderness area where vehicles are prohibited. While they provide easier access to the interior parts of the region, the special qualities of the wilderness character of the region will be protected by the complete closure of the roads to motorized vehicles. Both of these roads are legally closed by DEC, but access is not yet blocked (April 2012).

All bodies of water within the Pharaoh Lake Wilderness Area are trout waters with special regulations. No more than five trout may be taken per day, and the use of fish as bait is prohibited.

This section is bounded on the N by NY 74, on the E by Lake George, on the W by Schroon Lake, and on the S by NY 8. The trails on the periphery by Ticonderoga and Schroon Lake are well worth hiking to help give a broader perspective on the whole Adirondack region.

❈ Trails in winter: Snow conditions can vary considerably in the eastern Adirondacks. In years when "nor'easters" come up the Atlantic coast, there can be powder snow on the ground most of the winter. However, when the storms travel down the St. Lawrence valley, this region is on the warm side of them, and rain and ice are the result. When the snow is good, all the trails in the region are great for snowshoeing, and all those except for the mountain climbs are excellent ski routes. Specific suggestions for certain trails are included in the trail descriptions.

Suggested hikes in the region:

SHORTER HIKES:
Gull Pond—0.5 mi (0.8 km). An easy hike to a pretty little pond with rock ledges dropping down to the water.

Rogers Rock—1.1 mi (1.8 km). A short but quite steep climb to a great outlook over northern Lake George.

MODERATE HIKES:
Pharaoh Mt. from Crane Pond—4.3 mi (6.9 km) from the parking lot on the wilderness perimeter. A nice moderate climb with fine views from open areas on top.

HARDER HIKES:
Clear Pond Trail (trail 21) counterclockwise to Treadway Mt. Trail (trail 29) and back to Putnam Pond on the Grizzle Ocean Trail (trail 30)—11.5 mi (18.5 km). A loop of four ponds plus a spectacular mountain.

	Trail Described	*Total Miles (one way)*		*Page*
12	Crane Pond Rd.	2.0	(3.0 km)	41
13	Goose Pond	0.6	(1.0 km)	41
14	Long Swing Trail to Crane Pond Rd.	2.8	(4.5 km)	42
15	Tubmill Marsh Trail	6.4	(10.2 km)	43
16	Crab Pond Spur to Glidden Marsh Trail	0.4	(0.6 km)	43
17	Pharaoh Mt. Trail (from Crane Pond to Pharaoh Lake)	6.2	(9.9 km)	44
18	Lean-to Spur Trail	0.2	(0.3 km)	44
19	Glidden Marsh to Pharaoh Lake	4.4	(7.0 km)	45
20	Otter Pond	0.3	(0.5 km)	46
21	Clear Pond Trail	4.0	(6.4 km)	47
22	Rock Pond Spur	0.5	(0.8 km)	47
23	West Clear Pond Trail	0.6	(1.0 km)	47
24	Putnam Pond to Clear Pond Trail	0.6	(1.0 km)	47
25	Bear Pond Trail	2.8	(4.5 km)	48
26	Rock Pond to Lilypad Pond	1.9	(3.0 km)	49
27	North Rock Pond Trail	0.8	(1.3 km)	49
28	South Rock Pond Trail	0.7	(1.1 km)	49
29	Treadway Mt. Trail	2.1	(3.5 km)	50
30	Grizzle Ocean Trail	5.2	(8.4 km)	51
31	Grizzle Ocean Circuit Trail	1.1	(1.8 km)	51
32	Berrymill Flow from the North	2.0	(3.2 km)	53
33	Berrymill Flow from the South	3.2	(5.1 km)	53
34	Lost Pond	2.6	(4.3 km)	54
35	Pharaoh Lake via Mill Brook	2.5	(4.0 km)	54
36	East Shore of Pharaoh Lake	2.4	(3.8 km)	55
37	Springhill Ponds	4.4	(7.0 km)	56
38	Springhill Ponds from the South	3.0	(4.8 km)	58
39	Whortleberry Pond	0.3	(0.5 km)	58
40	Sucker Brook and Desolate Brook Trail to Pharaoh Lake	7.5	(12.1 km)	59
42	Spectacle Pond	1.7	(2.9 km)	60

43	Gull Pond	0.5 (0.8 km)	61
44	Cook Mt.	1.7 (2.7 km)	61
	Rogers Rock (unmaintained)	1.1 (1.8 km)	62

12 Crane Pond Rd.

Trails Illustrated Map 743: S28

The Crane Pond Rd. is one of the major northern access points for the Pharaoh Lake Wilderness. Within a reasonable distance from the parking lot are trails to Pharaoh Mt., Pharaoh Lake, and many of the interior ponds. At present (2012) this road is considered closed to motorized vehicles by DEC, but access is not blocked.

▶Trailhead: From the intersection of US 9 and NY 74 at I-87 Exit 28, just N of Schroon Lake, head S on US 9. Take the first L (E) on Alder Meadow Rd. (indicated by the sign for the airport). Go 2.2 mi to a L (E) fork in the road and continue another 2.4 mi on a narrow road to the Crane Pond parking lot. The road beyond this point is in classified Wilderness and most likely will at some time be blocked to vehicular traffic. The section of the road from the parking lot to Crane Pond isn't plowed in the winter.◀

From the parking lot (0.0 mi), the road to Crane Pond changes minimally in elevation. At 0.9 mi is the trailhead for the Goose Pond Trail (13) on the R (S). Some sections of the road from here to Crane Pond are quite rough, with "Wilson Hill" claiming numerous mufflers each year. At 1.6 mi, the NE end of Alder Pond may be flooded. A yellow-marked foot trail heads L just before the hairpin turn before the flooded area of road. At approx. 1.7 mi the Long Swing Trail (trail 14) from NY 74 comes in from the L. The W end of Crane Pond is reached at 2 mi.

🐾 Distances: Parking lot to Goose Pond (trail 13), 0.9 mi; to Long Swing Trail, 1.7 mi; to Crane Pond, 2 mi (3 km).

13 Goose Pond

Trails Illustrated Map 743: S28

▶Trailhead: The Goose Pond trailhead is on the S side of Crane Pond Rd. 0.9 mi from the Crane Pond parking lot at the wilderness edge (see trail 12 trailhead description).◀

The trail leaves from the S side of the road (0.0 mi) and has yellow trail markers. Goose Pond is special trout water. (See regulations in the introduction to this section.)

At 0.1 mi, the trail crosses a high plank bridge over the outlet of Alder Pond. Upstream a beaver dam can be seen. At 0.2 mi, the trail crosses a mossy log bridge over a wet place and soon another mossy log bridge. Now the trail goes gently uphill over rocks and roots, leveling off at 0.3 mi, and rising again. This section

is heavily used and eroded down to mud and tree roots in places.
   The trail goes gently downhill and at 0.5 mi Goose Pond can be seen glistening through the hemlocks. At 0.6 mi, the trail reaches a campsite near the edge of the pond. Across the pond is a view of Pharaoh Mt. A trail to the L skirts a bay and loops back to the main trail. Mergansers and loons may be seen here.
   ᘒ Distance: Trailhead to Goose Pond, 0.6 mi (1 km).

14 Long Swing Trail to Crane Pond Rd.

Trails Illustrated Map 743: S28

▶Trailhead: From I-87 Exit 28, cross US 9 heading E on NY 74. Go 4.2 mi to a small parking area on the R with the DEC sign for Crane Pond. The trailhead is only 0.1 mi W of the Paradox Lake State Campground entrance.◀

The trail climbs up the bank from the parking area (0.0 mi) and enters woods. It goes back (W) parallel to the road, crosses a cedar log bridge over a stream, and soon turns L (S) onto an older trail, marked with blue trail markers. The woods are mature white pine, hemlock, sugar maple, and yellow birch.
   At 0.2 mi, a smaller hemlock grows so close to a giant white pine that they look like Mutt and Jeff. The trail now heads S away from the road and is quite level. At 0.3 mi, the trail crosses a bridge over the stream, under tall trees that include some enormous yellow birch.
   Now the trail heads uphill along the stream and under tall hemlocks. At 0.4 mi, it crosses the stream on rocks. The trail heads uphill, then levels off again at 0.5 mi and skirts a beaver flow on the R side of the flooded marked trail for a short distance.
   At 0.7 mi, a new beaver pond filled with dead trees opens up the sky. The trail crosses a bridge over the outlet, with Blue Hill in view ahead. It follows the edge of the pond, then gently ascends at 0.9 mi. At 1 mi, the trail starts to descend; at 1.1 mi, it heads down more steeply. At 1.2 mi, it levels out at two hemlocks with old gashes, possibly the original trailmarkers.
   At 1.7 mi, the trail crosses a stream on rocks, then climbs the bank and levels again. It continues to climb until it levels at 1.9 mi. After passing some giant maples at 2 mi, the trail continues uphill through dense hemlock, beech, and birch. At 2.3 mi, near its northern limit, there is an enormous red oak.
   Now the trail goes gently downhill. At 2.8 mi is a T intersection with the narrow dirt road to Crane Pond (trail 12). Turn L to walk another 0.3 mi to Crane Pond and the trailhead to Pharaoh Mt.
   ᘒ Distances: NY 74 to beaver pond, 0.7 mi; to Crane Pond Rd. (trail 12), 2.8 mi (4.5 km). To Crane Pond, 3.1 mi (5.1 km).

15 Tubmill Marsh Trail
16 Crab Pond Spur to Glidden Marsh Trail

Trails Illustrated Map 743: S29

This trail from the N leads in to the Pharaoh Lake Wilderness and connects to the trails leading to the many ponds in the northern Pharaoh region. It also connects directly with some of the interior trails for easy access to Pharaoh Lake and Pharaoh Mt. for nice hiking and backpacking loops through the region.

▶Trailhead: A large trailhead sign on the R (S) side of NY 74, 8.1 mi E of Exit 28 on I-87, marks the start. The trail has blue markers; the spur from Crab Pond to Glidden Marsh (trail 16) is marked in red.◀

From the parking lot (0.0 mi), the trail heads E, parallel to the road, above a wetland with beaver activity, then uphill through woods of cedar, oak, birch, hemlock, and white pine, reaching the Eagle Lake dam at 0.3 mi. After crossing a bridge, the trail turns R (W) and follows the S side of the outlet stream. The fairly level trail soon crosses concrete culverts at 0.6 mi and then heads gradually uphill at 0.8 mi. After leveling off for a bit, the trail begins a long gradual decline until it reaches an intersection at 1 mi with two private trails from the Pyramid Lake Camp.

Bearing L (SW) around the base of Ragged Mt., the trail soon begins ascending through the pass between Ragged Mt. on the L (E), and Bear Mt. on the R (W). At 1.8 mi, it reaches the top of a triple col between Ragged Mt., Bear Mt., and Potter Mt. at about 1300 ft. After a descent along a side hill, the side trail for the Tubmill Marsh lean-to departs R (W) at 2.2 mi. The lean-to is 0.1 mi on this spur, and it's about 500 ft downhill to the marsh from the lean-to. This is a great place to see wildlife and is pretty when the blue flags are blooming in summer.

A sign indicating the way to Honey Pond is at 2.4 mi. After crossing a couple of streams, the trail cuts up along a ridge to a beaver pond at 2.9 mi. Across the beaver pond is a view of Big Clear Pond Mt., elev. 2000 ft, about 500 ft above the beaver pond.

The trail soon crosses a stream and turns away from the pond.

At 3.2 mi, the trail turns R and goes around Honey Pond and along a high ridge into a stand of birches. At 3.4 mi, it reaches the jct. with the trail to Lilypad Pond (trail 26) coming in from the L (E). It is 1.8 mi along this trail to Rock Pond; the Lilypad Pond Lean-to is very near the intersection.

Continuing S, the trail climbs for a short distance and then passes an old indistinct side trail for Treadway Mt. at 3.8 mi. The trail soon crosses the outlet of a small pond, and at 4.2 mi Horseshoe Pond comes into view. Soon there is an anglers' trail to the R, across an old beaver dam. The trail descends along the outlet of the pond and then crosses the inlet to Crab Pond, which is soon visible through the hemlocks.

The trail crosses another inlet stream and continues along the S side of the pond, reaching a jct. at 4.9 mi. L is the Crab Pond Spur Trail (trail 16), a direct route 0.4 mi S from Crab Pond to the Glidden Marsh Trail (19). It is marked with red markers.

Continuing straight (W) around the outlet of Crab Pond, the trail reaches Oxshoe Pond at 5.4 mi and the Oxshoe Pond Lean-to at 5.6 mi. It's a pretty view from the lean-to with rock ledges and pines around the shore of the pond.

At 5.9 mi, the trail reaches the shoreline of Glidden Marsh and intersects with the W end of the Glidden Marsh Trail (trail 19). Turning R, the trail heads NW, away from the shoreline, and enters a nice hemlock forest. After crossing a bridge, the trail climbs slightly and intersects the Pharaoh Mt. Trail (trail 17) at 6.4 mi. From here it is 0.7 mi to the end of the road at Crane Pond (trail 12).

🥾 Distances: Parking lot at NY 74 to Tubmill Marsh lean-to cutoff, 2.2 mi; to Rock Pond/Lilypad Pond Trail (trail 26), 3.4 mi; to Crab Pond jct., 4.9 mi; to Oxshoe Pond lean-to, 5.6 mi; to Glidden Marsh Trail (trail 19), 5.9 mi; to Pharaoh Mt. Trail (trail 17), 6.4 mi (10.2 km). Distance of Crab Pond Spur Trail (trail 16), 0.4 mi (0.6 km).

17 Pharaoh Mt. Trail (Crane Pond to Pharaoh Lake)
18 Lean-to Spur Trail

Trails Illustrated Map 743: R–S28

Pharaoh Mt. is a very dominant feature when looking across Schroon Lake from the Northway into the Pharaoh region. It rises sharply from the landscape with its steep rock faces on the W side. It's a pleasant mountain to climb, and the views offer a panoramic perspective on the eastern Adirondack region.

▶Trailhead: The red-marked trail starts at the W end of Crane Pond, at the end of Crane Pond Rd. (trail 12).◀

Leaving Crane Pond Rd. (0.0 mi), the trail crosses a plank bridge at the outlet of Crane Pond. A trail register is a short distance along the trail past the bridge. It follows an old tote road through a pretty woods of tall evergreens. At 0.7 mi, the trail reaches a jct. with the Glidden Marsh Trail to Pharaoh Lake (trail 19). The trail to Pharaoh Mt. bears R by an old cellar hole. It soon passes a beaver pond, Glidden Marsh on the L, and big white pines.

The trail begins ascending at 1.9 mi, soon bearing R and becoming steeper. At 2 mi, it crosses a stream (dry in late summer). Now the trail is fairly steep and eroded down to rock. At 2.8 mi, at a good view, the trail is on an open ridge of bare rock. The top isn't far away.

The trail soon reaches the site where the observer's cabin once stood and then at 2.9 mi the open rock summit where the fire tower once stood. The actual summit is just a short distance to the N of the observer's cabin site.

There are great views to the High Peaks and Hoffman Notch Wilderness across Schroon Lake from the rock ledges on the W side of the summit. By exploring the summit to the N and E it is possible to view the High Peaks, the NE Adirondacks, Lake Champlain and Vermont, Pharaoh Lake, and the mountains of the

Pharaoh Lake Wilderness. Try to pick out Crane Mt. to the SW and the Tongue Mt. Range to the SE.

The route continuing across the summit and down the E side of the mountain is a pleasant, lightly used trail. From the site of the old observer's cabin, the trail heads E across the summit. After a couple of short, steep descents, at 3.2 mi (mileage from Crane Pond) the route crosses a stream, soon comes to an opening, then crosses the stream again. At 3.5 mi there is an outlook to the rocky face of Treadway Mt. to the NE. There are blueberries here, in season, along the open rock, as well as trailing arbutus which is on the State of New York list of protected plants.

At 3.7 mi, the clearing ends and soon Pharaoh Lake can be seen below. After crossing and then re-crossing a stream, the trail goes over a couple of bridges and wooden walkways, coming close to the shoreline of Pharaoh Lake at 4.5 mi. Turning R (S) along the shore of the lake, the trail parallels the shoreline, passing over a couple of streams, then a wetland on the L, and reaches a jct. with a side trail at 5.3 mi. This Lean-to Spur Trail (trail 18) leads to Pharaoh lean-to 5 and the point that protrudes into the lake. There are great views from the tip of the point, 0.2 mi from the main trail.

Continuing along the main trail, lean-to 6 is visible through the trees at 5.7 mi. The outlet of the lake and the jct. with the Mill Brook Trail (trail 35) are at 6.2 mi. It is 2.5 mi to the parking lot at Mill Brook and 3.6 mi to the parking lot by the wilderness boundary via trail 35.

❋ Trail in winter: This is an excellent ski-shoeing route in the winter, skiing in on the road and part way up the trail, then snowshoeing to the summit. A group could return the same way, or continue down the other side, skiing out the Pharaoh/Mill Brook Trail (trail 35) to another car parked at the end of the access road.

🐾 Distances: Crane Pond Rd. (trail 12) to Glidden Marsh Trail (trail 19), 0.7 mi; to summit, 2.9 mi; to shore of Pharaoh Lake, 4.5 mi; to side trail to lean-tos, 5.3 mi; to Pharaoh Lake via Mill Brook Trail (trail 35), 6.2 mi (9.9 km). Ascent from Crane Pond, 1470 ft (448 m); ascent from Pharaoh Lake, 1390 ft (424 m). Elevation of Pharaoh Mt., 2551 ft (778 m).

19 Glidden Marsh to Pharaoh Lake

Trails Illustrated Map 743: R28–29

This trail connects the Crane Pond area with the Pharaoh Lake area and the Grizzle Ocean Trail (trail 30). This makes it possible to hike from the Crane Pond area to the Pharaoh Lake area, then up to the Putnam Pond area (trail 24), and back to Crane Pond via Crab Pond and Oxshoe Pond (trails 26 and 15) without having to retrace many of your steps. It's a long route, but it would make a nice two- to four-day backpacking trip (depending on how much time you have to relax and enjoy or explore).

▶Trailhead: The yellow-marked Glidden Marsh Trail begins along Glidden

Marsh at a jct. with the Tubmill Marsh Trail (trail 15), 0.4 mi E of the Pharaoh Mt. Trail (trail 17), and 1.1 mi from the end of Crane Pond Rd. (trail 12). Glidden Marsh is a great place to see wildlife. Herons and other waterfowl frequent this area and there is a lot of beaver sign. ◀

At the jct. with the Tubmill Marsh Trail (trail 16) (0.0 mi), the trail heads SE along the shore of Glidden Marsh. The trail soon begins a gradual ascent and at 0.6 mi reaches a jct. on the L with the Crab Pond Spur Trail (trail 16). There is a sign here for Crab Pond 0.4 mi to the L.

The trail now climbs very gradually through the rolling woods on the E side of Pharaoh Mt., crosses a couple of streams, and passes a small pond. At 2.1 mi, it begins a fairly steep descent toward Pharaoh Lake, coming near the shoreline at 3.1 mi, where a sign indicates a turn L. The trail now follows to the E around Split Rock Bay on Pharaoh Lake, and then swings S along the bay toward a lean-to. At 3.7 mi, the trail reaches Pharaoh Lean-to 4 on a fine broad point with views of the lake.

Heading E, the trail soon crosses a stream and then heads more S and away from the lake. Passing a side trail for Wintergreen Point (0.3 mi, with some great views), the trail almost immediately comes to a jct. with the Grizzle Ocean Trail (trail 30) and the East Shore of Pharaoh Lake Trail (trail 36) at 4.4 mi.

🚶 Distances: Tubmill Marsh Trail (trail 16) to Crab Pond Spur Trail, 0.6 mi; to Pharaoh Lake, 3.1 mi; to Pharaoh Lean-to, 3.7 mi; to Grizzle Ocean Trail (trail 30) and East Shore of Pharaoh Lake Trail (trail 36), 4.4 mi (7 km).

20 Otter Pond

Trails Illustrated Map 743: S29

This is the only pond in this area that is open for public access. There have been serious trespassing problems here. The only legal public access is from the boat launch on Eagle Lake, since the shoreline on the S side of the road is privately owned. You may not drive your vehicle on the private road. There is no public access to Gooseneck Pond on this road. Be sure to follow the trail directions with absolute care.

▶Trailhead: On NY 74, approximately 9.5 mi E of I-87 Exit 28 (about 8 mi W of Ticonderoga), is a boat access site for Eagle Lake, just W of the causeway. It is a short canoe trip almost due S across the lake to the trailhead and sign for Otter Pond in a small cove on the SE shore of Eagle Lake. ◀

From the canoe landing (0.0 mi), walk L on the road along the shore for 0.1 mi to a low place on the R where two dark blue DEC trail markers lead into the woods. The trail is well marked, but the start is easy to miss.

Continuing on the level for a short time, the trail quickly goes uphill. It climbs steeply through a draw on a N-facing slope of hemlocks and boulders. The trail is so little used that you must depend on the trail markers. At 0.2 mi, the trail levels, curves L, and goes gently uphill to Otter Pond at 0.3 mi. Trail markers on the trees here show that the beavers are busy at work. To the R at about 100 ft is a beaver dam at the outlet.

🚶 Distance: Canoe landing to Otter Pond, 0.3 mi (0.5 km).

21 Clear Pond Trail
22 Rock Pond Spur
23 West Clear Pond Trail
24 Putnam Pond to Clear Pond Trail

Trails Illustrated Map 743: R–S29

This trail circles around the Putnam Pond area and provides access to the several small ponds W of Putnam Pond. When the Clear Pond trail is combined with a portion of the Grizzle Ocean Trail (trail 30), it's possible to make a complete circuit of Putnam Pond.

▶ Trailhead: Drive 13.3 mi E on NY 74 from I-87 Exit 28 (Ticonderoga–Paradox) to a large sign on the R for Putnam Pond State Campground. Drive S 3.8 mi to the entrance. Day-use fees are charged in season. A boat launch is just beyond on the R and the parking lot is at 4.2 mi (0.4 mi from the entrance). From the parking lot, walk along the entrance road 0.4 mi to the entrance booth, then another 0.4 mi to the campground where the trailhead is at campsites 38 and 39. The trail is marked with yellow markers to the end of Clear Pond, and then blue markers from Clear Pond to its jct. with the Grizzle Ocean Trail (trail 30). ◀

Starting at campsites 38 and 39 (0.0 mi), the trail heads N toward Heart Pond. It crosses and re-crosses a stream, reaching the jct. with Bear Pond Trail (trail 25) at 0.4 mi. Continuing L to the S of Heart Pond, at 0.5 mi the trail passes a spur to the N that goes to a point that overlooks this pretty little pond.

The trail continues W over rolling terrain, follows the N shoreline of North Pond, and crosses a bridge at 1.1 mi. At 1.5 mi, the trail reaches the shore of North Pond. (North Pond is actually a long extended bay to the N of Putnam Pond.) The trail heads W, climbs up and then descends over a hill, and reaches a jct. with the Rock Pond Spur Trail (trail 22) at 1.7 mi.

Turn L (S) at this jct. for the main trail and the shortest route to Clear Pond, as well as the Little Rock Pond Lean-to. The trail crosses a stream and comes to the lean-to at 1.9 mi, meeting up with the Rock Pond Spur Trail again at 2 mi.

[The Rock Pond Spur Trail (22) heads straight (W) at the jct. at 1.7 mi to a jct. with the Rock Pond to Lilypad Pond Trail (26) at Rock Pond in 0.2 mi. Turn L (S) at the trail 26 intersection to follow S along the E shore of Rock Pond, passing the Rock Pond Lean-to at 0.4 mi and meeting up with the Clear Pond Trail at 0.5 mi. This spur is 0.5 mi long, or 0.1 mi longer than the parallel section of the main trail.]

From the jct. at 2 mi, trail 21 continues S, with Rock Pond to the W and Little Rock Pond to the E. It crosses an isthmus that separates the two ponds, and then comes to another jct. at 2.1 mi. The trail to the R (W) is the S route of the Rock

Pond to Lilypad Pond Trail (trail 26).

Trail 21 continues on to the S, ascending and then descending to the trail jct. at the head of Clear Pond at 2.7 mi. Here again there's a choice, to go around the E or the W side of Clear Pond. The West Clear Pond Trail (trail 23), at 0.6 mi long, is the shorter by about 0.1 mi. It heads R at this intersection, following the W side of Clear Pond and rejoining the main trail.

The main trail heads L around the E shoreline of Clear Pond, reaching the Clear Pond Lean-to at 3.1 mi. Behind the lean-to is the Putnam Pond to Clear Pond Trail (trail 24), running 0.6 mi to Putnam Pond. Continuing on the main trail at the outlet of Clear Pond, the jct. with the trail along the W side of the pond is at 3.4 mi.

Trail 21 continues S and E past Mud Pond to an intersection with the Treadway Mt. Trail (trail 29) at 3.6 mi. Continuing S across the intersection, the trail soon meets the Grizzle Ocean Trail (trail 30) at 4 mi. The trail L (E) leads to the Putnam Pond parking lot in 1.4 mi.

🚶 Distances: Putnam Pond campsites 38 and 39 to Bear Pond Trail (trail 25), 0.4 mi; to trail to Little Rock Pond and Rock Pond, 1.7 mi; to Little Rock Pond Lean-to, 1.9 mi; to Rock Pond Lean-to, 2.1 mi; to Clear Pond Lean-to and side trail to Putnam Pond, 3.1 mi; to Treadway Mt. Trail (trail 29), 3.6 mi; to Grizzle Ocean Trail (trail 30), 4 mi (6.4 km). Length of trail 22 spur, 0.5 mi (0.8 km); length of trail 23, 0.6 mi (1 km); length of trail 24 spur, 0.6 mi (1 km). Complete circuit of Putnam Pond with return via Grizzle Ocean Trail (trail 30) to parking lot, 6.2 mi (9.9 km).

25 Bear Pond Trail

Trails Illustrated Map 743: S29

This is a trail to one of the special trout waters in the Pharaoh Lake Wilderness area. (See the regulations in this section's introduction.) The trail connects with the Clear Pond Trail (trail 21) at Heart Pond at the E end and the North Rock Pond Trail (trail 27) on the W end. There is no public access other than the Clear Pond Trail.

▶Trailhead: The easiest access to this trail is via the Clear Pond Trail from Putnam Pond campsites 38 and 39 (see trail 21). It is 0.4 mi N on the Clear Pond Trail from the campsites to the beginning of the Bear Pond Trail. The trail is marked with blue markers. ◀

Leaving the Heart Pond jct. with the Clear Pond Trail (trail 21) (0 mi), the trail heads N along the E shore of Heart Pond. At 1 mi, it crosses open rocky places with blueberry bushes before descending a small hill to a L (S) turn near Bear Pond at 1.2 mi. Here an unmaintained trail leads to private land.

The trail soon leads over a small knoll to a campsite on the E shore of Bear Pond. There are lots of signs of beaver activity around the pond. Heading S, the trail soon reaches the edge of Bear Pond and then follows along a narrow, rocky path. The trail passes along the marshy SE corner of the pond with rocky cliffs on the L, crosses an inlet stream, and soon leaves the pond at 1.5 mi.

The trail gradually heads uphill, up and over Bear Pond Mt., reaching height of land at 2.2 mi, elevation approx. 1750 ft, 350 ft above Bear Pond. The trail is rather washed out for a while, then levels off on a hemlock-studded hillside before descending gradually along some rock cliffs. At 2.7 mi, it drops more steeply to Rock Pond, now visible through the trees. At 2.8 mi, the trail reaches the Rock Pond to Lilypad Pond Trail (26). L is the Rock Pond Spur Trail (22) in 0.2 mi. Across the pond are Peaked Hill and Little Clear Pond.

🐾 Distances: Heart Pond jct. on Clear Pond Trail to Bear Pond, 1.2 mi; to height of land, 2.2 mi; to Rock Pond to Lilypad Pond Trail, 2.8 mi (4.5 km).

26 Rock Pond to Lilypad Pond
27 North Rock Pond Trail
28 South Rock Pond Trail

Trails Illustrated Map 743: S29

This trail, besides being the connector trail between the Putnam Pond area on the E and the Crab Pond and Crane Pond area on the W, is a pleasant trail to hike. There are fine views from the shoreline of Rock Pond, and it's a nice walk along Rock Pond Brook to Lilypad Pond Lean-to. It's also possible to make a loop around Rock Pond using part of the Clear Pond Trail (trail 21).

▶Trailhead: From its E end, this red-marked trail begins at the SE corner of Rock Pond, near Little Rock Pond at a jct. with the Clear Pond Trail (trail 21).◀

From the Clear Pond Trail (trail 21) near Little Rock Pond (0 mi), trail 28 heads W around the S shore of Rock Pond. It soon follows the shoreline and heads N along the W shore, passing a campsite on a nice promontory on the W side of the pond. At 0.7 mi it meets trail 27 (see below) on the S side of Rock Pond outlet.

Heading W from the jct., trail 26 parallels the outlet stream for some distance. At 1.2 mi, a waterfall is heard off to the R. In a short distance the trail descends to the waterfall, where there is a short side trail leading to the falls. The trail now begins following along a wetland until at 1.8 mi it climbs and reaches Lilypad Pond Lean-to at Lilypad Pond. From the lean-to it's a short distance to the jct. with the Tubmill Marsh Trail (trail 15) at 1.9 mi.

Trail 27 starts from the NE corner of Rock Pond, on the Rock Pond Spur trail (22) at a point 1.9 mi from the Putnam Pond State Campground. It heads along the alluring N side of Rock Pond. At 0.2 mi, the Bear Pond Trail (trail 25) intersects on the R. Shortly after a turn R, there is a cave-like entrance to an old graphite mine with some brownish water seeping from it.

The trail climbs steeply uphill to a bluff on the L that overlooks the pond. A side trail leads to a rock point with some blueberry bushes and several large white pines on the end.

Pharaoh Lake from Treadway Mt. Jeffrey Trubisz

The trail soon passes a campsite with a fireplace, then follows the shoreline, climbs steeply to some more open rock at 0.4 mi, and drops steeply once again to the shoreline. At 0.7 mi there is another campsite on a huge open rock. It may be easy to lose the trail here because of the rock. Continue straight through the clearing to the trail, which crosses the outlet of Rock Pond to trail 26 at 0.8 mi.

🐾 Distances: Clear Pond Trail (trail 21) to jct. with trail 27 at Rock Pond outlet, 0.7 mi; Lilypad Pond lean-to, 1.8 mi; to Tubmill Marsh Trail (trail 15), 1.9 mi (3 km). Length of trail 27, 0.8 mi (1.3 km).

29 Treadway Mt. Trail

Trails Illustrated Map 743: R29

This is a unique mountain with large, open rocky spaces on top and an interior trail that winds along a U-shaped summit. Trailing arbutus and blueberries grow profusely along the upper parts of the trail. There are good views of Treadway's more popular neighbor, Pharaoh Mt., and surrounding points, as well as the High Peaks and more mountains to the W, S, and E. It is possible to cross Putnam Pond by canoe to the Treadway Mt. trailhead, which removes 3.6 mi from a round-trip.

▶Trailhead: The trailhead is 1.4 mi S on the Grizzle Ocean Trail (trail 30) from Putnam Pond State Campground, then 0.4 mi N on the Clear Pond Trail (trail 21). At a jct. at this point, the Treadway Mt. Trail goes L; R leads 0.2 mi to the landing for the canoe shortcut. To reach the Treadway Mt. trailhead on Putnam Pond by canoe, put in at the boat launch on the E shore near the Putnam Pond parking lot (see trail 21). Then canoe W and S to a small point on the W shore of Putnam Pond. The trail starts by a small stream in the cove behind the point. The trail is marked with red markers.◄

From the Clear Pond Trail (trail 21) (0 mi), the red-marked trail proceeds 0.1 mi to a deadwood swamp called Mud Pond. Wintergreen grows along the edge of the trail, which follows the S side of Mud Pond. At 0.2 mi, the trail crosses a stream on a log with a beaver dam downstream, turning L along the stream. At 0.3 mi, it crosses the stream and soon re-crosses it. Now it climbs moderately and can be wet. It is a wide old tote road through hemlocks, with a stream on the R, and then mixed hardwoods.

At 0.9 mi, the trail comes to a swamp with bright green grass and moss. It becomes steeper at 1.1 mi above a swampy stream. At 1.2 mi, it becomes rocky, winding above a ravine to the L. Then it arrives at the first bare rock with trailing arbutus and a cairn at 1.3 mi. It is important to follow the red paint blazes on the rock. In early July, bright pink sheep laurel blooms here.

At 1.5 mi, the trail climbs through a chimney and arrives in a thick growth of blueberry bushes. At 1.6 mi, it goes into woods again; at 1.7 mi is the first view to the E. At 1.8 mi, the trail comes to the bottom of a dip. Then at 2 mi it reaches a false summit and after another dip arrives at the true summit at 2.1 mi.

This mountain deserves more attention; it has a varied and satisfying climb and fascinating summit trail over its open rocky top. Views are excellent.

❄ Trail in winter: This would make an excellent snowshoe trip and enjoyable, advanced-level ski trip. Some distance could be saved by cutting straight across Putnam Pond to the trail, as can be done in summer with a canoe.

🐾 Distances: Clear Pond Trail to cairn, 1.3 mi; to chimney, 1.5 mi; to summit, 2.1 mi (3.5 km). Parking lot to summit, 3.9 mi (6.5 km). Ascent, approx. 900 ft (275 m). Summit elevation, 2240 ft (683 m). By canoe: paddle approx. 1 mi across Putnam Pond from boat launch SW to a small point. Walk on trail with red markers 0.2 mi to a jct., then straight to summit at approx. 2.3 mi (3.8 km).

30 Grizzle Ocean Trail
31 Grizzle Ocean Circuit Trail

Trails Illustrated Map 743: R29

This fairly easy trail connects the Putnam Pond and Pharaoh Lake areas.

▶Trailhead: The trail begins on the W side of the parking lot at Putnam Pond State Campground. For directions to the parking lot, see the Clear Pond Trail (trail 21). The trail has yellow markers.◄

The trail immediately crosses a pair of bridges. A side trail goes R to Putnam Pond. At 0.3 mi the trail crosses a muddy place, and then crosses a brook. At 0.7 mi, the trail goes downhill through hemlocks with a mossy cliff on the L and soon crosses an inlet to the pond on a plank bridge. At 1.2 mi, it reaches a jct.

(An unmarked side trail R goes to the S edge of Putnam Pond.) The trail crosses a brook on a plank bridge. At 1.4 mi it reaches a stream with a bridge. On the other side a trail R leads via Clear Pond Trail (trail 21) back to Putnam Pond State Campground, circling Putnam Pond.

The main trail heads L (S) to Grizzle Ocean. At 1.6 mi it crosses the stream on rocks, and at 1.8 mi reaches a height of land. (The Grizzle Ocean Lean-to spur goes L 0.2 mi, following blue trail markers. The lean-to is set back under pines from the edge of Grizzle Ocean, a pretty, shallow pond in spite of its name.)

From the lean-to spur, the trail continues to a long wooden walkway, which crosses the outlet of Grizzle Ocean at 2 mi. The trail turns L at the end of the walkway and at 2.1 mi reaches a jct. with the red-marked Grizzle Ocean Circuit Trail (trail 31).

Grizzle Ocean is on the L. [This trail circles the pond and reaches the lean-to in 0.9 mi. It is 0.2 mi from the lean-to following yellow markers back to the Grizzle Ocean Trail for a total of 1.1 mi (1.8 km) around the E side of Grizzle Ocean. Turn R to continue to Pharaoh Lake.]

At 2.2 mi, the trail reaches a miniature pond on the R. At 2.5 mi, it crosses a small stream on rocks and soon crosses the stream again. At 2.8 mi, it reaches a wet place which is the start of a stream under high maples, and begins to follow the stream downhill. This is the divide between Putnam Pond and Pharaoh Lake. It is also a pass between Grizzle Ocean Mt. to the N and Thunderbolt Mt. to the S.

At 3.3 mi, the trail comes to a very muddy spot, then a couple of streams. It goes along a hillside with hemlocks and maples at 3.7 mi, then crosses a bridge. At 3.8 mi, it reaches a small stream tumbling down through rocks, from Devil's Washdish. At 3.9 mi, the trail passes Wolf Pond on the L, seen through the trees. It reaches an inlet to Wolf Pond at 4 mi, and another at 4.1 mi.

Now the trail goes along a fern-filled hillside above a swampy area. It follows a ridge, and then passes through a grove of hemlocks. It descends and at 4.4 mi travels over some rolling terrain.

At 4.6 mi, the trail reaches the top of another small hill and at 4.8 mi it reaches an algae-filled bay. At 5.1 mi, it crosses a stream that feeds into Pharaoh Lake and then passes under a tall stand of red pines; a waterfall is audible down to the L.

At 5.2 mi, the trail reaches an intersection at Pharaoh Lake. The Glidden Marsh Trail (19) R goes to Wintergreen Point and to Pharaoh Lean-to at Split Rock Bay. The East Shore of Pharaoh Lake Trail (trail 36) L goes along the E shore of Pharaoh Lake. Just before this trail jct. it is about 100 ft downhill through the woods to a view of the waterfall. From the jct. it is 0.1 mi L to a good plank bridge directly below the waterfall. This is a good place for a rest stop and picnic, with a good view of Wintergreen Point and its shallow bay filled with pond lilies.

🥾 Distances: Putnam Pond State Campground parking lot to Clear Pond Trail (trail 21), 1.4 mi; to Grizzle Ocean Lean-to jct, 1.8 mi; to watershed divide, 2.8 mi; to Pharaoh Lake, 5.2 mi (8.3 km); to waterfall and plank bridge, 5.3 mi (9.1 km).

32 Berrymill Flow from the North

Trails Illustrated Map 743: R29

▶Trailhead: The trailhead is near the exit of the parking area in the Putnam Pond State Campground (see trail 21). Maps, including the one used as the base map for this book, identify the flow as Berrymill Pond, but trail signs, and consequently this book, refer to it as Berrymill Flow.◀

The trail starts uphill on an old tote road, crosses a stream, and soon enters a straight section, following blue markers. At 0.4 mi, the road goes up along the brook on the R. At 0.6 mi, it crosses a stream and then travels at a gentle pace through the woods. At 1.5 mi, the trail crosses a clearing and another stream where there may be some beaver activity. The marked side trail R (W) to the pond and the lean-to is at 2 mi, near the outlet of this sinuous body of water.

❋ Trail in winter: This is ideal as a gentle ski or snowshoe trip.

𝄞 Distance: Parking lot to pond and lean-to, 2 mi (3.2 km).

33 Berrymill Flow from the South

Trails Illustrated Map 743: Q–R30

▶Trailhead: This trailhead is reached from the town of Hague. Turn R (N) onto Summit Dr. from NY 8, 3 mi W of Hague (0 mi). At 0.8 mi, take the sharp R curve. The road soon joins with West Hague Rd. and at 1.4 mi passes May Memorial Cemetery on the R (E). At 2 mi there is a small trailhead parking lot and sign for Berrymill Flow on the L (W) side of the road. The trail follows yellow markers for 0.3 mi and then forks R with blue markers. Maps, including the one used as the base map for this book, identify the flow as Berrymill Pond, but trail signs, and consequently this book, refer to it as Berrymill Flow.◀

From the parking lot (0.0 mi), the trail starts uphill and at 0.3 mi there is a jct. with the Springhill Ponds from the South Trail (trail 38) on the L. Bear R and continue the gradual climb. The trail becomes steeper at 1.2 mi, and then levels off at 1.3 mi. It passes a wetland at 1.5 mi, then crosses a couple of bridges and a stream and beaver flow with uprooted trees at 2.2 mi. A spring is passed at 2.6 mi, just before a bridge. The jct. on the L for Berrymill Flow is at 3 mi, with the shore of the pond at 3.1 mi. Turning R, there is an old lean-to site at 3.2 mi. After a knoll of white and red pine, the trail reaches the end of this point at 3.4 mi. Blueberries grow in abundance here, as do trailing arbutus and ladyslippers. There are signs of beaver activity in the cove to the R, where there is also a lean-to.

To reach the lean-to, go back to the jct. at 3 mi. Head L (N) about 100 yd to another jct., with a sign for Putnam Pond (1.9 mi away) to the R and Berrymill lean-to to the L. Another 100 yd to the L (W) is the lean-to on the cove.

❋ Trail in winter: Suitable for snowshoeing.

𝄞 Distances: W. Hague Rd. parking to wetland, 1.5 mi; to first Berrymill Flow jct., 3 mi; to lean-to, 3.2 mi (5.1 km).

34 Lost Pond

Trails Illustrated Map 743: R29–30

▶Trailhead: From NY 74 at Chilson, turn S onto the road with a large sign for Putnam Pond State Campground and drive 3.3 mi to the trailhead sign for Lost Pond on the L. The trail is an old tote road with yellow markers. This is a well-used trail popular with campers and anglers. The pond's outlet is underground for a quarter mile adjacent to the trail.◀

Departing from the trailhead sign (0.0 mi), at 0.3 mi the old road enters a stand of hemlocks. There are lots of Indian pipes growing here in July. At 0.4 mi, the trail forks L from the old road. There are exposed roots of beech and maple trees. At 0.5 mi, the trail goes over a knoll, into a dip, and then up another knoll. Here it levels off. At 0.7 mi, it navigates a muddy seep.

At 0.9 mi, the trail descends gently before going through woods of maple, beech, and huge birches. At 1 mi, it reaches a plank bridge over a stream with huge boulders. A beaver swamp is down to the L. White orchids may be seen growing here on the R in July. The trail passes the outlet of the pond at 1.1 mi, then a private trail on the L over a stream. At 1.2 mi, the trail crosses the stream, continuing uphill.

At 1.3 mi, the trail levels out among mature maples. At 1.4 mi, Lost Pond is in sight, and soon the trail reaches a jct. for a trail around the pond.

Continuing R around the pond, yellow markers are very helpful since the path is sometimes faint. There has been a fair amount of beaver activity at this pond. At 1.7 mi, the trail comes along a mossy cliff on the R, then crosses a rocky stream at 1.8 mi. At 1.9 mi, the trail comes around one of the end lobes of the pond. At 2 mi, it reaches an outcropping of boulders. This is a good picnic spot. Trout fishing is quite good. Chickadees, warblers, thrushes, and veeries sing their various songs along the edge of the deep forest.

In a few hundred yards there is a campsite with a fire circle. Another campsite is at 2.2 mi. Blueberries are thick along the trail here in summer.

Now the trail climbs steeply up through boulders along Abe's Hill. At 2.5 mi, it reaches another campsite, and at 2.6 mi it ends at a trail jct. where the loop around the pond began.

❉ Trail in winter: Suitable for snowshoeing and skiing, with one steep hill.

🏃 Distances: Putnam Pond State Campground road to plank bridge, 1 mi; to Lost Pond, 1.4 mi; to boulders, 2 mi; complete loop around pond, 2.6 mi (4.3 km).

35 Pharaoh Lake via Mill Brook

Trails Illustrated Map 743: Q28

This is the easiest and most popular trail into the Pharaoh Lake Wilderness from the S. The trail is a nice walk directly to the S end of Pharaoh Lake, from where there is access to the rest of the Pharaoh region via the Pharaoh Mt. Trail (trail

17) and the East Shore Trail (36).

▶Trailhead: From Exit 25 on I-87, head E on NY 8 to the NE end of Brant Lake. After following the main part of the lake, take the first L (N) onto Palisades Rd. (around the N end of the lake), 0.0 mi. After passing a nice old stone barn on the L where there is an L bend in the road, and then the Point O'Pines Farm Rd. soon after on the R, take the next R at 1.5 mi onto Beaver Pond Rd. At 2.6 mi, on a bend, the dirt Pharaoh Lake Rd. cuts off to the R. At 3.1 mi, the road reaches the wilderness boundary and a parking lot. From this point the DEC considers this road closed to vehicular traffic, but access is not denied. At some time in the future, this point may be the trailhead. It is another 1.1 mi over a very rough road to the trailhead at Mill Brook. This last section of the road is not plowed in the winter.◀

From the Mill Brook parking lot (0.0 mi), the trail heads N across Mill Brook on a nice plank bridge; however, the open area on the other side of Mill Brook may often be flooded with knee-deep water for about 300 ft. The trail register (which is sometimes missing) is in the woods along the trail just after the wet area ends. The trail soon follows an old tote road on a gradual grade NE through attractive woods.

At 1.2 mi, the trail bears R and crosses a bridge over a stream. A spur before the bridge to the L leads to an evergreen knoll with an informal campsite that overlooks the beaver pond and large wetland. After crossing the bridge the trail swings L and uphill on the tote road again, with occasional views of Pharaoh Mt. to the N. At 2 mi, the road begins descending, soon joining a stream on the L.

An unmaintained footpath enters on the R at 2.4 mi. To the L but poorly marked at this point is the end of the Sucker Brook Trail (trail 40) from Adirondack. The footbridge at the outlet of Pharaoh Lake is reached at 2.5 mi. The Sucker Brook Trail spur foot trail intersects just beyond the bridge. This is also the intersection with the Pharaoh Mt. Trail (trail 17) and the East Shore Trail (36).

❋ Trail in winter: Flat, wide, and excellent for skiing and snow-shoeing.

🀄 Distance: Mill Brook to bridge and campsite spur, 1.2 mi; to Pharaoh Lake outlet trail, 2.5 mi (4 km).

36 East Shore of Pharaoh Lake

Trails Illustrated Map 743: R28–29

This is a fine trail along the E shore of Pharaoh Lake with some great views of the lake and the surrounding mountains. It passes by three lean-tos and the trails to Whortleberry Pond (trail 39) and Springhill Ponds (trail 37). It's also the connector trail between Mill Brook and the Putnam Pond and Crane Pond area via the Grizzle Ocean Trail (trail 30) and the Glidden Marsh Trail (19).

▶Trailhead: The trail starts at the jct. with the Mill Brook Trail (35) and the Pharaoh Mt. Trail (trail 17) by the outlet bridge at the S end of Pharaoh Lake. The trail is marked with yellow markers.◀

From the trail jct. (0.0 mi), the trail goes uphill to the R, crossing the clearing and into the woods on the E side of the lake. At 0.4 mi, Lean-to 1 is on the lakeside. From the lean-to are nice views across the lake to Treadway Mt. At the top of the hill beyond the lean-to on the main trail on the R side is the unmaintained side trail for Whortleberry Pond (trail 39).

The trail soon crosses open bedrock with bracken, blueberry bushes, reindeer moss, and trailing arbutus. At 0.7 mi, Lean-to 2 is set back in the woods on the L. The trail is now narrow and alluring with views of the lake and Pharaoh Mt. In a short distance, at 0.8 mi, the cutoff for Springhill Ponds (trail 37) is on the R. Bear L to continue around the shore of the lake. In about 500 ft, the trail reaches a spur to a small point on the lake. Lean-to 3 used to be here, but has been moved over a mile farther along the trail.

The main trail heads R and soon crosses a couple of rocky bluffs with nice views across the lake. After climbing over a huge rock, the trail drops and crosses a bridge. Soon after going along another high bluff that faces a cove and some islands, the trail reaches another promontory at 1.3 mi. From this point there is a beautiful panorama of the lake, the islands, and the surrounding mountains. The trail then enters woods of cedars, hemlocks, and pines. After contouring along a steep hillside with red pines, the trail reaches an informal path to Lean-to 3 on the L at a point at 1.9 mi. There's good swimming and great views of the lake and surrounding mountains from the ledge beyond the lean-to.

Turning R, the trail follows a large bay, crosses an inlet, and then wanders through some boulders. After crossing a rocky stream near the shoreline, it crosses the bridge over the outlet from Wolf Pond at 2.3 mi. From here there's a fine view of Wintergreen Point across the water lily-filled bay. At 2.4 mi the trail reaches its N end at the jct. with the Glidden Marsh Trail (trail 19) straight ahead and the Grizzle Ocean Trail (trail 30) on the R.

🐾 Distances: Outlet at S end of Pharaoh Lake to Lean-to 1, 0.4 mi; to Springhill Ponds Trail (trail 37), 0.8 mi; to Glidden Marsh trail (19) and Grizzle Ocean Trail (trail 30) at NE end of Pharaoh Lake, 2.4 mi (3.8 km).

37 Springhill Ponds

Trails Illustrated Map 743: Q–R29

Springhill Ponds is an interesting destination and a desirable one for those who wish a bit more solitude than the usually popular Pharaoh Lake area affords. The round-trip from the Pharaoh Rd. parking lot at Mill Brook is 15.4 mi, so it is not a casual or late-start trip. It would be more feasible for a party camped at one of the Pharaoh Lake lean-tos or as a camping destination itself. Hikers should be prepared for wet going in many places and occasional overgrown sections. With less human presence, opportunities for observing wildlife are much improved and signs of their activity are more evident than in the Pharaoh Lake vicinity.

▶ Trailhead: The Springhill Ponds trail departs R from the yellow-marked trail around the E shore of Pharaoh Lake (trail 36), 0.8 mi from the outlet bridge (and

3.3 mi from the trail register at Mill Brook), by Lean-to 2 near the lake. ◀

Leaving the East Shore of Pharaoh Lake trail (36), the trail is initially well marked with red markers. It zigzags around in an E direction to find the driest ground. After 0.2 mi, the trail crosses a small stream and starts to ascend. At this point it is a wide path through an attractive hemlock forest and shows few signs of heavy use by man or beast.

Continuing to ascend, the trail now enters a shallow divide with a rock outcropping on the R. At 0.5 mi, it reaches a height of land and a wet area. The trail is now harder to follow. Bear along the L side among the rocks. Soon afterward it begins a gradual descent through deciduous growth, still traveling E. When leaf cover is light the rocky bulk of Thunderbolt Mt. is visible through the trees, slightly to the L.

After 1 mi, the trail enters a glen of conifers where new growth narrows the path, giving it a more intimate feel. Soon afterwards, it crosses a stream and turns to the SE. It now climbs steeply but briefly above the stream and resumes an E direction.

In a now familiar pattern, the trail once again descends to a wet area. It edges around to the S and at 1.5 mi crosses the largest stream since leaving Pharaoh Lake. In spring or other wet periods, the crossing may result in wet feet. Easier crossing is to be found downstream rather than upstream.

Leaving the stream, the trail ascends gently, going from evergreens into a mature deciduous growth. Occasionally the open rocks along the length of Thunderbolt Mt. can be seen more closely to the NE.

The trail has been showing progressively less and less usage and by now the secondary growth is often waist-high and footsteps less secure. After climbing gradually for some distance, the trail enters a cozy glen of hemlocks and a shallow depression. It emerges at a large bog and follows its R bank. The going is level now and offers easy and soft travel over pine needles.

Leaving the bog, the trail parallels a nice feeder stream on the L at roughly 2.1 mi. Several rocks offer good resting spots with the murmur of the stream as background music. Continuing S, the path again becomes quite overgrown. At 2.7 mi, it passes through a cut made in a fallen tree. The walking becomes more level now and, unfortunately, wetter. As the trail climbs slightly, a stream enters from the L and crosses the trail.

Not long afterward the sound of a larger stream is heard. Follow it upstream to the E. The route is now on an old road, which becomes gullied ascending to a crossing with a small set of falls on Spuytenduivel Brook. At 3.5 mi, the path is narrow again and ascends quite steeply from the brook, with thick undergrowth. At the top, the trail is quite indistinct. Turn R and cross a feeder stream. The path bears L shortly and passes through another wet area where trail markers are few and far between amid much low growth.

Turning R and due E, the trail follows a washed-out roadbed steadily uphill and reaches the turnoff for Springhill Ponds on the L (N) at 4 mi. The yellow trail to West Hague Rd. (trail 39) goes straight ahead here.

The remaining 0.4 mi to Springhill Ponds involves three more stream crossings, the last being the hardest. Looking upstream from the last one, a very large beaver dam can be seen. After a final rise, the trail descends to the SE shore of the larger Springhill Pond at 4.4 mi. A smaller pond is to the E. An informal fisherman's trail continues around the E shore. On its W end, an attractive rocky promontory with pines overlooks the pond.

🚶 Distances: Pharaoh Lake to small stream, 0.2 mi; to large stream, 1.5 mi; to falls on Spuytenduivel Brook, 3.5 mi; to Springhill Ponds from the South Trail (trail 38), 4 mi; to larger Springhill Pond, 4.4 mi (7 km). Distance from Pharaoh Rd. parking lot at Mill Brook to Springhill Pond, 7.7 mi (12.9 km).

38 Springhill Ponds from the South

Trails Illustrated Map 743: Q29–30

This is a new trail which branches from the Berrymill Flow from the South Trail (33). There is a maze of old logging roads near its start, so be certain to keep your eyes on the yellow trail markers. At its W end, it joins the red-marked trail from Pharaoh Lake to Springhill Ponds (trail 37) to reach these secluded bodies of water.

▶Trailhead: At 0.3 mi on the Berrymill Flow from the South Trail (33).◀

Leaving trail 33 (0.0 mi) to the L at a "Wilderness Area" sign, the yellow-marked trail narrows and parallels a brook to the R and then crosses it on mossy rocks at 0.5 mi. Crossing several smaller watercourses, the trail becomes brushier and continues steadily uphill with the yellow markers.

The trail follows a ridge and crosses a small grassy knoll at 1.4 mi and a moss-covered rock face on the R. Watch carefully for trail markers along this twisty section before descending slightly to join a narrow woods road at 2.3 mi. Bear to the R (the L heads to private land), up and over the ridge to the jct. with the red trail from Pharaoh Lake at 2.7 mi. The yellow trail ends here as the route forks R, following the red markers to the Springhill Ponds (see trail 37).

Trail in winter: Suitable for snowshoeing; skiing would be quite viable except on the middle twisty and steep sections.

🚶 Distances: Trail 33 to grassy knoll and rock face, 1.4 mi; to fork with narrow road, 2.3 mi; to jct. with red trail (trail 37), 3 mi (4.8 km). Continuation to Springhill Ponds via trail 37, 3.4 mi (5.5 km).

39 Whortleberry Pond

Trails Illustrated Map 743: Q28–29

▶Trailhead: The path begins on the East Shore of Pharaoh Lake Trail (36), 120 ft E of a lean-to on the L and privy on the R at the loop trail's 0.4 mi mark. The Whortleberry Pond Trail turns R (S) off the loop trail; coming from the E, one can see a yellow-painted arrow on a hemlock at the start of the path; there are occasional faint yellow paint blazes along it. The large hemlocks have carpeted the forest floor with their needles, so there is no underbrush. This trail is not maintained by DEC, but is easy to follow.◄

Leaving the East Shore Trail (0.0 mi), at 0.2 mi the route turns R above the pond, reaching an inlet brook. Turn L here and follow the trail along the inlet and through the woods to the water's edge at 0.3 mi. Hemlocks and white pines line the shore. A lovely point across the pond on the E side has a bog on its N side. A great blue heron, crows, blue jays, ravens, chickadees, and woodpeckers are among the resident species. Stevens Mt. (elev. 2103 ft) and Little Stevens Mt. are visible S. Bushwhacking is not difficult in these open woods. This secluded pond is a birdwatcher's paradise.

🐾 Distance: East Shore of Pharaoh Lake Trail (36) to Whortleberry Pond, 0.3 mi (0.5 km).

40 Sucker Brook and Desolate Brook Trail to Pharaoh Lake
Trails Illustrated Map 743: Q–R27

▶Trailhead: From the Adirondack General Store in the hamlet of Adirondack on the E shore of Schroon Lake, drive E 0.5 mi on Beaver Pond Rd. to a large sign for the Pharaoh Lake Horse Trail. Turn L at the sign, drive 0.2 mi to a T, then L again for 0.6 mi to a parking lot at a dead end. This is a horse trail marked with yellow markers. A long, remote trail, it may be difficult to follow.◄

An old road leaves the Pharaoh Lake Horse Trail parking lot (0.0 mi) and rises gently, heading N through beautiful woods. At 0.9 mi, the road crosses a stream. Then it goes through a cedar grove. Another small stream intersects the road at 1 mi, and another at 1.3 mi. At 1.4 mi, another old road enters on the L. Continuing straight ahead, the road steadily climbs at a gentle grade.

At 1.6 mi, an old driveway goes up to the R with a stone wall opposite. On the R is the foundation of a farmhouse with a deep cellar. Now the road goes down again. At 1.7 mi and 2.1 mi it crosses streams.

A beaver pond is visible down to the L at 2.5 mi. It is interesting to walk downhill through the woods over an old dump of bottles, cans, and an old cast iron stove to get a better look at the pond. A huge beaver house is along the close shore to the L. This pond is a wide place in Sucker Brook.

Now the old road ends and walking becomes more difficult after a R turn (E) to follow the pass that Sucker Brook flows through. It is necessary to thread your way through the woods on a narrow trail that crosses Sucker Brook at 2.6 mi and again at 2.7 mi, then winds up and over the N side of Orange Hill. At 2.9 mi, the trail starts down again, then up and downhill some more. At 3.3 mi, it crosses Sucker Brook again, generally following the valley of the brook.

At 4.7 mi, the trail makes the first of several turns down the N side of No. 8

Hill, first R, then L, until crossing Desolate Brook at 5 mi.

At 5.1 mi, the trail crosses another branch of Desolate Brook, aptly named, for these are dark, dank woods. Huge hemlocks and maples tower above. A carpet of bunchberry covers the barely discernible trail. At 5.4 mi, it climbs a short hill, with the brook occasionally visible, winding a sinuous course down to the L.

At 5.6 mi, the trail turns R and at 5.8 mi climbs around a low shoulder on the SW side of Pharaoh Mt. At 6.1 mi it starts downhill, crossing a muck hole and climbing briefly before beginning a steep descent through beech woods. The trail crosses a small brook at 6.4 mi in a level stretch among incredibly tall, straight trees.

In the next 0.5 mi the trail crosses several small streams. At 7.1 mi, it goes more steeply uphill, soon leveling out. At 7.4 mi, the trail becomes an old road going downhill to a clearing. The horse trail goes R and then L to a wet crossing of Pharaoh Lake Brook. It meets the Mill Brook Trail (35) at 7.5 mi. On trail 35, it is a few hundred feet L to the picturesque outlet of Pharaoh Lake, the first long-distance view of the trip, and an intersection with the Pharaoh Mt. Trail (trail 17) and the East Shore Trail (36).

A drier crossing of Pharaoh Lake Brook is possible via the foot trail spur at a L turn in the clearing at 7.4 mi. It is a short distance to the bridge on the spillway at the Pharaoh Lake outlet.

A good cross-country ski run would be a trip on the old road from Adirondack to the beaver pond, a round trip of 5.1 mi.

🐾 Distances: To cellar hole, 1.6 mi; to beaver pond, 2.5 mi; to No. 8 Hill, 4.7 mi; to Mill Brook trail (35) and Pharaoh Lake, 7.5 mi (12.1 km). To parking lot at Mill Brook, 10.1 mi (16.9 km).

42 Spectacle Pond

Trails Illustrated Map 743: R27

This is a beautiful and relaxing walk in deep woods.

▶Trailhead: From I-87 Exit 25 (Chestertown–Hague) turn E onto NY 8, then L (N) immediately after the northbound entrance ramp at a brown and yellow sign for Adirondack. After 8 mi, turn L at a T then take the first R at Adirondack General Store. After 5 mi there are State Forest Preserve signs on trees. After another mile there is a wide turnout on the R for the trailhead. A sign says Spectacle Pond, 2 mi. Actually, the walk is a little shorter, at 1.7 mi.◀

There is a yellow DEC trail sign here at the start of this old logging road (0.0 mi), which bends L. At 0.1 mi the trail crosses Spectacle Brook on a bridge. At the end of May there is a profusion of wildflowers in these rich woods: ladyslippers, foamflower, clintonia borealis, jack-in-the-pulpit, and violets. At 0.2 mi, the trail crosses a second bridge over the stream and at 0.5 mi a third bridge.

At 0.6 mi, the trail begins to climb. The stream provides a pleasant companion with its many small cascades, twists, and turns around moss-covered rocks. At

0.9 mi, the trail crosses a small stream. At 1 mi, it passes a wetland, then turns L at 1.2 mi and reaches the foot of Spectacle Pond at 1.3 mi.

At 1.4 mi, the trail comes to beaver dams above and below a bridge over the outlet of the pond. After crossing the bridge, the trail turns L and follows a ridge that ends as a rocky promontory in the pond at 1.7 mi, giving an excellent view of Pharaoh Mt.

※ Distances: Trailhead to third bridge, 0.5 mi; to foot of Spectacle Pond, 1.3 mi; to promontory, 1.7 mi (2.9 km).

43 Gull Pond

Trails Illustrated Map 743: R27

▶Trailhead: Drive N from the Adirondack General Store (see trail 42) 7.1 mi. This is 1.1 mi N of the trailhead for Spectacle Pond (trail 42). The trailhead parking area for Gull Pond is off the road on the R.◀

From the parking area (0.0 mi), the trail goes through deep woods, wet in places, until it climbs a rocky outcrop overlooking Gull Pond at 0.5 mi. This is a jewel of a pond with sheer rock cliffs across on the E side. There are blueberry bushes on the rocks. No camping is permitted at the lookout.

※ Distance: Trailhead parking lot to Gull Pond, 0.5 mi (0.8 km).

44 Cook Mt.

Trails Illustrated Map 743: R31–32

This is the northernmost hike in the Lake George Basin region. From the top are views S to Anthony's Nose, Lake George, and Rogers Rock, with Black Mt. and the Tongue Mt. Range off in the distance. To the E is Mt. Defiance, with Lake Champlain and the Green Mountains beyond. The Cook Mt. Preserve is owned and maintained by the Lake George Land Conservancy and is open to the public for recreational, educational, and scientific purposes. For more information, please contact them at PO Box 1250, Bolton Landing, NY 12814, phone 518-644-9673.

▶Trailhead: Approximately 1 mi S of the monument and traffic circle in Ticonderoga on NY 9N, turn E onto Alexandria Dr. At about 1.2 mi, turn R (S) onto Baldwin Rd. The trailhead is 1.5 mi S on Baldwin Rd. on the R at a gate on an old logging road with Lake George Land Conservancy signs. Just beyond on the L is a state historical marker referring to this area as "Abercrombie's landing, where 15,000 men landed to attack Ticonderoga which was successfully defended by Montcalm in July 1758."◀

From the gate (0.0 mi), the trail follows a grassy old road W toward Cook Mt. In just 0.1 mi a very active beaver flow with several ponds and lodges is on the R. Branches of the trail go on either side of the flow, meeting on the far side. The road soon turns L (S) and begins climbing. At 0.3 mi, it turns R at a Y and then

R again at the next intersection.

In a short distance, an unmarked path leads to the L. Stay straight ahead on the old road, until at 0.5 mi, the trail, marked with red markers, heads sharply L at a sign that says Summit Trail.

From here the well-marked trail climbs at a steady pace up terrain that varies from gradually to moderately steep, ascending a series of small ridges up the side of the mountain through a lovely open hardwood forest of oak, beech, and maple. At 0.8 mi, the trail joins what appears to be an old logging road and turns R (NW), then soon heads more westerly again. A level plateau is at 1 mi, but the trail soon swings L with some rock cairns near a posted private land boundary.

Climbing moderately again, the trail reaches an open area at 1.2 mi. It's pretty here with a variety of mosses, junipers, and pines, and a view to the N above the trees. Before reaching the S end of this open area, the trail takes a sharp L into the woods. From here the hiking is much more gradual. Climbing over a series of small ledges, the trail turns to the R and proceeds in a SE direction up over more small ledges.

The rocky top is at 1.3 mi, with the trail marked mostly by rock cairns. Here there are great views to the S and E above the scrub oaks.

The trail continues S across the rock toward the main part of Lake George, descending gently on an almost indistinct path with red markers, then soon turns R in a more SW direction at 1.4 mi, to a small open ledge S at about 1.7 mi. For the adventurous, the reward is a great outlook over the entire N Lake George basin, with nice views to the E from the open rocky areas along the way. There should be lots of blueberries in season.

❋ Trail in winter: With adequate snow cover, this is a great snowshoe, though rather steep in a few spots. Snowshoe crampons are recommended. Views are great without leaves on the trees.

🐾 Distances: Baldwin Rd. to Summit Trail sign, 0.5 mi; to high point, 1.3 mi; to open ledge at S end of summit, 1.7 mi (2.7 km). Ascent from Baldwin Rd., 895 ft (273 m). Elevation, 1230 ft (375 m).

Rogers Rock *(unmarked footpath, see page 14)*

Trails Illustrated Map 743: Q–R31

This trail is not marked or maintained by DEC, and hikers are advised to proceed at their own risk. It is a very steep trail, so it is not recommended for small children. The view is spectacular.

▶Trailhead: From the hamlet of Hague on Lake George, drive N on NY 9N 4 mi to Rogers Rock State Campground. There is also a beach and boat launch site here. There is a day-use fee in spring, summer, and fall.

After the entrance booth, take a sharp L and drive 1.2 mi to a turnoff on the L for campsites. The trail starts at campsite 210. There is no sign and no markers.◀

Lake George from Rogers Rock. Carl Heilman II

From campsite 210 (0.0 mi), a small, well-defined path climbs gradually past a Private Land sign on a tree, through hemlock, pine, and oak woods. At 0.2 mi it turns L (N) at a boulder slope and follows a small gully along the base of the mountain. At the top of the gully by a boulder on the L, the trail angles R up the face of the mountain. At 0.3 mi, it climbs up a steep ledge.

The first view opens as the trail continues up steeply, with Cooks Bay below on Lake George. From 0.5 mi to 0.7 mi there is a succession of fantastic views along the ridge and, in summer, plenty of blueberries. Now the trail ducks into oak and white pine woods. In season, pale corydalis blooms in the shallow soil on top of the rock shelf. At 0.9 mi, the trail reaches another outlook, then descends to an open rock face at 1 mi. Continue along this rock until the end of the trail at 1.1 mi. It is possible to walk a little farther, but trees obstruct the view and then there is no further passage.

There is a maze of paths across the broad summit N and E of the lookouts. If you try these paths, head W on them until you reach the steep, rocky scramble you came up. Robert Rogers struggled to put on his snowshoes backwards near here and then beat a hasty retreat, successfully fooling the Indians pursuing him. They concluded from the snowshoe tracks that Rogers had fallen to his death over the cliff.

From this perch one can see E to Vermont, S down Lake George, and W to the southern Adirondacks. Along the E shore of Lake George are Anthonys Nose jutting into the lake, Record Hill, South Mt., Spruce Mt., Elephant Mt., and Black Mt.

❄ Trail in winter: This is a steep trail, even for snowshoes. The snow can often be crusted or icy so it's important to have crampons on the snowshoes, or to be able to switch over to just crampons.

🥾 Distances: Campsite 210 to steep ledge, 0.3 mi; to level ridge, 0.5 mi; to Rogers Rock, 1.1 mi (1.8 km). Elevation of Rogers Rock, 1027 ft (313 m).

Cat Mountain. Carl Heilman II

Northwestern Lake George Wild Forest Section

This region is a fairly extensive area with a combination of old roads and some motorized access, and some fine hiking trails. It is bounded by NY 8 on the N, US 9 on the W, and the Warrensburg/Diamond Point area on the S. The shoreline of Lake George forms the E boundary. Along this section of Lake George is the Tongue Mt. Range and some great hiking, with fine views looking into the wildest parts of the lake. While parts of the Tongue Mt. Range are heavily used, more isolated areas, both on Tongue Mt. and in the rest of this region, see very minimal use through the year. Access to some of the region is over very messy 4WD roads, which diminishes the experience at the destination.

A number of the roads in this region head toward good fishing ponds and are great for portaging in a small ultralight canoe. While some of the snowmobile trails are suggested as foot trails, these trails are maintained for winter use and may be quite wet at some times in the spring, summer, and fall, particularly since they are used by ATVs. Trash dumping has gone along with this use, further degrading the setting. Since this is a Wild Forest area, these roads can also be used for mountain biking. Many of them are rather rough and unimproved, so expect a good challenge, not a groomed surface.

The Tongue Mt. area is home to the endangered eastern timber rattlesnake. The snakes are not aggressive and are seldom seen; however, please observe the cautions in the trail descriptions that mention the snakes and remember that this is their home, not ours.

❉ Trails in winter: This region has some nice skiing and snowshoeing possibilities. Most trails, with the exception of the Tongue Mt. region, are great for skiing when there's adequate snow. There is snowmobiling on some of the old roads, and there are snowmobile routes through the region, so you may not have the trail to yourself. These routes, though, are not too heavily used, except sometimes on holiday weekends. Some fresh powder on top of a packed snowmobile trail can make for fine skiing.

The Tongue Mt. area can be pretty rugged for skiing, but most of the trails have gentle, flatter sections. There is some good snowshoeing over the mountains, but be sure to carry crampons for poor snow conditions and ice.

Suggested hikes in the region:

SHORT HIKE:

Deer Leap—1.1 mi (1.8 km) from the Tongue Mt. trailhead to an overlook above Lake George. This is a heavily traveled trail because it is near the road, with views of the lake at the end.

MODERATE HIKE:
Northwest Bay Trail—5 mi (8.7 km) one way. Very pretty and mostly flat along the shoreline. One may hike as far as one chooses and then return to the trailhead.

HARDER HIKE:
Tongue Mt. Traverse—11.8 mi (17.9 km). From NY 9N on the N to Montcalm Point on the S, this is one of the most strenuous and spectacular routes in the eastern Adirondacks. With the Fifth Peak lean-to midway, this can be a fine backpacking trip, or a one-day trip. It's possible to be picked up by boat from Montcalm Point, or one can return to the Clay Meadows trailhead via the Northwest Bay trail for a total of 16.2 mi.

	Trail Described	Total Miles (one way)		Page
46	Lily Pond from Grassville Rd. to NY 8	3.8	(6.1 km)	66
47	Round, Duck, and Buttermilk Ponds	3.8	(6.1 km)	68
48	Buttermilk Loop Trail	2.1	(3.4 km)	70
49	Long and Island Ponds	1.5	(2.4 km)	70
50	Wardsboro Rd. N to S	5.6	(9.0 km)	71
51	Wardsboro Rd. Side Trail	1.5	(2.4 km)	71
52	Jabe Pond	1.0	(1.6 km)	73
53	Tongue Mt. Range Trai	11.2	(17.9 km)	73
54	Deer Leap	1.1	(1.8 km)	76
55	Northwest Bay Trail from Clay Meadow	5.0	(8.7 km)	77
56	Five Mile Point	3.3	(5.3 km)	78
57	Northwest Bay Brook	0.2	(0.3 km)	79
58	Up Yonda Farm Environmental Education Center	various		80

Cat and Thomas Mt. Preserve

59	Thomas Mt. Trail	1.5	(2.4 km)	80
59A	Thomas Mt. Blue Trail	1.0	(1.6 km)	81
60	Cat Mt. Trail	2.6	(4.5 km)	81
61	Richard Hayes Phillips Trail	2.3	(3.7 km)	82

46 Lily Pond from Grassville Rd. to NY 8

Trails Illustrated Map 743: O28

This route is a nice walk, and a great ski in the winter, especially when it's linked with further exploration to Round Pond and Buttermilk Pond via the Round, Duck, and Buttermilk Ponds Trail (47). Some sections of this route are old town roads, open to automobiles, while other sections are snowmobile trails closed to all other motorized vehicles. The area is in theory not traveled by ATVs, though their use is apparent. It's also a great route for an adventurous mountain biker.

There have been plans to upgrade the road into Lily Pond, so this area may see more traffic. The State gained, in 2005, a State Supreme Court ruling that motorized access be stopped. Enforcement of the road closure is an outcome devoutly to be wished, and restoration of the ATV-caused mud wallows and attendant trash dumps along these trails would take a long effort at cleanup by Mother Nature and her offspring.

This description proceeds from the highest trailhead (S) to the lowest for the benefit of skiers.

▶Trailhead: From the Horicon Fire Dept. (0.0 mi) in the hamlet of Brant Lake, follow NY 8 E. At 2.3 mi, turn R (S) onto Grassville Rd. At 1 mi, follow the road sharp R. At 1.9 mi, the road becomes dirt. A small camp, barn, and clearing are at 3 mi. If parking on the private land just past the camp, be sure to ask permission, or park just along the road. It may be better to park along the wider section of road just before reaching the camp. This is the S access.◀

The N trailhead along NY 8 is 3.7 mi beyond Grassville Rd. (6 mi from the Horicon Fire Dept.). After an S-turn on NY 8 with a 25 MPH suggested speed limit, the dirt road to Lily Pond is on the R, just before a fair-sized stream. On the L (N) are cabins along the shore of Brant Lake. The camp named Tak-it-E-Z is just beyond the access road on the L (N), and 0.3 mi past it is Palisades Rd. on the L (N), which winds around the N shoreline of Brant Lake. A small gray garage is on the R (S) side of NY 8, just to the L of the road to Lily Pond. At some time a small parking lot may be built here, but at present (2012), parking is on the shoulder of NY 8.

From the clearing, just beyond the camp (0.0 mi), the road heads gradually downhill. In a short f distance a small stream crosses. At 0.3 mi, another stream crosses along a rock water bar. At 0.4 mi, a DEC trail marker indicates Grassville Rd. to the L. Avoid the L though, as this travels over private lands back to the sharp R turn on Grassville Rd. Follow to the R for the trail to Lily Pond.

The road climbs gradually uphill, then at 0.6 mi drops back down again on a moderate grade. The keen observer will pick out remnants of the long-abandoned homesteads all through this area. At 0.9 mi, the road begins a long gradual descent, passing a snowmobile trail (a wet route in the summer) to Island Pond on the R (S) at 1 mi, and reaching the S shore of Lily Pond at 1.1 mi. Here there is an informal campsite and fire ring at a nice lookout over the pond. Continuing on the road to the E, there is a bridge over an inlet stream, with a lot of beaver activity visible. At a jct. at 1.2 mi, the road to NY 8 heads L (N). The road straight ahead is the Round, Duck, and Buttermilk Ponds Trail (47).

Turn L to go along the E shoreline of the lake on the wide path. In a short f distance the path splits, then rejoins again soon. The L route more closely follows the shoreline, with some nice views of the pond along the way.

After passing over a couple of informal campsites, the trail joins the dirt road from NY 8 at 1.5 mi. Here it is just about 100 ft to an open area on the L overlooking Lily Pond. The pond is pretty, but the foreground has been littered extensively.

Turning R, the dirt road follows but is out of sight of the E shoreline. At 2 mi, it crosses over the outlet of the pond. There has been a lot of beaver activity here in the past, and this section has often been flooded.

The road gradually begins to descend and at 2.3 mi crosses a bridge over the outlet stream, re-crossing it again at 2.5 mi, after passing an old beaver pond. At 2.7 mi, the stream may be heard on the R. From here the road drops steadily at a gradual to moderate rate, then reaches a jct. with an old road joining on the L (W) at 3.1 mi. At 3.5 mi, the road descends again, past a yellow Forest Preserve sign on the R, at a moderate rate almost the whole way to the unmarked jct. with NY 8 at 3.8 mi.

❋ Trail in winter: While this route is frequented by snowmobilers, it can be a delightful ski trip. Additional routes can be included by going to Buttermilk Pond or taking the cutoff to Island Pond (a snowmobile trail not described because of its wet character in the summer).

❋❋ Distances: Grassville Rd. to jct. L to private lands, 0.4 mi; to first outlook over Lily Pond, 1.1 mi; to the Round, Duck, and Buttermilk Ponds Trail (47), 1.2 mi; to road to NY 8, 1.5 mi; to Lily Pond outlet, 2 mi; to NY 8, 3.8 mi (6.1 km).

47 Round, Duck, and Buttermilk Ponds
Trails Illustrated Map 743: O–P28

This can be an enjoyable, though sometimes wet, walk (or bike) to a couple of nice fishing ponds in the Brant Lake area. The terrain is rolling, and the route uses mostly old roads in the area. Evidence of ATV use abounds and is testimony to the destructive power of these machines.

▶Trailhead: This trail begins at the 1.2 mi point on the Lily Pond Trail (46) and heads E along the old road.◀

Continuing straight ahead from the Lily Pond Trail (0.0 mi), the road climbs steadily uphill and at 0.1 mi reaches a jct. The L fork is the Buttermilk Loop Trail (trail 48), a pleasant alternative route to Buttermilk Pond; it rejoins trail 47 and is described below as part of the return loop in this description. To skip Round and Duck ponds for a slightly shorter and drier hike, turn L at this fork and take trail 48 only to Buttermilk Pond.

Continuing straight ahead, the road is now marked with orange DEC snowmobile trail disks. At 0.3 mi a small stream can be heard on the R, and the trail crosses the stream on a bridge at 0.4 mi at a wide, shallow place.

At 0.7 mi, the trail reaches the top of a rise and then starts downhill. At 0.8 mi, it curves L from E to N and goes slightly uphill. At 0.9 mi, it reaches a pile of stones on the L. At 1 mi, the road forks L through a very wet intersection. Stay straight.

After climbing, the trail goes downhill again toward Round Pond. At 1.1 mi, the trail makes a sharp curve L. (A foot trail that is unmarked and unmaintained by DEC but has painted blazes on trees heads off to the R.) The trail heads L and downhill, passing the intersection of the cutoff trail, which branches L at the wet intersection.

Still winding downhill, the trail arrives at lovely Round Pond at 1.3 mi. This is an attractive pond with some rocky shoreline. Minnows warm themselves in the shallows and giant dragonflies patrol the air. A pair of ravens may come flying and squawking overhead.

A small foot trail slightly L goes on to Duck Pond at 1.5 mi after crossing through muddy ruts and blowdown in a cedar swamp. There is a large, flat rock here for a rest and picnic.

Retracing your steps to the jct., turn L at 1.7 mi on another narrow trail marked with snowmobile markers. This leads into a swamp with rotten corduroys. There have been cedars cut (perhaps for a bridge?) near a flooded corduroy with floating logs. It is important to keep watch for the orange snowmobile trail markers since the trail is faint.

At 1.8 mi, the trail crosses a stream on stones. It soon reaches a wooden snowmobile trail sign pointing S.

At the intersection with the snowmobile sign, the route L connects to the trail to Buttermilk Pond. The trail goes through cedars following orange snowmobile trail markers. At 2.4 mi, it reaches open rock with moss, bracken, and young balsam firs. At 2.6 mi, the faint trail is in a low, dark, and wet cedar swamp with a rocky hill on the R. At 2.7 mi, it curves R and into a birch grove. Now the path is barely discernible.

At 2.8 mi, the trail recombines with the Buttermilk Loop Trail (48). The L route turns NE and then swings SW toward Lily Pond. R is Buttermilk Pond. The snowmobile signs are orange.

The road heads uphill through a pass. At 3 mi, the trail reaches a crest. It is growing over with beech and striped maple saplings. Now the trail goes level through huge ferns, birch, beech, and maple. At 3.4 mi, it turns abruptly L after descending from the end of the ridge, and then crosses a stream. Now it turns sharply R downhill along the stream.

The trail passes two small ponds R and leads through a glade of hay-scented ferns. At 3.7 mi, Buttermilk Pond can be seen ahead, and moments later the trail reaches the S end of the pond. To the L is an unmarked ATV path along the shore. At 3.8 mi there is a huge beaver lodge along the shore. A small point to the L with huge white pines and a large rocky bluff on the opposite shore make this a picturesque and peaceful spot.

❀ Trail in winter: Suitable for snowshoeing and cross country skiing, but snowmobile use may be heavy.

❀ Distances: To W end of Buttermilk Loop Trail (trail 48), 0.1 mi; to Round Pond, 1.3 mi; to Duck Pond, 1.5 mi; to E end of Buttermilk Loop Trail, 2.8 mi; to Buttermilk Pond, 3.8 mi (6.1 km).

48 Buttermilk Loop Trail

Trails Illustrated Map 743: O-P28

This trail is an "express" route to Buttermilk Pond, bypassing Round and Duck Ponds. Because it provides a variation on the return hike from Buttermilk Pond, it is described here in that direction (E to W).

▶Trailheads: Interior trail, with trailheads at 0.1 mi (W end) and 2.8 mi (E end) on the Round, Duck, and Buttermilk Ponds Trail (47). The trail is described from E to W.◀

An unnamed pond glistens on the R just before the E trailhead. Just past this jct., where there is bare rock for the roadbed (a pleasure after several miles of faint and wet trails), one can walk 300 ft to the R on a small trail to the edge of this pond. Brush around the edge obscures the view, but it might be a good place to fish.

The trail, in fact an old road, heads first NW (there are pink ladyslippers here in early June) and then SW through lovely woods. It is marked with yellow snowmobile markers and is a bit less marred by the ruts from 4WD vehicles than is trail 47. At 0.8 mi, the road is bare rock after passing a square stone foundation R.

At 1 mi, the road crosses a bridge of stone slabs and goes through an old farm clearing with an apple tree. The walking is level. At 1.9 mi, the road passes a large old apple tree and then a pile of rocks on the L. At 2.1 mi, it rejoins Round, Duck, and Buttermilk Ponds Trail (47). Turn R here to reach the Lily Pond Trail (46) in 0.1 mi.

❊ Trail in winter: Suitable for cross-country skiing and snowshoeing.

🐾 Distances: E trailhead to stone slab bridge, 1 mi; to W trailhead, 2.1 mi (3.4 km).

49 Long and Island Ponds

Trails Illustrated Map 743: O28

Long Pond is a good fishing spot, but swimming is not recommended because of leeches. They range in size from 1/16 inch to 5 inches and are quick to establish a relationship. The pond is used mostly by anglers. Beavers are quite active here. A short connector trail leads from Long Pond to Island Pond, where in winter a snowmobile trail leads from the NW corner of the pond up to Lily Pond.

▶Trailhead: From Brant Lake Fire Station, drive E 1.7 mi on NY 8 to Duell Hill Rd. on the R. Turn up this steep road and continue on it for 3.1 mi, passing Orin Duell Rd., Jim Youngs Rd., Streeter Pond Rd., Harris Rd., and Granger Rd. Now turn L. This is called the Padanarum Spur Rd. After 1 mi, the road reaches a green camp called "Cirlew." Here the road turns to a narrow track that is not maintained from December 1 to April 1. Continue another 0.8 mi down this narrow dirt road to the trailhead for Long Pond on the L. (0.0 mi.) It is an old road going uphill to a gate, an orange DEC snowmobile disk, a trail sign for the two

ponds, and a DEC fishing sign. There is a small space to park on the L just before the gate. ◀

From the trailhead (0.0 mi), the old road on the L (N) goes straight uphill along a washed-out section for 0.1 mi. The trail levels out, and then there is a series of huge mud holes made by vehicles. At 0.3 mi, a new wide side trail has been cut on the L around a large wet area, the first of several similar detours.

At 0.5 mi, the road descends gently to another wet spot, and then climbs into pines. At 0.8 mi, it goes up, then at 0.9 mi levels off in birch, white pine, hemlock, balsam, and maple woods.

At 1 mi, the road curves L 90 degrees. At 1.1 mi, there is a trail sign L to Island Pond (see below). The R fork leads in 0.1 mi to the S end of Long Pond, after a descent of 250 ft. Beavers have raised the pond level considerably. There is an informal campsite here.

The continuation to Island Pond is interrupted by a beaver flow (2012) on the trail. At 1.5 mi, it reaches a flooded edge of pretty Island Pond, which seems to be completely filled in, perhaps the work of beavers. Both ponds are fun to explore in a small ultralight canoe.

🚶 Distances: Padanarum Spur Rd. to Long Pond spur, 1.1 mi; to Island Pond, 1.5 mi (2.4 km). Round trip spur to Long Pond, 0.2 mi.

50 Wardsboro Rd. from N to S
51 Wardsboro Rd. Side Trail

Trails Illustrated Map 743: P29–30

This trail follows an old road that passes through some nice wild land in the NE part of this region. The N section travels through some private lands, including some timber lands, but there is a public easement to use the road. Approximately the first half mile has been built up to a hard road surface for logging trucks, but the road becomes more of a trail after this. This is a great route for skiing (park a car at both the N and S ends of the trail). There is no public access to Swede Pond or Swede Mt.

▶Trailhead: The N trailhead is on NY 8, 1 mi E of the E end of North Pond (approx. 10 mi E of the firehouse in the hamlet of Brant Lake and about 1 mi W of the hamlet of Graphite). Soon after North Pond, a rock painted to resemble an elephant is on the R. A posted logging header is on the R. In about 0.1 mi, take a sharp R onto Fly Brook Rd. Park on the R side of Fly Brook Rd.

To reach the S trailhead, drive 5 mi E from I-87 Exit 24 to NY 9N, then turn L (N) and drive 6 mi. to Padanarum Rd. (dirt) on the L. At 1.8 mi, cross a bridge, then turn R onto Wardsboro Rd. and drive to a parking turnout across from a red cabin at 3.4 mi. The old Wardsboro cemetery can be seen here. Be sure to respect the private property here.◀

From the N trailhead (0.0 mi), walk along Fly Brook Rd. past an intersection on the R with the gated logging heading. Continue ahead, walking gently uphill to a L (S) turn onto a side road at 0.4 mi. This is the N end of the Wardsboro road.

The logging is soon left behind and the road becomes less rutted. Bear L up the hill, until at 0.9 mi the road reaches the top of the hill and bears R (S). At 1.1 mi, at a fork, the main trail is on the R, while the Wardsboro Rd. Side Trail (trail 51) heads to the L (see below). Stay on the main trail.

The road soon heads downhill and comes to a stream on the L at 1.6 mi. At 2.2 mi, there is a large detour around a big beaver pond, and a second jct. with trail 64A is at 2.3 mi.

The Wardsboro Rd. Side Trail (trail 51) heads L from its N jct. with the main trail (0.0 mi), and descends gradually at first, then more steeply. At 0.4 mi, there is a jct. with an old road on the L. Heading to the R, the road becomes eroded and then soon levels off at 0.7 mi. The road descends again to the jct. with the main trail by the beaver pond at 1.5 mi. It is 0.3 mi longer than the equivalent section of trail 50.

From the S jct. of trails 50 and 51, below the beaver pond, the road passes over some rolling terrain with some wet sections and reaches a stream at 2.7 mi. The road varies from level to muddy to rolling, and passes occasional beaver handiwork.

At 3.8 mi, there is another stream crossing. The road descends on a gradual grade and at 4.3 mi reaches a cabin on the L. There are some signs of logging, and then the road descends alongside a hill with a pretty glen down to the L at 4.6 mi.

After a stone bridge over the outlet of Spectacle Ponds, a small green house on the R is at 5 mi. At 5.4 mi, orange markers on the trees on the L announce that the stream is a nursery for Atlantic landlocked salmon. The old Wardsboro cemetery is just ahead at 5.6 mi.

🥾 Distances: Parking along Fly Brook Rd. to L turn onto Wardsboro Rd., 0.4 mi; to N jct. with trail 51, 1.1 mi; to S jct. with trail 51, 2.3 mi; to cabin, 4.3 mi; to Wardsboro cemetery, 5.6 mi (9 km). Length of trail 51, 1.5 mi (2.4 km).

52 Jabe Pond
Trails Illustrated Map 743: P30

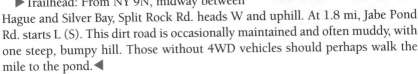

Jabe Pond is a fairly recent and nice addition to the Forest Preserve and has 4WD access.

▶ Trailhead: From NY 9N, midway between Hague and Silver Bay, Split Rock Rd. heads W and uphill. At 1.8 mi, Jabe Pond Rd. starts L (S). This dirt road is occasionally maintained and often muddy, with one steep, bumpy hill. Those without 4WD vehicles should perhaps walk the mile to the pond. ◀

The pond has good canoeing, with a twisty shoreline and islands to explore. It is surrounded by low mountains in a lovely setting. There are designated campsites, and small motors of 10 horsepower or less are allowed on boats. An old road on the W shore leads to a herd path with Little Jabe Pond 0.3 mi away.

❄ Trail in winter: Jabe Pond Rd. is not plowed in winter, providing good snowshoe or ski access to the pond.

🥾 Distance: Split Rock Rd. to Jabe Pond, 1 mi (1.6 km).

53 Tongue Mt. Range Trail
Trails Illustrated Map 743: M–N29

This trail traverses the rugged backbone of the Tongue Mt. Range, which extends into the mid-section of Lake George, bounded by the shoreline of Northwest Bay on the W and the narrows of Lake George on the E. Views from open rocky sections along the trail looking to the lake and the mountains beyond are quite inspiring. The streams in the lower sections of this trail are seasonal. The trail can be quite dry for its entire length. Be sure to carry plenty of water.

This region is also home to the eastern timber rattlesnake, a threatened species in New York State. It's a treat to be able to see them in their natural habitat in one of the few places in the state where they may be found. They are not aggressive, and are seldom seen, but it's wise to take a few precautions. Wear high-top boots and use caution when approaching rocky ledges and warm sunny places. Remember, though, that rattlesnakes can be found anywhere on the mountain. It's important never to tease or corner a rattler. If you give them a wide berth and leave them alone, they'll leave you alone. Because its range and population are limited, the timber rattlesnake is protected under New York State law. It is illegal to kill, take, or possess this species without a special DEC permit.

Winter on Tongue Mt. James Appleyard

▶Trailhead: From I-87 Exit 24, drive 5 mi E to NY 9N. (Just before NY 9N, there are great views from the road of the Tongue Mt. Range, Lake George, and the surrounding mountains.) Driving N on NY 9N (0.0 mi), the Clay Meadow trailhead is at 4.7 mi on the R. Continue N on 9N until at 9.5 mi the N trailhead for the Tongue Mt. Range appears on the R (E). There are blue markers along this trail.◀

From the parking area along the road (0.0 mi), the trail at first heads W, somewhat parallel to NY 9N. In about 500 ft, the trail turns L, away from a tote road, and soon begins to climb. Some of this section is eroded and may be wet. At 0.6 mi, there is a jct. with the yellow-marked Deer Leap trail (54) on the L.

The trail continues climbing steadily, up and over Brown Mt., and reaches an overlook just off the trail at 1.7 mi. The forest varies from hardwoods to hemlocks as the trail reaches a small clearing at 2 mi. At 2.4 mi, the trail follows rock cairns across a stretch of open rock, enters the woods, and then begins climbing again across more open rock with cairns. The Tongue Mt. Camp lean-to is at 2.6 mi. There is a fine view from the lean-to area.

Past the lean-to, a couple of good views look N and W. There's much more open rock underfoot, and there are lots of blueberries in season. Cairns mark the trail.

The trail passes through some red pines, descends to a ridge, and at 3.3 mi reaches a small clearing. The trail soon climbs up and over the ledges near the top of Five Mile Mt., reaching the top at 3.5 mi. Summit elevation, 2258 ft.

From the top, the trail descends slightly and then climbs over a couple of rocky outcrops. There are occasional views to the E, S, and W. Be sure to keep in mind the rattlesnakes, and be careful where you put your hands. The trail continues its descent, passing a couple of interesting boulders along the way, reaching a stream (maybe dry) at 4.4 mi. After a couple of small level sections, and some downhill switchbacks, the trail crosses another small stream just before the intersection at the Saddle at 5.2 mi. The E/W trail is the Five Mile Point Trail (56). From this point it is 1.9 mi W along the Five Mile Point Trail to the Clay Meadow trailhead, and 1.7 mi E to the shoreline of Lake George.

Heading straight ahead (SW) toward Fifth Peak, the trail climbs slightly, descends into a glen, and then winds, heading E and then S again. Soon some old stonework along the trail is a reminder of the old CCC days. The trail is cut into the hill and rises steadily along a steep hillside, reaching the yellow-marked uphill spur trail for the Fifth Peak Lean-to at 5.6 mi. The fairly new lean-to is about a quarter mile off the main trail. It faces away from the fabulous view as protection from the winds. There's a great view to the E, S, and W, with a view of French Point Mt. farther down the trail.

The main trail continues S, passes a steep rock face, and soon heads uphill more steeply. At 5.8 mi, it passes a small pool at the base of a cliff, and soon traverses a fairly level enclosed ridge. At 6 mi, it passes the site of a fire in the summer of 1985. The undergrowth has pretty well taken over again.

The trail heads downhill at a stone outcrop and soon comes to a good view of the lake and Black Mt. on the E side. French Point Mt. is to the S with First Peak farther S and to the R.

After passing a rock cairn, at 6.3 mi the trail makes a sharp L at a burned-out tree, and soon reaches a lookout with a good view of Northwest Bay. The trail soon drops sharply W and then follows downhill along a rock wall.

At 6.5 mi, there is a sign to turn R. An old unmarked trail used this col from E to W at this point. The range trail follows the sign to the R and goes uphill through hemlocks. Black Mt. is visible across the lake once again.

The trail climbs steeply again, and at 6.7 mi reaches the top of Third Peak. After crossing some open rock ledges facing S, the trail reaches a precipitous drop and then another outlook. After heading down past a L arrow with a white marker and passing a rock cairn, the trail heads into some beeches and then begins to switchback up French Point Mt., reaching the top at 7.5 mi. The summit elevation is 1739 ft. A short f distance to the S on the trail there's a great view of The Narrows of Lake George, and the whole southern panorama.

The trail heads S over bare rock with faint, light blue paint blazes and soon reaches another lookout. At 7.8 mi, the trail crosses open rock with ledges on the E, with some fine views. It passes a tiny pond and another S outlook, and continues following the blue-blazed rock, heading directly SW toward Northwest Bay.

At 8 mi, the trail descends steeply through a boulder field. After traversing toward the E, it soon turns and heads W and drops steeply to a small stream before climbing again. The trail passes through some huge oaks, comes to another lookout, then undulates up to the top of First Peak at 8.9 mi.

The trail switchbacks down the S side of First Peak through some scrubby oaks and soon comes to a grassy section with a view of the Point of Tongue at 9.6 mi. The route passes another couple of fine views, then turns W through some junipers and at 10 mi goes through a narrow cleft of rock with a slanted side before leveling off for a short f distance. After passing a rocky opening with a good view, the trail descends a steep pitch before climbing to a fine view to the E from the top of a flat rock.

The trail descends to another outlook and then enters the deep woods. It begins to level off and soon reaches the jct. with the Northwest Bay Trail (trail 55) at 10.8 mi. Turning L to go to the tip of the point, at 11 mi there's a trail jct. for the state boat dock. Turning R, the trail reaches Montcalm Point at 11.2 mi. From here it's a nice boat ride back to the "mainland," or a 5 mi walk back from the jct. to the Clay Meadows trailhead via the Northwest Bay Trail (trail 55).

❄ Trail in winter: Novice skiing as far as the Deer Leap jct. except for one fast hill on the return; easy snowshoeing. Advanced-level skiing and moderate snowshoeing as far as Five Mile Mt. Beyond Five Mile Mt., both skiing and snowshoeing become strenuous and are best as part of a multi-day trip.

🐾 Distances: NY 9N trailhead to Deer Leap Trail (54), 0.6 mi; to Tongue Mt. Camp Lean-to, 2.6 mi; to summit of Five Mile Mt., 3.5 mi; to Five Mile Point Trail (55), 5.2 mi; to cutoff for Fifth Peak Lean-to, 5.6 mi; to French Point Mt., 7.5 mi; to Northwest Bay Trail (trail 55), 10.8 mi (17.2 km); to Montcalm Point, 11.2 mi (17.9 km). Elevation at trailhead, 1065 ft (325 m); Five Mile Mt., 2256 ft (688 m); Fifth Peak, 1813 ft (553 m); French Point Mt., 1756 ft (535 m); Lake George, 320 ft (97.5 m). Total trail ascent from N to S, approx. 2680 ft (817 m).

54 Deer Leap

Trails Illustrated Map 743: N–O30

This is a short spur trail that leads from the Tongue Mt. Range Trail (trail 53) to some nice lookouts over the mid-Lake George area. There are many more spectacular views from along the Tongue Mt. Trail, but the advantage of this trail is its short length. This is a fairly heavily used trail. The same cautions about rattlesnakes as described at the beginning of trail 53 pertain here, too.

▶Trailhead: The yellow-marked trail begins at 0.6 mi S of the NY 9N trailhead for the Tongue Mt. Range Trail (trail 53).◀

From the jct. with the Tongue Mt. Range Trail (0.0 mi), the trail heads E. After reaching an outlook at 0.3 mi, it rolls up and down over a couple of hills. After crossing an oak meadow at 0.8 mi, it arrives at a rocky opening overlooking Lake George at 1.1 mi. Here there's a view across the lake to the hamlet of Huletts Landing on the E shore, with Sugarloaf Mt. above it and Black Mt. looming to its R.

❄ Trail in winter: Excellent snowshoeing; several narrow, twisty hills make deep snow a must for advanced skiers.

🐾 Distance: Trail 53 to Deer Leap, 1.1 mi (1.8 km). Elevation of Deer Leap, approx. 1100 ft (335 m).

55 Northwest Bay Trail from Clay Meadow

Trails Illustrated Map 743: M–N29

This is an extremely pleasant section of trail that is not used much. It often borders the lake and was originally built as a horse trail by the CCC, but that plan was abandoned once rattlesnakes were discovered. Please read the caution regarding rattlesnakes at the beginning of trail 53.

▶Trailhead: From I-87 Exit 24, drive 5 mi E to NY 9N. The steep hill down to NY 9N gives a good view of the undulating ridgeline of Tongue Mt. to the NE. Drive 4.7 mi N on NY 9N to a parking area on the R at an old quarry. (When this lot is full, you may find additional parking space a short f distance N on the R.) About 100 ft (S) downhill along the road is the Clay Meadow trailhead for Tongue Mt., with a register. The trail is marked with blue markers. ◀

Timber Rattlesnake. Cheryl Miller

From the register (0.0 mi), the trail goes downhill through a grove of white pines planted by the CCC in the 1930s. It crosses a long plank bridge over a stream at 0.2 mi, alongside a beaver dam. At 0.4 mi, it reaches a jct. Straight ahead is the Five Mile Point Trail (56) to The Saddle, Fifth Peak Lean-to, the Ridge Trail and Five Mile Mt. Point on the E side of the mountain. The Northwest Bay Trail to Point of Tongue is to the R.

At 0.5 mi, the trail crosses a bridge over a stream with moss-covered rocks. At 0.7 mi, it begins to go up gradually, crossing a stream on stones, then heads uphill and into a hemlock grove alongside another picturesque stream, which it crosses. The trail becomes steeper and washed out at 0.9 mi. It reaches the top of the steep pitch at 1.1 mi, then goes downhill and crosses a plank bridge over another beautiful stream. At 1.5 mi, it goes downhill through a deeply shaded hemlock glen.

At 1.7 mi, the trail reaches the marshy head of Northwest Bay. At 1.8 mi, it crosses a stream on another plank bridge. Then it goes up alongside a hill by the shoreline under large hemlocks with a fantastic mossy cliff on the L. At 2 mi, a spur trail R goes 200 ft to Bear Point, where there is a nice view into Northwest Bay and down Lake George. At 2.1 mi, the trail reaches a high bluff where people have camped. Then it comes downhill and crosses another stream on a bridge at 2.2 mi.

At 2.4 mi, the trail passes a point with a fire circle. At 2.5 mi, it crosses a dry stony brook, then climbs steeply up and then down along a mossy cliff, crossing a bridge. It reaches a small point with a fire circle at 2.6 mi, then goes uphill and under hemlocks, almost level with the lake shore. This is a beautiful stretch of trail, close to the water.

At 2.7 mi, there is a nice rock to swim from. At 3.1 mi, the trail reaches an opening along the shore with a fire circle. This is also a good place for swimming. At 3.2 mi, it crosses on a log over a stream that cascades 12 ft down huge mossy blocks of rock.

At 3.4 mi, the trail crosses another stream on rocks. At 4 mi, it goes uphill, then down steeply to cross a muddy stream and then through a large wet area. At 4.2 mi, it descends a hill and crosses a seasonally dry brook.

The very narrow trail goes along a steep hillside just above the shore. At 4.5 mi, the trail cuts away from the clear lake and goes steeply uphill among jumbled rocks. Then it comes down steeply at 4.7 mi. At 4.8 mi, there is an opening on the shore. At 4.9 mi, the trail crosses a small stream.

At 5 mi, the trail reaches a jct. with the Tongue Mt. Range Trail (trail 53). To the L, French Point Mt. is 2.9 mi, Fifth Peak Lean-to is 6.2 mi, and the Tongue Mt. trailhead is 11.4 mi. Point of Tongue is straight ahead.

At 5.2 mi, the trail divides. A state dock is about 80 yd to the L on the E side of the point. There is a lovely view of The Narrows from here, as well as islands and Black Mt. and Shelving Rock Mt. (see Southeastern Lake George Wild Forest Section). S is Dome Island (a bird sanctuary owned by The Nature Conservancy), and SW is the elegant Sagamore Hotel on Green Island. Point of Tongue is a good place for a picnic and a swim at 5.4 mi (8.6 km).

❄ Trail in winter: Mostly wide and smooth, for easy and delightful snowshoeing. Intermediate skiers will be challenged only by a few fast, twisty hills.

🎿 Distances: Clay Meadow trailhead to Five Mile Point Trail, 0.4 mi; to Bear Point, 2 mi; to log bridge, 3.2 mi; to Tongue Mt. Range Trail, 5 mi; to state dock, 5.2 mi; to Point of Tongue, 5.4 mi (8.6 km).

56 Five Mile Point

Trails Illustrated Map 743: N29

This is a pretty route that connects with the Tongue Mt. Range Trail (trail 53) for reasonable-length climbs of Five Mile Mt. and French Point Mt. It then continues down the E side of the Tongue Mt. Range to the shoreline of Lake George. This is a great place to swim on a hot summer day. There are many wildflowers along the trail, and blueberries in season (around open rocky sections). Please read the caution about rattlesnakes at the beginning of the description of trail 53.

▶Trailhead: The start is at a jct. with the Northwest Bay Trail (trail 57) 0.4 mi E of the Clay Meadow trailhead. The trail has red markers.◀

From the jct. (0.0 mi), the trail heads directly uphill. In a short f distance, a side trail branches R to a pretty waterfall that drops more than 100 ft over a series of boulders and ledges.

Continuing up, after crossing a stream at 0.3 mi, the trail becomes steep again. The trail crosses and then recrosses a stream on a couple of plank bridges, and at 0.9 mi begins a series of switchbacks up a steep and rocky hemlock-covered hill.

The trail reaches a plateau at 1 mi, but turns abruptly uphill again at 1.2 mi. At 1.3 mi, the grade moderates along the brook, still on the L. After a level along a moss-covered cliff with overhanging polypody ferns, there's yet another switchback before The Saddle intersection at 1.6 mi, 1180 ft above Lake George. The N-S trail is the Tongue Mt. Range Trail (trail 53). Five Mile Mt. is 1.7 mi to the L (N), and French Point Mt. 2.4 mi to the R (S).

Continuing straight ahead across the intersection, the trail is fairly level, passing a marshy section at 1.7 mi by hugging the R shoreline. The trail soon turns R and begins descending, leveling off briefly at 2.5 mi. It swings N, passes a small brook, and then turns S again.

Descending through a grassy area, there are views to Black Mt., Mother Bunch Islands, and Huletts Landing, with another lookout at 2.6 mi, just off the trail. The trail now descends through shrub oaks, junipers, and some cedars along an old horse path that was built up with some fine stonework. After a short, steep descent along some ledges and steep rock, the trail levels and enters a stand of maples and oaks. The descent is now much more gradual with lots of wildflowers along the grassy trail.

After crossing a small stream, the trail swings L and reaches Five Mile Point at 3.3 mi. The rock that descends into the lake can be nice for swimming, and makes a good landing place for a boat. Black Mt. seems to rise directly out of the water, Erebus Mt. is to the R of it, and Hatchet Island is straight ahead. To the N are the Harbor Islands, Sabbath Day Point, the cliffs of Deer Leap, and Spruce Mt.

❋ Trail in winter: The route has enough steep, twisty sections to make it a challenging snowshoe trip and an expert-level ski trip.

❀ Distances: Northwest Bay Trail (trail 55) to Tongue Mt. Range Trail (trail 53), 1.6 mi; to Five Mile Point, 3.3 mi (5.3 km). Total f distance from Clay Meadow trailhead, 3.7 mi (6 km).

57 Northwest Bay Brook

Trails Illustrated Map 743: N29

This brook has some steep cascades just before it joins Northwest Bay. The short walk through a grove of pines planted by the CCC in the 1930s is pleasant.

▶Trailhead: After parking at the quarry for the Clay Meadow trailhead (see trail 55), walk across NY 9N and downhill 100 ft to a wooden gate with a stop sign.◀

From the gate (0.0 mi), the route goes under tall pines on a wide path, continuing 0.2 mi to the edge of a steep hill and then down about 50 ft to a waterfall on Northwest Bay Brook. Herd paths border a nice long flume below the falls; they head back E toward the highway, so a short loop is possible to and from the parking area.

❀ Distance: NY 9N to Northwest Bay Brook, 0.2 mi (0.3 km).

58 Up Yonda Farm Environmental Education Center

Trails Illustrated Map 743: M28

This 73-acre preserve and environmental education center is run by the Warren County Parks and Recreation Department. It has a small museum, a maple sugaring house, perennial and butterfly gardens, year-round nature programs, and a half-dozen short trails (up to a mile long) through the woods and fields of the former farm. Trail maps and descriptions are available at the center, which can be reached by telephone at 518-644-9767 or at www.upyondafarm.com.

Directions: From I-87 Exit 24, head E toward Bolton Landing, and follow Co. Rt. 11 for 5 mi to NY 9N. Turn R (S) and travel 0.5 mi toward Bolton Landing. Up Yonda Farm is on the R across from the Candlelight Motel. From Lake George Village, take NY 9N and travel N for 9 mi, passing the second stoplight in Bolton Landing. Travel N 1 mi more; Up Yonda Farm is on the L.

CAT AND THOMAS MOUNTAINS PRESERVE

Trails Illustrated Map 743: L–M27

This Lake George Land Conservancy preserve opened in 2004. It comprises 1900 acres with two summits and the rolling land between, and is located W of Bolton Landing on the W shore of Lake George. Much of the land was logged before the establishment of the preserve, so access is by old logging roads, on which three of the four trails are laid out. The preserve protects the watershed of Edgecomb Pond, which is Bolton Landing's water source. There are wonderful views of the south basin of Lake George, and the forest is recovering from the logging.

Additional information and a map can be found in the Lake George Land Conservancy brochure titled Cat and Thomas Mountains Preserve. This brochure can be obtained from ADK or the Lake George Land Conservancy; at the trailhead kiosk (often but not always); or downloaded from www.lglc.org/NaturePreserves/Cat_and_Thomas_071120.

▶Trailhead: From I-87 Exit 24 head E on Co. Rt. 11 for approx. 2 mi. Turn R (S) on Valley Woods Rd. The preserve parking lot is almost immediately on the R, with a kiosk and register.◀

59 Thomas Mt. Trail

See Cat and Thomas Mountains Preserve above

This is a 1.5 mi long road to an overlook below the top (which is private) of the Thomas Mt. ridge, where there is a small cabin and a stupendous view to the S. It is marked with orange disks, with two at each bend and four on a post at the fork with the Cat Mt. Trail (60).

Heading L (S) from the kiosk and trail register (0.0 mi) past a gate and along a road slightly downhill, the route winds up past a large excavation (trail 59A forks R just beyond this clearing) on the R to a fork in a clearing with a disk-marked post indicating the jct. with the Cat Mt. Trail (trail 60) at 0.7 mi. Take the R fork uphill steadily to a R hairpin at 1 mi. Continuing up the road into the fringe of unlogged hemlock woods, the trail ends at the cabin and lookout on the L at 1.5 mi. The summit is to the N; it is on private land and is not accessible.

❅ Trail in winter: Excellent for snowshoeing and superb for skiing.

👣 Distances: Kiosk to Cat Mt. Trail (trail 60), 0.7 mi; to hairpin, 1 mi; to cabin and lookout, 1.5 mi (2.4 km). The Blue Trail (59A) and the Richard Hayes Phillips Trail (61) meet here near the cabin. Ascent, 780 ft (238 m). Elevation, 1980 ft (604 m).

59A Thomas Mountain Blue Trail

See Cat and Thomas Mountains Preserve, p. 80

This trail opened in early 2012 as an alternate route up Thomas Mt. It crosses the wooded summit and has several wonderful viewpoints along the ridge, before linking with the orange-marked Thomas Mt. Trail (59) and the Richard Hayes Phillips Trail (60) near the cabin on the southerly summit of the mountain.

Heading L (S) from the kiosk and trail register (0.0 mi) past a gate and along a road slightly downhill, trail 59A forks R at a trail sign just after the former excavation site. Trail 59 continues to the L. Taking the R onto 59A, the blue-marked route enters dark wood, winds its way across a stream, and climbs a fairly steep section of hardwood forest. It levels out near the base of a small, wet rock slide (a former logging road laid out too directly up the mountain).

The trail ascends with the rutted wet skidder trail on the R, and then crosses it, zig-zagging along some small ledges until it reaches a grassy section beneath pines. This is the summit ridge. The trail crosses the flat grassy summit and descends on a short spur to a lookout of wonderful views W from blueberry ledges. The Northway is directly below, but almost inaudible. As the trail continues S on the W side of the ridge, it winds up and down and then back into boreal woods before reaching the intersections with trails 59 and 60 just before the cabin and lookout toward Cat Mt.

❅ Trail in winter: Excellent for snowshoeing; too steep, narrow, and twisty for skiing.

👣 Distances: From the intersection with orange-marked Thomas Mt. trail just past excavation area, to intersection with Richard Hayes Phillips Trail near cabin, 1 mi (1.6 km).

60 Cat Mt. Trail

See Cat and Thomas Mountains Preserve, p. 80

This starts as a rolling roadway, mostly on a sidehill, which runs from the fork and post at 0.7 mi along the Thomas Mt. Trail (trail 59), past a small pond and to a gate, where it eventually narrows to a trail as it ascends Cat Mt. It is marked

View from Cat Mt. summit. Carl Heilman II

with blue markers.

At the marked fork on the Thomas Mt. Trail (trail 59) (0.0 mi), bear L, straight ahead and downhill out of the clearing, following yellow markers. This rolling road crosses a small stream, ascends to a clearing, and proceeds to the open shore of a small pond at 1 mi. Cat Mt. is visible to the SW over the pond. The trail continues across the outlet of the pond, through a darker hemlock woods, to a gate at 1.3 mi.

Past the gate, the route becomes more of a trail, marked with yellow disks (be alert to the yellow markers; intersecting woods roads can lead you astray). Leaving the gate, the route heads R (W) uphill, then zigzags down, up L, and down R across a double pipe culvert that feeds a pond full of standing dead trees at 2 mi. Another flooded wood is immediately on the R, as the road, becoming narrower, winds more steeply up the mountain. The Richard Hayes Phillips Trail (61) crosses the route and provides a more direct path L to the summit. The main route begins to bear generally S in a series of switchbacks to a lookout to the SW and the open summit at 2.8 mi. The terrific view extends from Tongue Mt. in the NE, over Lake George, and around to Crane Mt. in the W.

❊ Trail in winter: Very suitable for snowshoeing and skiing, advanced-level past the gate.

🐾 Distances: Thomas Mt. Trail (trail 59) to pond, 1 mi; to gate, 1.3 mi; to culvert, 2 mi; to summit lookout, 2.8 mi (4.5 km). From trailhead, 3.5 mi (5.6 km). Ascent from trailhead, 756 ft (230 m). Elevation, 1956 ft (596 m).

61 Richard Hayes Phillips Trail

See Cat and Thomas Mountains Preserve, p. 80

This trail, marked with blue disks, begins W of the cabin site at the top of the orange-marked Thomas Mt. Trail (59). It connects the two main summits in the Preserve, and is a backcountry alternative to the logging road approach (60) to Cat Mt. Veteran trail builder Richard Hayes-Phillips designed the trail, which follows the summit ridge, meandering up and down through clearings, past vernal pools, and over small lookouts. There are several remnant logging roads along the route, but they are gradually blending into the landscape.

The Thomas Mt. summit cabin is the starting point (0.0 mi). The cabin is unlocked; please take good care of it. From there, the Summit Trail begins a steep descent R through a cleft and along ledges in the rocks. The trail crosses a logging track in a grassy area and winds up and down over several rocky and grassy outcroppings and past a vernal pool on the L. It then zigzags across the ridge, follows a logging road briefly, and bears L away from it. A vernal pool is on the R, then a logging road descends amidst brambles to the L. The trail follows this road and then bears R off of it on a sidehill. It follows the sidehill past some yellow paint blazes on trees, then ascends slightly to a jct. marked with cairns. A side path R leads 100 yd to a nice lookout to the W at 1.8 mi.

The main Summit Trail turns left and down, over rocks and past a few more cairns, and then steadily climbs the N side of Cat Mt. It crosses an old road, passes several interesting boulders, and then crosses the yellow-marked Cat Mt. Trail (60) before continuing to the top. It winds through a grassy area of rocks and evergreens before reaching the summit lookout of Cat Mt. at 2.6 mi. The 180-degree view over Lake George and toward the south is magnificent!

❋ Trail in winter: Very suitable for a snowshoe trip, but too winding and narrow for skiing.

❀ Distances: From the cabin site to lookout marked with cairns, 1.8 mi; to intersection with the yellow-marked Cat Mt. Trail (60), 2.3 mi; to summit of Cat Mt., 2.6 mi (4.2 km).

Summit cliffs of Sleeping Beauty Mountain. James Appleyard

Southeastern Lake George Wild Forest Section

This region to the E of Lake George contains quite a network of trails. Bounded by the Huletts Landing area to the N and West Fort Ann on the S, this area contains a nice mix of mountains, ponds, pleasant forests, and breathtaking shoreline views. Black Mt., to the N in this section, is the highest mountain with a trail in the whole eastern Adirondack region (2646 ft).

Since this is a Wild Forest area, there is an overlapping mix of hiking trails, horse trails, and snowmobile trails. Many of the trails in this section are part of a large network of carriage paths and trails that were once part of the Knapp Estate (see below). Several of these were logging roads that were improved by the men who worked for Mr. Knapp in the early 1900s. Most were stabilized with some fine stonework and are suitable for a variety of activities. These paths and trails switchback up the mountains and form a maze of paths all through the Shelving Rock area. It's a great area for the hiker, as well as the mountain biker. At present (April 2012), there are limited restrictions on mountain biking in Wild Forest regions. Mountain biking is only prohibited on certain mountain trails. On the SE side of Lake George, mountain biking is prohibited on the trails leading to the summits of Black, Buck, and Sleeping Beauty mountains, and on the other side of the lake the trails leading up Tongue Mt. will eventually be off limits. Due to the very rough nature of these trails, for the most part, they are not suitable for mountain biking. Unfortunately, DEC signs indicating these restrictions are often removed illegally.

To the NE of Shelving Rock are some lovely, little-used ponds that would be great for exploring in a small ultralight canoe. The trails quite near to Shelving Rock see intensive use, particularly on holiday weekends. You don't have to go too far away, though, to find lesser-used areas and solitude during even some of the busiest times.

At one time, the Knapp Estate, at the end of Shelving Rock Rd., consisted of 9500 acres and 75 miles of roads and trails. The people who built these roads and trails left a wonderful legacy for hiking. To learn more of the history of this area, read *Sweet Peas and a White Bridge* by Elsa Steinbeck (North Country Books, 1974), filled with anecdotes about the summer hotel visitors and staff, local characters, and customs. Also of interest is *From Then 'Til Now* by Fred Stiles (Washington County Historical Society, 1978). The original estate house on a lower slope of Shelving Rock Mt. burned in 1917. Today the family owns about 75 acres with several camps on Pearl Point. Be sure to respect the boundaries of their land, as there is no public access through the Knapp Estate.

The state owns the remainder of the land, including Black Mt., Erebus Mt., Shelving Rock Mt., Sleeping Beauty Mt., and seven ponds (all with trail access and described in this section). Hiking is possible on most of the network of roads that remains.

❊ Trails in winter: Though this area is marked for snowmobiles in the winter, there's not a lot of use, so there is some great snowshoeing, cross-country skiing, and ski-shoeing potential. Remember though, if parking near the Dacy Clearing area, that most of the trails head downhill to Lake George and have to be climbed on the way back out at the end of the day. With the exception of the mountain trails, all the trails in the region are fine for skiing, and the mountains are great snowshoe tours, especially when combined with a ski in on the more level approach routes. Specific suggestions for certain trails are included in the trail descriptions.

Suggested hikes in this region:

SHORTER HIKES:
Inman Pond—0.8 mi (1.3 km). This is a pleasant walk on an old woods road to a picturesque pond.

Lapland Pond—3 mi (4.8 km). A walk on an old woods road to a pond with a lean-to and a lot of wildlife.

MODERATE HIKES:
Sleeping Beauty Mt. Loop—7.6 mi (11.4 km) (total round trip f distance). From Dacy Clearing; great mountain views from Sleeping Beauty, and then a descent to Bumps Pond and return.

Black Mt. from the E—5 mi (8 km) round trip. Some fine views are a good reward for this climb with some steep places up to the communications tower at the summit.

HARDER HIKES:
Black Mt. via Shelving Rock Mt.—6.6 mi (10.6 km) one way. This route climbs first over Shelving Rock Mt., then follows the old woods road along the Lake George shoreline, and then ascends steeply up the spectacular W route to the summit of Black Mt.

	Trail Described	Total Miles (one way)	Page
62	Prospect Mt.	1.7 (2.9 km)	88
63	Lake George Recreation Area	various	89
65	Overlook Trail	3.9 (6.3 km)	89

Berry Pond Preserve
65A	Berry Pond Loop Trail	1.7 (2.7 km)	89
66	Lichen Ledge Preserve	various	92
67	Old Road on the Shoulder of Pilot Knob	1.0 (1.6 km)	92

Pilot Knob Preserve

68	Orange Trail	1.3	(2.0 km)	94
69	Blue Trail	0.9	(1.5 km)	94
70	Butternut Brook Trail	2.8	(4.5 km)	94
71	Inman Pond	0.8	(1.3 km)	95
72	Buck Mt. Trail from Pilot Knob	3.3	(5.3 km)	96
73	Buck Mt. Trail from Hogtown	2.3	(3.7 km)	97
74	Buck Mt. Connector Trail	0.5	(0.8 km)	98
75	Shelving Rock Falls Lakeshore Loop	2.0	(3.2 km)	99
	Shelving Rock Falls Trail *(unmaintained)*			
76	West Shelving Rock Falls Connector Trails	0.3	(0.5 km)	102
77	East Shelving Rock Falls Connector Trails	0.6	(1.0 km)	102
78	Hogtown Trailhead to Fishbrook Pond via Dacy Clearing and Bumps Pond	4.6	(7.4 km)	103
79	West Fishbrook Pond Trail	0.7	(1.1 km)	104
80	Sleeping Beauty	2.1	(3.4 km)	105
81	Old Farm Rd.	1.8	(2.9 km)	106
82	East Old Farm Rd. Leg	0.7	(1.1 km)	107
83	West Old Farm Rd. Leg	0.6	(1.0 km.)	107
84	Shortway Trail	2.4	(4.0 km)	108
85	Longway Trail	2.5	(4.1 km)	109
86	Longway Spur	0.2	(0.3 km)	110
87	Bumps Pond Spur	0.9	(1.4 km)	111
88	Erebus Mt. Trail	3.4	(5.4 km)	111
89	First Ridge Spur	0.7	(1.1 km)	113
90	Second Ridge Spur	0.3	(0.5 km)	113
91	Big Bridges Trail	0.9	(1.5 km)	113
92	Shelving Rock Mt. Trail	1.5	(2.4 km)	114
93	Shelving Rock Mt. to Lakeside Trail	1.0	(1.6 km)	115
94	Ridge Trail	3.9	(6.2 km)	116
95	Lakeside Trail to Black Mt. Point	3.5	(5.6 km)	118
96	Red Rock Bay Trail	1.4	(2.2 km)	120
97	Fishbrook Pond from Lake George	2.8	(4.5 km)	121
98	Black Mt. Point to Black Mt.	2.8	(4.5 km)	122
99	Black Mt. from the East	2.5	(4.3 km)	124
100	Lapland Pond Trail	3.0	(4.8 km)	125
101	Black Mt. Ponds Trail	1.0	(1.6 km)	127
102	Greenland Pond	1.2	(1.9 km)	128

Gull Bay Preserve

103	Blue Trail	0.3	(0.5 km)	129
104	Orange Trail	1.5	(2.4 km)	129
105	Yellow Trail	1.0	(1.6 km)	130

Last Great Shoreline Preserve
106   Lake George View Trail   1.3   (2.1 km)   130
106A   Green Mountain and Ticonderoga
       Overlook Trail   0.4   (0.6 km)   131

62 Prospect Mt.

Trails Illustrated Map 743: I27

This trail would be best rerouted up the mountain with a more gradual rate of ascent and some switchbacks. (A new trail is planned, with an approach from the S, but has not yet been approved or marked.) As it is, it is a steep, rocky trail, but a fairly short climb. The current trail will only become more badly eroded as time goes on. There are no vistas along the way.

▶Trailhead: Turn N off US 9 in Lake George village at LaRoma Restaurant. Pass three churches (the Episcopal Church has a youth hostel in summer) and then turn R onto Cooper St. Go one block, turn L onto West St., then L onto Smith St. The trail starts at the end of Cooper St., but there is no place to park there. On Smith St. there is space for about five cars at the base of the stairway leading to the trail bridge over I-87, the Adirondack Northway.◀

The stairway (0.0 mi) is the equivalent of about four stories of steps; it and the bridge account for 0.1 mi of hiking. On the far side, the trail markers are red. The trail goes steadily up on a wide rocky path to 0.2 mi, where it makes a gentle L and becomes more moderate. An old foundation on the R has a set of stone steps. More foundations from the inclined railway that once went up the mountain are soon passed.

At 0.3 mi, the trail resumes a fairly steady upward climb. At 0.6 mi, it crosses

Buck Mt. from summit of Prospect Mt. Carl Heilman II

the toll road to the peak. After crossing the road, the trail is badly eroded. It turns R at 0.7 mi, up onto bare rock, and then makes a L. At 0.8 mi, it comes to a large sloping rock wall on the R. The trail goes off to the L from this wall, then levels off until at 0.8 mi it turns R and heads uphill again. At 0.9 mi, a small stream can be heard to the L as the trail climbs steeply over bare slabs of rock.

At 1 mi, the trail makes a level L turn, then resumes climbing again. At 1.2 mi, it becomes even steeper, but soon moderates, then goes level through huge hemlocks and white pines. At 1.4 mi, it passes through maples and beeches as it bends S onto a ledge with a partial view E to Lake George.

The trail turns R here and arrives at the toll road at 1.5 mi, near the summit. Turn R up the road, then L into the picnic area at 1.6 mi. Uphill across the road, which has been blasted out of the summit, are the remains of the fire tower at 1.7 mi. In season there are many people on the top, including those from tour buses. The view from Prospect Mt. includes Lake George Village and the lake to the E, and the mountains of Vermont off in the f distance.

※ Distances: Smith St. to first jct. with toll road, 0.6 mi; to second jct. with toll road, 1.5 mi; to summit, 1.7 mi (2.9 km). Ascent, approx. 1600 ft (489 m). Elevation of Prospect Mt., 2041 ft (622 m).

63 Lake George Recreation Area
Trails Illustrated Map 743: 127

This municipal facility includes several athletic fields and a network of hiking/biking/ski trails. Several of the trails lead to the access to the Berry Pond Preserve (65, 65A). There is a kiosk with a trail map at the parking area.

▶Trailhead: At I-87 Exit 21, take NY 9N W past ADK Headquarters on the L for 0.5 mi to Transfer Road on the R. Follow it for 0.6 mi past intersections L to a gravel pit and R to the Transfer Station, to the Lake George Recreation Center in a field at the top of the hill. There is a cabin and a football field on the R and parking with a trail kiosk on the L.◀

BERRY POND PRESERVE
Trails Illustrated Map 743: 127

The Berry Pond Preserve was purchased in 2008 by the Lake George Land Conservancy and protected from likely second-home development. The 1400-acre tract contains its namesake pond, several low mountains, and the headwaters of West Brook, one of the major tributaries of Lake George. The Conservancy and other local groups have been working hard to mitigate sediment flow into the lake, so protection of uplands along such watercourses has become one of their high priorities.

Some of the tract has been logged in the past, and much of the loop trail follows a gravel roadway; several other woods roads intersect the trail, and there are frequent snowmobilers' signs along the western swing of the loop. The recovering woods have an interesting mix of hemlocks, pines, and hardwoods, including an extensive S-facing oak forest. Highlights are the lookouts along the N spur of the trail, and Berry Pond, whose shore is passed along the western orange-marked loop. The shallow pond is a haven for beavers and herons. The hiking is generally moderate with some steep pitches, and the Blue Trail loop rises in the N to lookouts at a high point of about 1700 ft. There is no camping allowed on these lands.

▶Trailhead: At I-87 Exit 21, take NY 9N W past ADK Headquarters on the L for 0.5 mi to Transfer Road on the R. Follow it for 0.6 mi past intersections L to a gravel pit and R to the Transfer Station, to the Lake George Recreation Center in a field at the top of the hill. There is a cabin and a football field on the R and parking with a trail kiosk on the L. The route follows the LGRC ski trail network (trail 63) for a half-mile before heading W toward the Berry Pond loop. It is worth closely perusing the posted trail map before starting out, as the ski trail network can be confusing. A check on the Lake George Land Conservancy website and a look at the Berry Pond preserve map, at http://www.lglc.org/NaturePreserves/BerryPond/ will lessen the confusion.◀

65 Overlook Trail

See Berry Pond Preserve, p. 89

This trail is an up-and-down adventure over a small notch and a small mountain with two very nice lookouts. The climbing and descents are steady and fairly steep. The route begins as a half-mile approach over LGRC ski trails to the boundary of the Berry Pond preserve.

Following blue Lake George Land Conservancy markers, cross a small clearing behind the kiosk, and head R downhill on Guard Help Way. Turns in the route are shown with two or more markers. It begins as a gravel woods road before turning L through hemlocks and crossing a stream on a culvert. Continue behind a small log lean-to on the R. Avoid the bridge and bear to the L to follow the zigzag trail uphill to a three-way intersection with Wolf Den. Follow the second R onto Wolf Den uphill on a cobbled surface. Cross an intersection with Sylvan continuing slightly L but generally straight ahead on Wolf Den, passing an intersection with Barkeater on the R and Tomahawk on the L.

The trail is now called "204 Way", and it meets the blue-marked Bear Claw on the L. Follow Bear Claw as it curves uphill o the R, passing another unmarked intersection. The Thio Hero trail goes L at a yellow "one way" sign, and continues with blue LGLC disks. This meets the LGLC trail L connecting this network with the Berry Pond Preserve. After a half-mile of route finding through this maze, is the start of the connector trail to the Berry Pond Preserve. It is also marked with blue LGLC disks as it climbs up and through a saddle between two hills and reaches the Berry Pond Preserve. There are several unmarked logging roads on either side before a steep descent through dark hemlocks, to two intersections, at double blue and orange disks, with the two loop trails. One can turn either immediately R on the Blue Trail along an old logging road or just beyond, onto a recently maintained gravel roadway, marked with orange LGLC disks, at the start of the Orange Trail. Travel L, downhill on the gravel road, is prohibited.

The Blue Trail heads immediately and steadily uphill on an old logging road to the R, then jogs L on a level contour before climbing R, steeply up the roadway again. The oak and beech leaves everywhere can be very slippery! As it flattens out, the trail leaves the road and bends L toward the summit of a small mountain. There is a large clearing facing northeast over Lake George toward Black Mt., the highest peak above the lake. Islands and camps along the shore are also visible. Follow the trail to the L and another lookout that faces S and W. This view takes in Glens Falls out on a low plain and mountains and ponds at higher elevations.

At this summit, the trail rejoins a roadway that more gently winds its way down the NW side of the mountain to an intersection with a wider dirt road. Turn L, downhill, here, as the road levels and twists to a T intersection with the orange-marked trail. From this point, one may take the Orange Trail R to Berry Pond, or L and downhill, back to the junction with the Blue Trail and back toward the trailhead.

🚶 Distances: To end of Lake George Recreation Center trails and start of ascent on Conservancy Overlook Trail, 0.5 mi; over a notch and down to double blue and orange-marked intersections, 1 mi; up blue-marked Overlook Trail to twin overlooks, 1.65 mi; down to junction with dirt road, 1.36 mi; to intersection with Berry Pond Loop, 1.65 mi; back down to double intersection, 2.9 mi; back to parking lot, 3.9 mi (6.3 km).

65A Berry Pond Loop Trail

See Berry Pond Preserve, p. 89

This trail begins at the first junction, described above, with the blue-marked Overlook Trail (65). Cross a small bank and stream to the newer roadway, and head R gradually uphill, with a small stream on the L. The orange-marked trail crosses two level clearings before reaching an intersection L to Berry Pond. At this point, the Overlook Trail (65) comes in on the R, descending from its two mountaintop lookouts.

The roadway L is level and reaches the trail around Berry Pond, a pretty flow, on the R, in 0.3 mi more. Turn R at the orange markers, crossing the small ditch onto a woods road. This counter-clockwise route alternates between path and roadway, approaching the shore of the pond and veering away from it. Sharp beaver-chewed stumps, like Punji sticks, abound, so be careful where you step! Beaver lodges are visible from the shore, as are heron nests in the dead trees of the pond. At one point, the trail traverses the top of a small beaver dam, and it crosses numerous beaver paths leading away from the shore.

This very pretty and interesting trail winds around the W end of Berry Pond and zigzags to its S shore and away from it, as it returns to the dirt road at 1.5 mi. Turn L here and return along the road past the start of the pond loop and back to the upper intersection with the Overlook Trail (65). At this clearing, turn

R along the main roadway and downhill to the lower junction with the Overlook Trail and the return along it through the ski trails to the parking lot.

❉ Trail in winter: If there's ever again 2-3 ft of snow in the area, these old roads are terrific for advanced-level cross-country skiing, with several fast steep hills, plenty of width for turning and braking. (The trails in the Lake George Recreation Center on the way in are fine for those with more moderate skiing abilities.) Snowshoeing would likewise be great. Note that the Berry Pond Loop road, which includes part of the Orange Trail, is open to snowmobiles.

❈ Distances: From intersection with blue Overlook Trail (65) and L to Berry Pond, 0.6 mi; to intersection R around N side of Berry Pond, 0.8 mi; around pond and back to roadway, 1.5 mi; back to blue Overlook Trail intersection, 1.7 mi (2.7 km).

66 Lichen Ledge Preserve

Trails Illustrated Map 743: I-J28

This is a tiny Lake George Land Conservancy preserve of one acre, shaped as a sliver of pie, yet it provides a wonderful view of the south basin of Lake George from a ledge. The trail is short, only a few minutes walk from the car pullout to the ledge. Watch out for poison ivy!

▶Trailhead: There is a small pulloff, space for about 2 cars, parallel to NY 9L. It's 1 mi W of Dunham Bay's intersection of NY 9L and Bay Rd, 3.6 mi E of the intersection of 9L and US 9/9N in the Village of Lake George.◀

67 Old Road on the Shoulder of Pilot Knob

Trails Illustrated Map 743: K29

Many people take a wrong turn onto this road, thinking they are heading for the Buck Mt. Trail (72). This old road is a lovely deep-woods walk, a connector to Lower Hogtown, or the first part of a loop with return past the Buck Mt. Trail jct.

▶Trailhead: The route begins at 0.2 mi on the Buck Mt. Trail from Pilot Knob (trail 72). There are infrequent blue markers, but the road is easy enough to follow.◀

Leaving trail 72 (0.0 mi), the road begins to go uphill beside a stream to the R. At 0.2 mi, it rounds a wide curve to the L as it cuts into the side of a hill. The stream is farther below now. At 0.3 mi, a small trail goes R down to the stream. Now the road is cut into a steep bank and the grade increases.

The road crosses a dry streambed, continuing to climb through beautiful, high, deep woods. The streambed is now down to the L. At 0.4 mi, the road crosses a wet place beneath a huge slanting rock wall on the R partially covered with mosses and ferns. At 0.6 mi, the road crests a hill with a waterfall audible ahead and below on the L.

At 0.8 mi, the road crosses a rocky, steep, damp streambed. At 1 mi, it meets the Butternut Brook Trail (trail 70). Uphill to the R on trail 70, it is 1.9 mi to the Inman Pond trail (71), 2.4 mi to the Lower Hogtown trailhead, making a through trip from Pilot Knob of 3.6 mi.

Lake George night scene. Mark Bowie

❄ Trail in winter: Great snowshoeing and expert skiing, downhill from E to W.
🥾 Distances: Trail 72 to top of hill, 0.6 mi; to trail 70, 1 mi (1.6 km).

THE LYNN MONTAGNE SCHUMANN PRESERVE AT PILOT KNOB

Trails Illustrated Map 743: J–K29

This preserve opened in 2002 after a noteworthy fundraising campaign by the Lake George Land Conservancy to reclaim its lands. The Preserve's history is unique. It was the site of a house built illegally by a fugitive drug dealer in the early 1990s; its steep hairpin driveway is rumored to have cost $1 million, paid for in cash. The notoriety of these two construction projects drew the attention of the police, and a raid ensued. Subsequent owners gladly sold to the Conservancy, the house was razed, and the only remaining structure is a summit gazebo. It is a popular destination with wide views over south Lake George and the mountains beyond.

A loop trail marked with orange disks climbs from the parking lot to the lookout and gazebo and descends along the top of the driveway and back through the woods. Visitors are asked to come down the driveway only as far as the trail turnoff at a wide R-to-L hairpin, and follow the trail back to their cars. A second trail marked with blue disks begins at the high point of the Orange Trail and zigzags a mile to a waterfall, returning by the same route. There are numerous old paths and woods roads in the area, so be sure to follow the markers, which indicate a turn with two disks and a trail jct. with four disks.

▶Trailhead: Take Exit 21 off I-87 and head E to US 9. Turn L at the light on US 9. Turn R at NY 9L and follow it for 7.2 mi to Pilot Knob Rd. Turn L and drive 0.7 mi to the U-shaped trailhead parking lot on the R. There is a Preserve sign, a split rail fence, and a kiosk at the trailhead.◀

68 Orange Trail

See Pilot Knob Preserve, p.93

The trail heads uphill from the kiosk (0.0 mi) through mixed forest, bearing R and then L to cross a small sloping meadow, and arrives at a trail fork at 0.3 mi. Take the L fork up an old roadway, which steepens before the trail again bears R up into a clearing with expansive views and the gazebo at 0.5 mi.

The Orange Trail continues through the clearing S and down the gravel and asphalt driveway, to the fourth hairpin turn from the top at a wooden post and trail marker at 0.8 mi. The trail heads N across a grassy, wooded side-hill with one switchback before reaching the first fork again at 1 mi. It goes downhill to the parking lot at 1.3 mi.

❄ Trail in winter: Suitable for snowshoeing.

🚶 Distances: To first fork, 0.3 mi; to gazebo, 0.5 mi; to marked post on driveway, 0.8 mi; to parking lot, 1.3 mi (2.0 km).

69 Blue Trail

See Pilot Knob Preserve, p.93

This trail leaves the clearing and old house foundation behind and to the E of the gazebo on a small gravel incline. It crosses a small boardwalk, bearing R on an old woods road through hemlock and then grassy oak meadows. It heads downhill and turns L at a fork with markers at 0.3 mi, to ascend N through a forest of pole-sized trees.

At 0.5 mi, the roadway jogs R again uphill and then down across a wet spot. Take either the L or R fork at 0.7 mi to the waterfall. The L heads uphill and bears R over a rocky ledge and down onto a washed-out roadway, reaching the top of the falls at 0.9 mi. The R fork heads slightly downhill to cross the brook below the falls at 0.8 mi and then turns L to the top of the waterfall at 0.9 mi. These last two forks form a loop and can be hiked in either direction. There are other old roads in the area, so be sure always to follow the blue markers to return to the gazebo in the clearing.

❄ Trail in winter: Suitable for snowshoeing.

🚶 Distances: Gazebo to first L turn, 0.3 mi; to R turn, 0.5 mi; to L jct. with waterfall loop, 0.7 mi; to top of falls (either fork of loop), 0.9 mi (1.5 km).

70 Butternut Brook Trail

Trails Illustrated Map 743: K29–30

▶ Trailhead: Drive 6.3 mi on Buttermilk Falls Rd. N to the Lower Hogtown trailhead on the L just before Camp Little Notch, which is marked with a "CLN" sign. There is a wide turnout for parking on the L just N of the trailhead. Perhaps this old road was used by the farmers of Hogtown, to drive their hogs and carry vegetables to Lake George for the kitchens of the boarding houses and hotels along the lake. ◀

David Hough

This is a snowmobile and horse trail with only occasional blue markers. It might be a good route for cross-country skiing with a car at the Pilot Knob trailhead (see trail 67).

From the parking area (0.0 mi), the road starts gradually uphill past a hillside of jumbled rock on the R at 0.2 mi. At 0.5 mi, the trail reaches a new wooden bridge over a stream. Just before the bridge an old road goes R to Inman Pond (trail 71).

The trail crosses the bridge, follows a rocky, dry streambed, then crosses another stream. Now the road goes more steeply uphill, leveling off at 0.6 mi. Here there is a side road to the R, but the trail bends L, following snowmobile and horse trail markers. The road climbs another steep pitch to 0.7 mi, then goes downhill to the level. At 0.9 mi, the road starts uphill again, this time on solid bedrock. At 1 mi, an overgrown pond is visible below through the trees. The road crosses a stream, then another stream at 1.1 mi before it goes uphill again and then levels out.

At 1.4 mi, the road goes along a small ridge that appears to be an esker. Now it gently descends, coming alongside a beaver clearing and stream on the L. It crosses the stream at 1.5 mi, passing an informal path to the R, then passes through a fern-filled open hardwood gully. At 1.8 mi, it crosses another stream, and goes steadily downhill following horse and snowmobile trail markers.

(At 2.4 mi, trail 67 goes L 1 mi over the shoulder of Pilot Knob, joining the Buck Mt. Trail from Pilot Knob (trail 72) at 3.4 mi and reaching the Pilot Knob trailhead parking lot at 3.6 mi.)

The marked trail continues downhill to 2.8 mi, where it meets the Buck Mt. Trail from Pilot Knob (trail 72). A turn to the R would take you to the summit of Buck via yellow-marked trail 72. From the jct. the trail descends 1.2 mi to the Pilot Knob trailhead parking lot, making a through trip from Lower Hogtown of 4 mi.

❋ Trail in winter: A nice snowshoe trip. Skiing E involves a climb and gradual descent. Skiing W involves a steep, fast descent, requiring advanced skills.

🐾 Distances: Lower Hogtown to Inman Pond trail (71), 0.5 mi; to old road on the shoulder of Pilot Knob (trail 67), 2.4 mi; to Buck Mt. Trail (trail 72), 2.8 mi (4.5 km). To Pilot Knob trailhead via trail 72, 4 mi (6.8 km).

71 Inman Pond

Trails Illustrated Map 743: J–K29

▶Trailhead: This is a truly delightful walk and pleasing to the eye. It begins at 0.5 mi on the Butternut Brook Trail (trail 70), just before a wooden bridge over a stream.◀

Following red horse trail markers, the road diverges R from trail 70 (0.0 mi) and goes steeply uphill with a stream down to the L. It levels off at 0.1 mi, then curves up and L around the side of a hill through beech woods. DEC has indicated that this is not a horse trail.

At 0.2 mi, a path descends to the R. It is unmarked and apparently used by off-road vehicles. The road curves L and uphill, passing a "No Camping" sign on a large hemlock as it levels and splits to fork around Inman Pond at 0.4 mi.

Bearing L, the road crosses an outlet of the pond at 0.5 mi on giant logs. The pond is visible to the R. The trail passes through a corridor lined thickly with young balsams. It goes into the woods again, crossing a rusty pipe at a wet place.

At 0.7 mi, a wooden sign with "Trail" and an arrow pointing R is nailed to a maple. Snowmobile and horse trail markers are off to the R. This little-used trail leads through hemlocks and then downhill to a small bluff at 0.8 mi, overlooking this lovely pond. There is an informal campsite here as well as an abandoned beaver house in the bog that runs down the middle of the pond to just E of this bluff.

From the fork at 0.4 mi, the R road crosses another outlet with a pipe at 0.5 mi. There is an old beaver dam above the outlet. The view down the pond is fascinating since it holds a floating bog. At 0.8 mi, the road continues straight ahead, but to the L is a fire circle above the pond edge. This is the end of the official DEC trail. The owner of lands to the N has heavily posted the boundary of the Forest Preserve and the private lands.

❄ Trail in winter: A suitable destination for skiers or snowshoers.

🐾 Distances: Trail 70 to fork near pond, 0.4 mi; to S shore bluff, 0.8 mi; to N shore fire circle, 0.8 mi (1.3 km). Lower Hogtown trailhead to either terminus, 1.3 mi (2.1 km).

72 Buck Mt. Trail from Pilot Knob

Trails Illustrated Map 743: K29

Buck Mt. is an enjoyable climb with fine views from the open rock top on the lake side. It can be climbed from both the S (trail 72) and the N (trail 73). While the N route has less elevation gain, the more heavily used S route has a number of views along the ascent. The trail is marked with yellow markers.

▶Trailhead: To reach the Pilot Knob trailhead, drive 4.9 mi N on NY 9L from its intersection with NY 149. Turn R at a sign for Kattskill Bay and Pilot Knob and drive 3.5 mi to the Pilot Knob trailhead for Buck Mt. on the R.◀

From the trail register (0.0 mi), the trail heads E, passing various side paths, soon crosses a small brook, and reaches a fork at 0.2 mi. The unmarked old road R (trail 67) goes up a low shoulder of Pilot Knob and then joins the Butternut Brook Trail (trail 70 to Lower Hogtown).

Turning L at the fork, the trail passes through a forest of basswood, birch, white pine, oak, maple, sumac, and large grapevines. After crossing Butternut Brook at 0.4 mi, the trail turns L uphill. After another switchback, the trail climbs steeply, moderates briefly, and resumes the climb by a large boulder.

At 1 mi, the trail passes an old stone wall and then levels off. After crossing Butternut Brook again, the trail reaches a fork at 1.2 mi. The trail R is the Butternut Brook Trail (trail 70) to the Lower Hogtown trailhead. The yellow-marked trail to Buck Mt. heads L.

The route is steep again, with views through the trees of Lake George at 1.3 mi and the N side of Pilot Knob. The trail soon switchbacks to the L and at 1.6 mi crosses a stream. It briefly levels off, crosses a small stream at 1.8 mi, and then climbs steadily through a beech woods.

Past a large tree whose roots have enveloped a boulder, steep climbing begins again at 2.2 mi. The grade eases somewhat before another steep ascent at 2.4 mi. At 2.7 mi, the trail passes a small swamp, and then at 2.9 mi climbs another steep pitch to open rock with a view. At 3 mi, the trail ascends steeply up solid rock. Down to the SE is Crossett Pond, the site of a Boy Scout camp.

Just before the summit, the trail descends into a col where at 3.2 mi it meets the Buck Mt. Trail from Hogtown (trail 73). The summit is to the L at 3.3 mi. This rocky peak is understandably a favorite with its excellent view of Lake George and the surrounding mountains.

❊ Trail in winter: This is a great snowshoeing trail. It's good to carry instep crampons for the steeper sections and possible ice. It is negotiable as an advanced-level ski outing, requiring at least two feet of snow.

🐾 Distances: Pilot Knob trailhead to Old Road on the Shoulder of Pilot Knob (trail 67), 0.2 mi; to Butternut Brook Trail (trail 70), 1.2 mi; to summit, 3.3 mi (5.3 km). Ascent, 2000 ft (610 m). Summit elevation, 2330 ft (710 m).

73 Buck Mt. Trail from Hogtown

Trails Illustrated Map 743: K–L29

▶Trailhead: From the intersection of NY 9L and NY 149, drive E 1.6 mi to the intersection with Buttermilk Falls Rd. Turn L onto Buttermilk Falls Rd. In 3.2 mi, just after the jct. with Taylor Wood Rd. on the R, the road becomes Sly Pond Rd. and the pavement ends. Continuing straight ahead on Sly Pond Rd., at 8.7 mi Hogtown Rd. intersects on the R. Continue straight ahead on Shelving Rock Rd., which has a dead-end sign (this road continues on to the Knapp Estate on Lake George at 12.8 mi from NY 149). At 9.4 mi is the Hogtown trailhead and parking for the Lake George Trails System. Continue on to the L until at 9.9 mi there is a small parking lot and a sign on the L for Buck Mt.◀

Starting at the parking lot (0.0 mi), the trail soon crosses a stream on stones and then starts uphill. At 0.2 mi, the trail crosses another brook in a pleasant hemlock glade. After rolling up and down for a while, the trail passes a miniature pond at 0.5 mi. At 0.9 mi, the trail crosses a stream and then at 1 mi another; it then goes up a steep hill, leveling off at 1.2 mi.

The trail crosses a picturesque stream with shelving rocks, another stream at

1.4 mi, and then follows along water on the L at 1.5 mi. After crossing this stream twice, the trail heads steeply uphill with the stream on the R, passing three huge boulders at 1.7 mi. Now the trail is in a mature stand of hardwoods, and closely follows the stream up a steep pitch at 1.8 mi.

At 2 mi, the trail goes through a narrow pass of jumbled boulders and a mossy cliff with a stream cascading through its cleft. After a wet spell, water drips from the moss-covered rock. The trail soon narrows on a gentle grade overlooking the stream. At 2.1 mi, it becomes steep again, and crosses and recrosses the stream. Shortly the trail passes between two walls of boulders, levels out, and arrives at 2.2 mi at a jct. with the Buck Mt. Trail from Pilot Knob (trail 72), which continues down to the Butternut Brook Trail (trail 70) and Pilot Knob. Turn R and climb over bare rock to the summit at 2.3 mi.

The view from the open areas on top is quite fine. It includes a panorama of Lake George and the southern Adirondack mountains, including Tongue Mt., Shelving Rock Mt., Sleeping Beauty, and Black Mt. It's a fine place to relax and enjoy the view.

❄ Trail in winter: Buck Mt. is a great snowshoe trip from either side. Skiing would be suitable only on the approach to the climbing. Instep crampons are advised for poor snow conditions.

🥾 Distances: Parking lot to pond, 0.5 mi; to boulders, 1.7 mi; to Buck Mt. Trail from Pilot Knob (trail 72), 2.2 mi; to summit, 2.3 mi (3.7 km). Ascent, 1130 ft (345 m). Summit elevation, 2330 ft (710 m).

74 Buck Mt. Connector Trail

Trails Illustrated Map 743: L29–30

This short trail connects the N trailhead of Buck Mt. with the road to Dacy Clearing. It is not often used since most people park at the Buck Mt. trailhead to climb that mountain or at the Hogtown trailhead or Dacy Clearing. However, it can serve as the start of a very lovely walk or ski trip using other connector roads, providing a loop back to this spot.

▶Trailhead: The trail starts directly across from the N trailhead to Buck Mt. on the E side of Shelving Rock Rd., 0.5 mi NW of the Hogtown trailhead parking lot. A sign says, "Sleeping Beauty Mt., 3.4 mi; Fishbrook Pond, 5.2 mi." Light-blue horse trail markers help hikers stay on this little-used trail.◀

The trail leads gently downhill NE of the road, heading to a small brook, which it crosses. The trees are mostly beech, birch, and some hemlock. In October the forest floor is a brown and gold carpet.

At 0.1 mi, the trail descends to a pleasant hollow with the beginnings of a tiny stream. Woodpeckers tap and chickadees cheep busily.

Now the trail climbs up out of the hollow past maple and ash. A tan DEC marker with "67" on it is on a tree on this slope. The trail winds uphill around a small rock ledge and passes a few yellow DEC markers.

At 0.2 mi, the trail crosses a spring near an uprooted hemlock and passes a moss-covered ledge to the R. The trail continues gently uphill through beautiful woods of beech with some hemlock, oak, and ash, crossing another spring at 0.4 mi. At 0.5 mi, the trail meets the road to Dacy Clearing (trail 78) 0.5 mi from the Hogtown trailhead parking area.

❇ Trail in winter: Suitable for snowshoeing and skiing, though it gets steep at the bottom.

🐾 Distance: Shelving Rock Rd. at Buck Mt. trailhead to road to Dacy Clearing, 0.5 mi (0.8 km).

75 Shelving Rock Falls Lakeshore Loop
Shelving Rock Falls Trail (unmaintained)

Trails Illustrated Map 743: L29

This trail has a lot of variety in it. A nice way to do the trail is to park at one of the lower parking areas (see Trailhead below) and end the walk by passing Shelving Rock Falls. This route is the best way to see the falls, from a carriage pull-off near the top of the falls. An unmarked and unmaintained rugged path leads down to the bottom of the falls and then follows the gorge down to the bridge across Shelving Rock Brook.

This area is a popular place in the summer on weekends, especially holiday weekends, so it might be good to pick other times to visit. Camping in the Shelving Rock Falls area on the W side of Shelving Rock Rd. is restricted to 21 designated campsites in the level "pines" area along the road just N of the bridge over Shelving Rock Brook. Fires are permitted in existing fire rings. There is no parking after 9 PM in the parking areas along Shelving Rock Rd. near the Knapp Estate boundary (see section introduction). Parking is restricted to parking areas only; anyone parking along the road runs the risk of being towed away.

▶Trailhead: When traveling NW on Shelving Rock Rd. from the Hogtown trailhead (see trail 74), the E access to this trail is 2.5 mi from the trailhead on the L at the metal barrier gate, just before the bridge over Shelving Rock Brook. The N trailhead is 1.1 mi farther along (3.6 mi from the Hogtown trailhead) on the L side of the road, 0.1 mi before the private Knapp Estate, but the last parking is at the 3.4 mi point on the L. Five other trails (the first is back in the woods) with metal barrier gates are passed on the L when traveling from the E access to the N access.◀

At the N access, the trail begins on the L (0.0 mi). There are signs that read "No Horses Permitted" and "Motorized Vehicles Prohibited Except Snowmobiles." The trail begins heading downhill to the R, swings L, and then reaches a trail along the shore of Lake George at 0.1 mi. The R leg ends at a metal gate before a private land boundary in less than 0.1 mi. The public route turns L and passes a pretty rock point with great 180-degree views from N to S on the lake. The trail closely follows the shoreline, sometimes right along it and other times a short

Shelving Rock Falls. James Appleyard

distance inland. There are great views most of the way.

At 0.5 mi, the trail takes a sharp L away from the lake, then soon a sharp R to follow the shore again. It follows around a pretty little cove, then at 0.6 mi comes to a jct. The trail L is the main trail. (To the R a trail leads 0.1 mi to an old camping spot on the shore.) Here is a good view over to Log Bay Island and the shoreline beyond. There is good swimming off the ledges on a hot summer day.

The main trail contours around Log Bay, soon coming to a nice view S across a rocky point with the summit of Buck Mt. visible in the f distance. At 0.9 mi, the trail takes a sharp L inland to follow around a wetland in Shelving Rock Bay. A R turn here leads a short f distance onto a pine-covered point. Herons, beavers, and kingfisher all frequent this wetland.

At 0.9 mi there's a jct. with the West Shelving Rock Connector Trail (trail 76) straight ahead. Bear R, passing to the W side of an outhouse to continue on the main trail. In a short f distance another leg of trail 76 comes in on the L.

Following along the wetland, the trail comes to Shelving Rock Brook and crosses it on a plank bridge at 1.1 mi. Just across the bridge on the L (the S side of the bridge) is the end of an unmaintained foot trail from Shelving Rock Falls.

This area was used by Native Americans long before it was claimed by European settlers. Indian artifacts have been found in Shelving Rock Bay dating from 2700 BCE, including Vosburg points (named because this type was first found on the Vosburg farm near Albany). Pottery shards found here date from the Middle Woodland era, about 400 AD. Charcoal from a fireplace excavated near Harris Bay has been dated to 4200 BCE as documented by staff from the state museum in Albany.

After crossing the bridge, the trail continues along the wooded shoreline, until at 1.3 mi it takes a sharp switchback L and begins to ascend the side of the hill. (Straight ahead along the shore at this turn are an outhouse and an old campsite in about 100 ft.) This is the first of a series of switchbacks that continue up along the S side of the brook.

At 1.5 mi, the trail levels off in a forest of stately hemlocks, pines, and oaks. Staying level, the trail soon swings around to the top of the falls and a nice side lookout over the falls at 1.6 mi.

(A rugged, unmaintained foot trail leads from the L side of an old carriage pulloff to the bottom of the falls and then down the ravine to a plank bridge. **Warning: Many have been hurt here.** The dam at the top of the falls is algae-covered and slippery, and in the winter icy conditions make footing hazardous. Descending from just W of the pulloff just W of the top of the falls, this rocky path descends steeply to the base of the falls. This is a nice place to cool your feet in the water and enjoy the view of the falls. The route continues down through the rocky gorge past rushing rocky chasms and swirling pools under the dark, towering hemlocks. The route soon moderates, reaching the Loop Trail by a bridge near Shelving Rock Brook's entrance into the bay at 0.3 mi.)

Continuing E on the main trail, on the L are remnants of the old plank bridge that used to span the top of the falls. A crossing is not recommended here now.

The trail follows around the edge of an old beaver pond, and then reenters the woods following the pretty brook. The trail is mostly level to its jct. with Shelving Rock Rd. by a bridge at 2 mi. This is the E access to the trail.

❊ Trail in winter: The trail would be a good ski from E to N (with some tight turns from the falls down to the lake shore), and fine for snowshoeing. This trail is used by snowmobiles. Extra caution is advised around the falls in winter.

🚶 Distances: N trailhead to jct. with West Shelving Rock Falls Connector Trail (trail 76), 0.9 mi; to Shelving Rock Falls (top), 1.6 mi; to Shelving Rock Rd., 2 mi (3.2 km).

76 West Shelving Rock Falls Connector Trails
Trails Illustrated Map 743: L29

This is a pair of trails from Shelving Rock Rd. that meet by the Buck Mt. Connector Trail (trail 74). These trails form an angular crisscross in the Shelving Rock Falls area between the brook and the dirt road. They are each rather short, and help to form a variety of shortened loops that also utilize the Shelving Rock Falls Lakeshore Loop (trail 75).

▶Trailhead: From the Shelving Rock Mt. trailhead (see trail 92), after a short distance there's an "S" turn in Shelving Rock Rd. From here it is 0.2 mi to the trailhead and parking lot on the L. In another 0.2 mi (0.4 mi from Shelving Rock Mt. trailhead) is the second entrance, also on the L with a metal barrier gate. The last parking area on the road is just 0.1 mi past this trail.◀

Starting at the farthest E entrance, 0.2 mi from the Shelving Rock Mt. trailhead (0.0 mi), the trail parallels the road for a while and descends at a moderate grade. At 0.2 mi is the intersection with the other access trail from the R. From this intersection, each leg (straight ahead or L) connects with the Shelving Rock Falls Loop (trail 75) in about 250 ft.

From the intersection, turning R to return to the road, the trail follows along a wetland for a distance and climbs gradually. After a switchback, the trail heads across a stream and reaches the road at 0.1 mi. The last parking area is less than 0.1 mi to the NW.

🚶 Distance: W entrance to jct. with Shelving Rock Falls Loop and back to E trailhead, 0.3 mi (0.5 km).

77 East Shelving Rock Falls Connector Trails
Trails Illustrated Map 743: L29

▶Trailhead: From the pine knoll just past the bridge (0.0 mi), heading W on Shelving Rock Rd., is a pine grove. One entrance is to the L in the pines. A second entrance is by the gate on the L, 0.1 mi farther, and the third is 0.1 mi past the Shelving Rock Mt. trailhead (see trail 90) at the gate on the L.◀

The trail heads W through the pines, soon coming to a power line. The trail follows the power line and at 0.2 mi comes to a jct. with another entrance on the R. (The entrance is a bit over 0.1 mi away to the R on a level trail.)

The main trail descends slightly and then, just before dropping into a deep gully with a stream, reaches a T jct. at 0.3 mi. To the R is another entrance from Shelving Rock Rd. (The entrance is about 200 ft away on a mostly level trail.) Turning L, the trail parallels the stream, which is down a steep bank to the R. The forest is dark with many tall and stately pines and hemlocks.

At 0.5 mi, the trail reaches the top of the falls on the N side. With the bridge out the only way to reach the other side is by wading, or attempting to cross on a washed-out old beaver dam. Crossing here is NOT recommended. The view from the falls is better from the other side on the Loop Trail (trail 75). It's a nice walk, though, when doing the loop and heading back to the car.

❊ Trail in winter: good for snowshoeing.
🐾 Distance: Total trail distances, 0.6 mi (1.0 km).

78 Hogtown Trailhead to Fishbrook Pond via Dacy Clearing and Bumps Pond

Trails Illustrated Map 743: L30

This trail is a major N-S route up the E side of the Shelving Rock trail system. Since many trails intersect along the way, this isn't just a trail to a destination; it's also used in part for other routes in this quadrant. Using this trail as a base, any number of trips of varying duration can be planned that take in mountains or other ponds.

▶Trailhead: From the intersection of NY 9L and NY 149, drive E 1.6 mi to the intersection with Buttermilk Falls Rd. Turn L onto Buttermilk Falls Rd. (0.0 mi). In 3.2 mi, just after the jct. with Taylor Wood Rd. on the R, the road becomes Sly Pond Rd. and the pavement ends. Continuing straight ahead on Sly Pond Rd., at 8.7 mi Hogtown Rd. intersects on the R. Continue straight ahead on Shelving Rock Rd. with the dead end sign. At 9.4 mi is the Hogtown trailhead and parking for the Lake George Trails System. Sign the register here. In dry weather it is bumpy but possible to drive 1.5 mi beyond the register to Dacy Clearing, where the foot trail actually begins.◀

From the register (0.0 mi), the trail follows the narrow road N, reaching the Buck Mt. Connector Trail (trail 74) on the L at 0.5 mi. At 0.6 mi, one leg of the Old Farm Rd. (trail 82) branches off to the L. At 1.2 mi, the road passes through a small clearing on the R with a view up to the cliffs on Sleeping Beauty Mt. Soon the road goes through a larger clearing with hitching posts for horses and a jct. with the Shortway Trail (trail 84) on the L (W). The road bends around the foundations of the old Dacy farmhouse. The Dacy family supplied the Knapps with vegetables and also helped keep the roads clear.

After a bridge, the Longway Trail (trail 85) cuts off to the L. The road to Dacy

Clearing goes R past an old stone dam in a stream.

At Dacy Clearing, 1.6 mi, the trail bears R past a steel gate, following yellow markers, and begins a steady climb uphill. At 2 mi, a stream crosses the washed-out road. The trail soon crosses another stream and then levels out.

At 2.2 mi, the Sleeping Beauty trail (80) departs R. (This is a more spectacular but longer and more strenuous route to the N end of Bumps Pond.) The trail bears L, now following red markers. It follows the road, going uphill fairly steeply with few switchbacks, over loose rock. An overlook is at 2.4 mi, and another at 2.6 mi. Buck Mt. is to the S, and Lake George to the SW. It's often possible to see ravens and hawks here.

The trail soon begins to level off, and at 2.8 mi begins a gradual descent, reaching Bumps Pond at 3.1 mi. On the L is the old stone chimney of a former hunting lodge that was part of the Knapp Estate. This is now an informal campsite.

The trail soon comes to the jct. with the Bumps Pond Spur (trail 87) on the L at 3.2 mi. The trail curves E around the N shoreline of Bumps Pond, then heads N, reaching the jct. with the N end of the Sleeping Beauty trail (80) on the R at 3.3 mi.

Continuing straight ahead (N) for Fishbrook Pond, at 3.4 mi the trail passes an old beaver dam, and soon after an old beaver pond. The road is wet for a while, then levels at 3.6 mi and is drier. The trail soon begins its descent past blowdown and a beaver pond L toward Fishbrook Pond, reaching a rusted culvert at 4 mi. Before long, Fishbrook Pond is visible through the trees, and at 4.2 mi there is a turnoff to a pretty point with a fireplace. A lean-to is visible on the N shore. From this point it's possible to walk around either side of the pond.

The trail L is the West Fishbrook Pond Trail (trail 79). Heading to the R, the trail reaches the S lean-to at 4.3 mi. Just beyond is a rocky outcrop with a nice view of the pond and the lean-to.

The trail bridges the pond's outlet at 4.4 mi. Just beyond, an orange-marked snowmobile trail heads off to the R. The trail ends at a jct. with the Fishbrook Pond from Lake George Trail (trail 97) and the Lapland Pond Trail (trail 100) at 4.6 mi. The N lean-to is 0.2 mi W on trail 97. This lean-to is situated at a pretty spot on a rocky shelf that slopes into the pond. Great blue herons may be seen in the shallows at the edge of the pond, and owls can be heard through the night.

❄ Trail in winter: Excellent for snowshoeing and cross-country skiing.

🥾 Distances: Hogtown trailhead to Dacy Clearing and Longway Trail (trail 85), 1.6 mi; to S end of Sleeping Beauty trail (80), 2.2 mi; to Bumps Pond, 3.1 mi; to N end of Sleeping Beauty trail, 3.3 mi; to Fishbrook Pond, 4.2 mi; to Fishbrook Pond from Lake George trail (97) and Lapland Pond Trail (trail 100), 4.6 mi (7.4 km).

79 West Fishbrook Pond Trail

Trails Illustrated Map 743: L–M30

▶Trailhead: This trail begins at 4.2 mi on the trail from Hogtown trailhead and Dacy Clearing (trail 78). ◀

From the jct. at the point on Fishbrook Pond (0.0 mi), take the L trail past the privy. At 0.1 mi, the trail crosses an inlet stream and at 0.5 mi it reaches another inlet. At 0.7 mi, the trail ends at the Fishbrook Pond from Lake George trail (97). Turning R (E) on trail 97, it is 0.2 mi to the lean-to on the N shore of Fishbrook Pond, and 0.4 mi to the intersection with trails 78 and 100.

❄ Trail in winter: Suitable for skiing and snowshoeing.
🚶 Distance: Trail 78 to Trail 97, 0.7 mi (1.1 km).

80 Sleeping Beauty

Trails Illustrated Map 743: L30

With all the switchbacks on the trail to the summit, this is a moderate walk to a great destination. To return, either use the ascent route, or continue N to Bumps Pond and return via trail 78 along Bumps Pond to the Hogtown trailhead.

▶ Trailhead: The yellow-marked trail begins at 2.2 mi on the Fishbrook Pond Trail (trail 78) from the Hogtown trailhead. ◀

From the trail jct. (0.0 mi), the Sleeping Beauty trail bears R and after crossing a wet area on logs climbs along the shoulder of a hill at 0.2 mi. At 0.4 mi, it passes a cliff on the L and soon switchbacks to the R. After another switchback, the trail becomes steeper and more eroded at 0.7 mi. It soon levels off for a short distance and then makes a R turn around a red pine on solid rock.

Soon there is a view through the trees, and shortly after at 1.1 mi the trail reaches a Y jct. The trail R continues to Bumps Pond. The L turn is a spur to the summit at 1.2 mi. From the top are fine views of Lake George and the SE Adirondacks. A narrow trail follows another ledge to just below the summit for an even broader expanse of view. Visible are Buck Mt. to the S, Shelving Rock Mt. to the W, and the Tongue Mt. area to the NW.

To continue on to Bumps Pond, from the Y intersection (1.1 mi) head N on the moderately-used trail. At 1.4 mi the trail enters a hemlock grove and soon dips into a wet hollow. After winding uphill through some birches and hemlocks, the trail begins its descent at 1.6 mi. At 2.1 mi, the trail crosses the outlet of Bumps Pond and climbs up a short hill to the T intersection with trail 78. From here it's 3.3 mi

Sleeping Beauty. James Appleyard

S on trail 78 to the Hogtown trailhead, making a total loop length from the Hogtown trailhead of 7.8 mi, including the 0.1 mi detour to the summit.
* Trail in winter: Suitable for snowshoeing.
* Distances: Trail 78 to Y jct. near summit, 1.1 mi; to summit, 1.2 mi (1.9 km); via Y jct. to Bumps Pond, 2.1 mi (3.4 km). From Hogtown trailhead register to summit of Sleeping Beauty, 3.4 mi (5.4 km). Ascent, 1038 ft (316 m). Elevation, 2347 ft (715 m).

81 Old Farm Rd.

Trails Illustrated Map 743: L29–30

This is a pleasant old carriage path that is currently used by both horses and hikers. Motorized vehicles are prohibited, except for snowmobiles in the winter. This old road flows gracefully downhill through bouldery woods with many beech and hemlocks. While it has no real destination, it's a great connector trail for a number of loop possibilities.

▶Trailhead: The trail begins at a barrier on Shelving Rock Rd. 1.3 mi W from the Hogtown trailhead (see trail 78). There are yellow horse trail markers to the jct. with trail 82, then blue past it.◀

From the barrier at Shelving Rock Rd. (0.0 mi), the trail follows an old carriage path. It starts heading uphill, passing by some sizable oaks, a result of the moderating effect of Lake George on the local microclimate. Much rock work was done to stabilize this road many years ago. The trail continues at a moderate grade uphill and passes through a grassy clearing with huge maples and a rock pile on the L, remnants of farming days. The intersection with the East Old Farm Rd. Leg (trail 82) is at 0.6 mi.

From the intersection, the trail heads in a northerly direction over rolling terrain. As the trail straightens out, look to the R for an old stone wall about 100 ft in the woods.

The trail continues straight for a while through pines and past a couple of old clearings. Soon the trail follows around an S-curve in a mixed hardwood forest and then continues on a long, gradual straightaway. At 1.3 mi, it reaches the intersection with the Shortway Trail (trail 84). To the L it's 1.9 mi to Shelving Rock Rd., and to the R it's 0.5 mi to Dacy Clearing.

Continue straight ahead across the intersection, soon going downhill and crossing a brook. The trail curves uphill to the L along the hill, then turns R again after cresting the hill. At 1.7 mi, the trail crosses a small stream where there are several huge old hemlocks. In a short distance, the trail ends at a jct. with the Longway Trail (trail 86) at 1.8 mi. At this point it's 1 mi R to Dacy Clearing and 1.2 mi L to the Shelving Rock Mt. trailhead.

* Trail in winter: Excellent for skiing and snowshoeing.
* Distances: Shelving Rock Rd. to jct. with trail 82, 0.6 mi; to Shortway Trail (trail 84), 1.3 mi; to Longway Trail (trail 85), 1.8 mi (2.9 km).

82 East Old Farm Rd. Leg

Trails Illustrated Map 743: L29–30

Trailhead: This connector from trail 78 to Old Farm Rd. (trail 81) begins 0.5 mi N of the Hogtown trailhead on trail 78. It has yellow horse trail markers.

Heading W from the Hogtown trailhead to Fishbrook Pond Trail (78) (0.0 mi), the trail crosses an old stone culvert at 0.2 mi. The path is built up with stonework along the hillside and for nearly a half-mile runs almost level through the woods. Ground cedar, princess pine, ferns, and beech saplings grow in this pretty woods. The road rises and falls, generally meandering downhill. At 0.7 mi, it ends at Old Farm Rd. (trail 81).

✻ Trail in winter: Suitable for both skiing and snowshoeing.

🐾 Distance: Trail 78 to trail 81, 0.7 mi (1.1 km).

83 West Old Farm Leg

Trails Illustrated Map 743: I29–30

From the barrier at Shelving Rock Road (0.0 mi.), this trail follows another old carriage path. It starts uphill, passing by some sizable oaks, a result of the moderating effect of Lake George on the local microclimate. Much rock work was done many years ago, to stabilize this road The trail continues uphill and passes through a grassy clearing with huge maples and a rock pile on the L, remnants of farming days. The intersection with 82 is reached at 0.6 mi.

From the intersection of 82 and 83 at 0.0 mi, the trail heads in a northerly direction on rolling terrain. As the trail straightens out, look for an old stone wall about 100 ft back in the woods. The trail straightens for a while through pines and a couple of old clearings. Soon the route makes an S-curve before a long straightaway.

At 0.7 mi, the trail reaches the intersection with the Shortway Trail (84). To the L, it's 1.9 mi to Shelving Rock Rd., and to the R it's 0.5 mi to Dacy Clearing. Continue straight across the intersection, soon going downhill and crossing a brook. The trail curves uphill to the L along the hill, and then turns R again after cresting the hill. At 1.1 mi, the trail crosses a small stream where there are several huge old hemlocks. In a short distance, the trail ends at a junction with the Longway Trail (85) at 1.2 mi. From this point, it's 1 mi R to Dacy Clearing, and 1.2 mi L to the Shelving Rock Mt. trailhead.

✻ Trail in winter: Good for snowshoeing.

🐾 Distances: Trail 82: From junction with Hogtown/Fishbrook Pond Trail (0.0 mi) to jct. with trail 83, 0.7 mi (1.1 km). Trail 83: From Shelving Rock Rd. (0.0 mi) to jct. with trail 82, 0.6 mi. (1 km). From jct. of trail 82 and trail 83 to Shortway Trail (84), 0.7 mi (1.1 km); to Longway Trail (85), 1.2 mi (1.9 km). There is minimal elevation change except on trail 83, which ascends almost 400 ft (122 m) to its jct. with trail 82.

84 Shortway Trail

Trails Illustrated Map 743: L29–30

▶Trailhead: This old road starts from the first small clearing of the old Dacy farm (1.4 mi from the Hogtown trailhead on trail 78). Raspberries are filling in the clearing. It is quite probable this was a farm-to-market road down to boats at the lakeshore. It proceeds to the Shelving Rock Mt. trailhead, 3 mi W on Shelving Rock Rd. from the Hogtown trailhead, which is a good place to spot a car for a return trip to Hogtown trailhead or Dacy Clearing. The choices for backpacking and skiing are extensive.◀

Because of frequent vandalism, there is no sign at the clearing. Yellow horse-trail markers point L, while a red horse-trail marker points R to Dacy Clearing.

From the clearing (0.0 mi), walk L, downhill through the clearing into the woods. You are in for a treat. At 0.2 mi, the road reaches a lovely glen with a stream on the R and a stone fire circle on the L. Ahead is a barrier with a stop sign. Just beyond it is a bridge over the stream. This is an E branch of Shelving Rock Brook below the S slope of Sleeping Beauty Mt.

The road reaches a second bridge as the stream flows L to R, weaving its way downhill. At 0.3 mi, the road crosses a third bridge. Hobblebush flowers float gracefully over the stream in late May. Christmas fern and ostrich fern grow beneath a canopy of white birches, hemlock, beech, maple, and hop-hornbeam.

At 0.5 mi, the road reaches an intersection with Old Farm Rd. (trail 81). The trail L goes S, then splits W to Shelving Rock Rd. or E to Dacy Clearing Rd. A sign on the R points back the way you came, to "Dacy Clearing Short Way." Across a small culvert, a trail coming in on the R has a sign, "Dacy Clearing Long Way." Continue downhill, straight ahead.

The grade becomes steeper. At 0.7 mi, the road enters a hemlock glade. At 0.8 mi, it goes along a broad ridge with a stream gurgling at the bottom of the hill to the R. At 0.9 mi, it descends more steeply. As it bends L the stream comes into full view to the R below.

The road cuts across a hillside and then winds around the contour downhill to a sturdy wooden bridge with railings. A stream comes downhill from the L over a 50 ft expanse of moss-covered solid rock. Fringed polygala ("gaywings") bloom in bright pink profusion along here in late May. The small, tubular, tropical-looking flowers with dark green glossy leaves are an especially welcome sign after the long winter. Fringed polygala is on the state list of protected plants.

At 1.1 mi, a lovely gorge with an exquisite rocky chasm below is a great picnic and wading spot (after mosquito season). Just upstream 60 ft is a series of pleasant cascades.

At 1.3 mi, the road crosses a large wooden bridge. There is a jct. on the L at 1.4 mi with the Big Bridges Trail (trail 91). The road to the Shelving Rock Mt. trailhead continues straight ahead.

At 1.6 mi a trail to the R bears a sign for Mt. Erebus and Shelving Rock Mt. (trail 86). This route also leads back (E) to the large clearing at Dacy Clearing.

The road crosses another bridge, on the level, then ascends among mature hardwoods and white pines. More fringed polygala blooms in late May at 1.7 mi, near a large birch cut up along the road. One giant log is propped on two shorter ones to make a perfect bench for lunch, contemplation, nature study, or rest.

At 1.8 mi, a sign at an intersection says "Dacy Clearing 2.0 mi." Continue straight. In 100 ft is another jct. with a road on the R that continues N over Mt. Erebus (trail 88) and a narrower trail W up Shelving Rock Mt. (trail 89).

At 1.9 mi, a small seasonal stream crosses the road. There is a water pipe on the L. At 2 mi, there is a culvert under the road. Now the road is a carpet of golden pine needles with brown pine cones. A stream to the L 4 ft below the road is another tributary of Shelving Rock Brook.

At 2.3 mi, at a jct. with the Shelving Rock Mt. Trail (trail 92), a sign says "Dacey Clearing 2.3 mi. [Dacy seems to be spelled with or without an "e" on various signs], Shelving Rock Mt. 1.5 mi, Black Mt. Point 4.6 mi, Shelving Rock Road .25 mi." Continue straight ahead. At 2.4 mi, the route ends at Shelving Rock Rd.

❋ Trail in Winter: Good for snowshoeing.

𝕽 Distances: Small clearing at Dacy Clearing to trail 84, 0.5 mi; to trail 91, 1.4 mi; to Longway Trail (trail 85), 1.6 mi; to jct. with trail 88, 1.8 mi; to trail up Shelving Rock Mt. (92), 2.3 mi; to Shelving Rock Rd., 2.4 mi (4.0 km).

85 Longway Trail

Trails Illustrated Map 743: L29–30

This is another beautiful "hidden" walk in the Shelving Rock area. Since the route is popular with horseback riders there are places (steep and wet) where horses' hooves have created considerable erosion and quagmires. Nonetheless, it is rather enjoyable to see a group of horseback riders coming through the woods.

▶Trailhead: On the NW side of the large clearing at Dacy Clearing, a sign, "Stop—barrier ahead," and a horse trail sign indicate the start of an old road. This is 1.6 mi from the Hogtown trailhead (trail 78). Two privies are on the L. There is a stop sign on a steel barrier across the entrance to the road, barring vehicles.◀

From the barrier (0.0 mi), the trail heads NW, gently descending through the woods along a rock-strewn hill on the R. There are light-blue horse trail markers. The trail, often filled with rocks, undulates through mixed hardwoods and crosses several very small brooks that feed into Shelving Rock Brook.

At 0.5 mi, a rocky cliff appears to the R, on the S side of Sleeping Beauty Mt. Christmas fern, maidenhair fern, round-leaved hepatica, hobble bush, goldenrod, Dutchman's breeches, white aster, meadow rue, and violets combine to make this a wildflower lover's heaven for three seasons of the year.

The trail continues W underneath the sheer cliffs of Sleeping Beauty Mt. to the N. Polypody ferns look like a toupee on top of a huge boulder.

At 0.9 mi, the sky opens up above a small beaver meadow, a haven for birds.

The trail crosses a small outlet stream on rocks placed there, then meanders above the little stream gurgling below. In mid-October the forest floor is a carpet of golden, brown, and red maple and beech leaves.

At 1 mi, at a jct. with Old Farm Rd. (trail 81), turn R onto a yellow-marked horse trail continuing W to Shelving Rock. Now the trail goes more steeply downhill. Horses' hooves have churned it into a muddy mire.

After another small stream crossing, the trail goes uphill on more solid ground. Mature beeches have fallen to the ground, allowing hundreds of beech saplings to start the race for light and life.

The trail now descends a gentle pitch above a tiny feeder stream for Shelving Rock Brook. Then it crosses the boulder-filled brook on a wooden bridge on top of an old, ambitiously constructed set of stone cribwork. Huge ash trees tower over this glen. The lovely rocky stream winds downhill on the L, now guarded by hemlocks, maple, and ash.

Yellow horse trail markers direct hikers to a short re-route closer to the stream to avoid a mire. Hikers may ignore the detours marked with surveyor's tape, but horseback riders will want to follow them.

Soon the trail heads down again on a gentle diagonal with a hill to the L. There is a side route marked with yellow horse trail markers and red surveyor's tape. The detour goes over and down a hill to intersect at 1.8 mi with an old road marked with blue horse trail markers. Three small logs have been placed across the road L. The Longway Spur Trail (86) is R. A lovely brook heads downhill to the L. This is the northernmost branch of Shelving Rock Brook, coming off Erebus Mt. With several attractive cascades here, the intersection is a good spot for a rest and picnic by the brook.

The trail heads WSW from the jct. The rushing stream gathers strength and flows noisily through a lovely little gorge down to the R, providing another nice spot to explore and rest.

The old trail winds through a dark and beautiful hemlock glen with Shelving Rock Brook merrily flowing down at a steeper angle on the R. The trail and stream flirt with each other, then finally become partners as they pass through a narrow draw. The trail is almost level, thanks to considerable rock work on the R.

The trail crosses a small feeder stream on rocks 300 ft before the intersection with the Shortway Trail (trail 84) from Dacy Clearing and Shelving Rock Mt. trailhead at 2.5 mi.

❈ Trail in Winter:: Good for snowshoeing.

🐾 Distances: Dacy Clearing to Old Farm Rd., 1 mi; to Longway Spur Trail, 1.8 mi; to Shortway Trail, 2.5 mi (4.1 km).

86 Longway Spur

Trails Illustrated Map 743: L29–30

This short connector provides access from the Longway Trail (trail 85) to the Erebus Mt. Trail (trail 88). Leaving trail 86 at its 1.8 mi point (0.0 mi), it goes upstream 100 ft, then crosses the stream on rocks just above a small picturesque waterfall. It continues upstream with blue horse trail markers and the stream on the R. Then it winds around uphill to an intersection with a beautiful old road to the Erebus Mt. Trail (trail 88), marked with red horse trail markers, at 0.2 mi.

❋ Trail in Winter: Good for snowshoeing.

🐎 Distance: Longway Trail (trail 85) to Erebus Mt. Trail (trail 88), 0.2 mi (0.3 km).

87 Bumps Pond Spur

Trails Illustrated Map 743: L–M30

▶Trailhead: The S end connects with the Hogtown trailhead to Fishbrook Pond Trail (78), 3.2 mi from the Hogtown trailhead. The N end intersects the Erebus Mt. Trail (trail 88) 2.1 mi from the Shortway Trail (trail 84), and 1.3 mi from the Lake George to Fishbrook Pond Trail (97).◀

The trail begins on the W shore of Bumps Pond (0.0 mi). Heading through the grasses into the woods, it begins a very gradual climb, passing by an old spring in a short distance. At 0.2 mi, the trail begins to descend along the top of a wooded ridge and then soon reaches a sharp switchback to the R and continues on a moderately steep descent. At 0.4 mi, there is a sharp L switchback, soon followed by another switchback to the R.

The descent moderates and soon levels off to a pleasant walk as the trail winds through the forest. Soon after crossing a stream on a plank bridge, it ends at the Erebus Mt. Trail (trail 88) at 0.9 mi.

❋ Trail in winter: A short, easy snowshoe or ski section sandwiched between more difficult terrain.

🐎 Distance: Bumps Pond to Erebus Mt. Trail (trail 88), 0.9 mi (1.4 km).

88 Erebus Mt. Trail

Trails Illustrated Map 743: L–M30

This trail runs in a NE direction centrally across the Shelving Rock trail system and helps connect routes from both sides of the region. In particular, it connects with the Ridge Trail (trail 94) in two spots, more easily linking the Lake George E shoreline area with the interior trail system. The trail proves a pretty hike, following the brook that drains the S side of Erebus Mt. (pronounced locally "Air-a-bus" and in Greek mythology meaning "dark, unfriendly place close to Hell"). It shows little signs of use, by horses or by people, especially near its summit. While the trail doesn't lead directly to the top of Erebus Mt., those who enjoy a good bushwhack challenge might enjoy exploring the woods above the cliffs near the top of the mountain. When hiking this trail it is important to remember that this is designated as a horse trail and that some wet and muddy areas are not bridged or maintained as though it were a hiking trail.

▶Trailhead: The S end begins on the Shortway Trail (trail 84) 0.6 mi E of the Shelving Rock Mt. trailhead (see trail 84) along Shelving Rock Rd. The N end is on the Fishbrook Pond from Lake George Trail (97), 1.6 mi E of the Lakeside Trail to Black Mt. Point (trail 95), and 1.2 mi W of the intersection of trails 78 and 100 at the NE corner of Fishbrook Pond. This trail has red horse trail markers.◀

The trail bears L from the Shortway Trail (trail 84) (0.0 mi) and heads gradually uphill. Almost immediately is the jct. with the First Ridge Spur Trail (89) on the L. The Erebus Mt. Trail continues on a constant gradual grade uphill to 0.3 mi, where it levels off briefly, then begins climbing again. The forest along most of this trail is a nice mix of maturing mixed hardwoods and conifers.

At 0.4 mi, the trail levels once again and soon reaches a jct. with the Longway Spur Trail (86) going R at 0.6 mi. It crosses a streambed (which may be dry), then at 0.7 mi crosses a stream on a wooden plank bridge.

The trail continues to climb at a gradual to moderate grade along the L bank of a pleasant stream that bubbles its way along over rocks and then rests in small pools. Before long, another jct. on the L at 1.3 mi is the Second Ridge Spur Trail (90).

The Erebus Mt. Trail soon climbs somewhat steeply up around a beautiful series of cascades on the R. After a brief respite, the trail climbs steadily once again along a series of rock ledges on the L, with another set of cascades off to the R. This area has a primeval feel to it. The trail then moderates briefly, crosses a plank bridge over a stream (that may be dry), and then at 1.5 mi crosses the main stream on some extensive rockwork.

The trail now continues up the R bank of the stream at a gradual grade uphill, soon reaching another plank bridge at 1.7 mi that re-crosses the stream by a rocky and mossy cascade. After the bridge, the trail climbs steeply and then continues up on mostly gradual to moderate grades. The trail levels off after passing through some blowdown, and reaches the jct. with the Bumps Pond Spur trail (87) at 2.1 mi. Bear L here for the Erebus Mt. Trail.

The trail now is mostly level, wandering in and out of a streambed (mostly dry except after a rain) and through some wet and muddy areas. At 2.4 mi, the trail passes by a large rock face on the R and then follows the base of these cliffs for a while. It may be possible to catch a glimpse of the upper reaches of these cliffs through some openings in the leaves on the trees. The trail soon begins another moderate ascent, and at 2.7 mi reaches a plateau, which is the highest point on this trail. From here, the trail drops and then climbs briefly again, with glimpses of Black Mt. to the N, before undertaking a moderately steep descent over a rocky trail to a jct. with the Fishbrook Pond from Lake George Trail (97) at 3.4 mi.

❅ Trail in winter: This trail is fine for skiing up to its jct. with the Second Ridge Spur Trail (trail 90). From there the steeper sections are more suited to snowshoeing, particularly the descent from the top of the trail down to the jct. with trail 97.

🕱 Distances: Shortway Trail to trail 86, 0.6 mi; to trail 90, 1.3 mi; to trail 87, 2.1 mi; to 97, 3.4 mi (5.4 km). Ascent from Shortway Trail to highest point, approx. 1600 ft (488 m).

89 First Ridge Spur

Trails Illustrated Map 743: L29

This is the first connecting spur from the Erebus Mt. Trail (trail 88) to the Ridge Trail (94). It bears L about 100 ft after the Erebus Mt. Trail leaves the Shortway Trail (84). The trail has yellow horse trail markers and orange snowmobile markers.

Leaving the Erebus Mt. Trail (trail 88) (0.0 mi), the trail heads across a wet area, then soon ascends along a rocky ledge. It levels off at 0.2 mi and comes to a wetland at 0.3 mi. It swings around the perimeter of the wetland, then at 0.5 mi heads W up a moderately steep ascent through a hemlock forest. The trail becomes more gradual for a short distance, then begins a moderate ascent up through a rocky gully with ledges on both sides. At the top of the gully it begins to level, reaching the Ridge Trail (trail 94) at 0.7 mi.

❄ Trail in winter: Good for snowshoeing.

🕱 Distance: Erebus Mt. Trail (trail 88) to Ridge Trail (trail 94), 0.7 mi (1.1 km).

90 Second Ridge Spur

Trails Illustrated Map 743: L–M30

Leaving the Erebus Mt. Trail (trail 88) (0.0 mi) at its 1.3 mi point, this trail follows blue horse trail markers. The trail first heads W through a predominantly hemlock forest. Soon it swings to the R, then winds back and forth, climbing on gradual to moderate grades. After crossing a wet area, it meets the Ridge Trail (trail 94) at 0.3 mi.

❄ Trail In Winter: Good for skiing and snowshoeing.

🕱 Distance: Erebus Mt. Trail (trail 88) to Ridge Trail (trail 94), 0.3 mi (0.5 km).

91 Big Bridges Trail

Trails Illustrated Map 743: L29

▶Trailhead: This route, an old road, starts 2.6 mi W of the Hogtown trailhead parking area off Shelving Rock Rd., just 0.1 mi W of the bridge over Shelving Rock Brook (see trail 75). There is a V-shaped entrance to the road on the N side of Shelving Rock Rd., across from an informal camping area. A sign points E along Shelving Rock Rd. to Hogtown trailhead parking area and W along the road to Shelving Rock Mt. trailhead; however, there may not be a sign for the destination of the route heading N into the woods: it connects to the Shortway Trail to Dacy Clearing (trail 84), and to the Longway Trail (trail 85). This old road is popular with horseback riders, snowmobilers, and skiers, as well as hikers. It is marked with blue horse trail markers after a barrier with a stop sign.◄

Past the barrier (0.0 mi), the old road goes gently uphill, and then levels under tall hemlock, ash, maple, white pine, and beech. Chanterelle mushrooms may be found here in fall.

In 0.3 mi, after an almost level walk, the road crosses Shelving Rock Brook on a large wooden bridge under gigantic pines, then a smaller bridge 30 ft beyond. Now the road curves uphill above the beautiful brook below a towering cliff. Considerable rock work on the L holds the road into the hill above the brook. Another tributary cascades down the cliff before joining the brook.

The road goes more steeply uphill, continuing to follow the brook. The stream here tumbles down through a rocky ravine.

At 0.8 mi, the road crosses a wooden bridge with railings on top of a spectacular old hand-built stone abutment. This is a good place to rest and explore.

At 0.9 mi, the Big Bridges Trail meets the Shortway Trail (trail 84) between Dacy Clearing and the trailhead for Shelving Rock Mt. To the R (E) it is 1.4 mi on the Shortway Trail to the small clearing at Dacy Clearing. To the L it is 1 mi to Shelving Rock Rd.

🐾 Distances: Shelving Rock Rd. to bridge over Shelving Rock Brook, 0.3 mi; to Shortway Trail, 0.9 mi (1.5 km).

92 Shelving Rock Mt. Trail

Trails Illustrated Map 743: L29

Shelving Rock Mt. is a pleasant walk with partially obstructed views from the top. There also are some nice views along the way, along a well-built carriage road.

▶Trailhead: The trail starts on the Shortway Trail (trail 84) 0.2 mi from its trailhead on Shelving Rock Rd. The trail has blue horse trail markers and orange snowmobile markers.◄

The trail departs L from Shortway Trail (84) (0.0 mi) and proceeds on the level under huge white pines for 0.3 mi. It enters a hemlock glade where stonework holds the roadbed. After a couple of switchbacks, the trail moderates and heads in a more N direction. At 0.4 mi, the trail switchbacks L (W). A long, steep, rocky slope is up to the R with several walled switchbacks ahead. The trail climbs uphill over the switchbacks that get increasingly steeper, reaching the top of them at 0.7 mi.

Now the trail rolls up and down a bit and then heads gently downhill to a jct. at 0.9 mi. The R fork (trail 93) heads N to the Lakeside Trail (trail 95) and also leads to the Ridge Trail (trail 94). Continue straight to Shelving Rock's summit, now with yellow markers. The trail rises at an easy grade under hemlocks, swinging from N to W to S high above Lake George. At 1.1 mi, the trail makes a switchback to the J., and at 1.3 mi reaches an expansive terrace-like grassy pulloff and overlook W to Lake George and Tongue Mt.

At 1.5 mi, the trail reaches the summit, overgrown with oak and sumac. S along a narrow trail there's an overlook above the young trees in a grassy clearing. Sleeping Beauty Mt. is to the E, Buck Mt. to the S, and some of the S end of Lake George may be visible. The Knapps had a pavilion on the summit of Shelving Rock Mt. for afternoon tea parties and evening dances (see chapter introduction).

🕺 Distances: Shortway Trail to trail 93, 0.9 mi; to overlook, 1.3 mi; to summit, 1.5 mi (2.4 km). From Shortway Trail trailhead, 1.7 mi (2.7 km). Elevation, 1130 ft (344 m). Ascent, approx. 650 ft (198 m).

93 Shelving Rock Mt. to Lakeside Trail

Trails Illustrated Map 743: L29

▶Trailhead: This interior trail connects the Shelving Rock Mt. Trail (trail 92) and the Lakeside Trail (trail 95) on the Lake George shoreline. There is no public access through the Knapp Estate at the S end of the Lakeside Trail, so the only return to Shelving Rock Rd. is by retracing one's steps back up and over the shoulder of Shelving Rock Mt., or by designing any of several long loops out of the numerous trails on the slopes and ridges of Erebus Mt. and Shelving Rock Mt. (see map for these and more possibilities for even longer loops farther to the E, with the lean-tos at Fishbrook Pond as a possible overnight stop). This trail has red markers.◀

Heading N from the jct. (0.0 mi) with trail 94, 0.6 mi from its start on trail 84 and 0.8 mi from the Shelving Rock Rd. trailhead, the trail descends slightly, reaching a jct. in about 200 ft with a closed trail that leads to private land. The trail soon switchbacks up a ridge to the R, then heads E across the ridge. It soon turns L at a small knoll, then drops into a small col and reaches a jct. on the R at 0.3 mi with the Ridge Trail (trail 94).

The trail bears L through a notch and soon begins a steep descent. After a switchback, the trail descends steeply, moderates a bit, then gets steep again.

At 0.8 mi, the trail descends along a ravine with huge rock walls covered with polypody ferns. Still heading steeply downhill, it reaches the Lakeside Trail (trail 95) at 1 mi. From this jct., a L turn leads to a dead end at private land in 0.6 mi. A R turn heads N to Red Rock Bay and Black Mt. Point.

✻ Trail in winter: The upper parts of this trail are too steep for skiing, particularly the descent to Lake George. They would be fine for snowshoeing, but be sure to carry instep crampons for icy conditions.

🕺 Distances: Shelving Rock Mt. Trail (trail 92) to Ridge Trail (trail 94), 0.3 mi; to Lakeside Trail, 1 mi (1.6 km).

94 Ridge Trail

Trails Illustrated Map 743: L29

This route is a horse trail that follows the ridge line from Shelving Rock Mt. to the W flanks of Erebus Mt., before dropping down to the shoreline of Lake George. The rugged trail traverses mostly through deep, dense hemlock forests, but there are open hardwoods on some of the rocky ledges. The views from a couple of vistas are expansive and unique. The trail appears to be little used, by horses or people. It is maintained as a horse trail, so there are no bridges over wet areas or rock work to stabilize some of the loose areas.

A recommended hike is to head up Shelving Rock Mt. (trail 84 to trail 92), over the Ridge Trail to the Lakeside Trail (95), then S to the Red Rock Bay Trail (trail 96), and return via the Ridge Trail and the First Ridge Spur Trail (trail 89) and back to the trailhead via the Shortway Trail (trail 84). This sounds complicated, but once on the trails it comes together easily; see the map referenced above. Total elevation gain is about 2300 ft; distance is about 10 mi over some very scenic country.

▶Trailheads: This is an interior trail. Access is from the Shelving Rock Rd. trailhead via the Shortway Trail (trail 84), the Shelving Rock Mt. Trail (trail 92), and the Shelving Rock Mt. to Lakeside Trail (trail 93). It is 1.4 mi from the trailhead on Shelving Rock Rd. to the SW start of the trail via these three trails. This access is marked with blue horse trail markers and orange snowmobile disks. The N access is from the Lakeside Trail (trail 95), 1.2 mi S of Black Mt. Point and 2.2 mi N of the jct. of the Shelving Rock Mt. to Lakeside Trail (trail 93). This access is marked with yellow horse trail markers.◀

From the jct. at the small col with the red-marked Shelving Rock Mt. to Lakeside Trail (trail 93) (0.0 mi), the blue-marked horse trail heads E and switchbacks up a small ridge. Once on the ridge line, there is a rocky outcrop to the L from which there are some views of Northwest Bay and the Tongue Mt. area, partially obstructed by treetops.

The trail continues along the ridge, then soon takes a R turn to the ridge top. It bears L along the flat, wooded ridge top, then heads more N again. At 0.3 mi, the trail crosses the first of three wet spots in a nice hemlock forest. The trail here, as in much of the way along the top, is in a deep forest. If not for the wind blowing across the ridge it would be easy to imagine the trail following a secluded ravine.

At 0.5 mi, the trail passes to the N of a rock shelf, then soon turns L and switchbacks down into a small col, reaching a jct. at 0.8 mi with the First Ridge Spur to the Erebus Mt. Trail (trail 89) to the R. It's 1.2 mi back to the Shelving Rock Rd. trailhead via this connector and the Shortway Trail (trail 84).

Continuing straight ahead (NE), the main trail climbs and then switchbacks up the ridge, then follows the ridge for a while. At 1 mi, the trail makes a sharp switchback R, heading SW along the side of the ridge. It soon swings around S and then E, and comes to some open hardwoods on top of a small cliff. First there's a view through the trees, then at 1.2 mi the trail comes to an open ledge just off the trail that's covered with lichens, caribou moss, and grasses. There are great views from the ledge that overlooks the Shelving Rock Brook basin. To the E is Sleeping Beauty Mt.; to the S is Buck Mt.; SW are Lake George and Shelving Rock Mt.; and NW is the Tongue Mt. area. Crane Mt. is in the distance beyond other mountains surrounding Lake George. Ravens often frequent this spot, floating on the thermals not far from the cliff.

The trail heads up over ledges with more vistas, then heads N back into the woods. The trail is mostly level, passing a couple of wet spots, and wanders up and down through the hemlock forest. At 1.7 mi, a jct. with the Red Rock Bay Trail (trail 96) is in a wet area. A sign points L for the lakeshore, 0.8 mi; ADK's measurement showed it to be 1.4 mi instead.

Heading straight ahead (N), the main trail soon swings R (E) and then S. It winds around uphill to the ridge top heading NE, reaching a wooded rocky ridge at 2 mi. After one has walked in the hemlocks for so long, the open hardwoods here are like a breath of fresh air.

After following the ridge a short distance, the trail circles around a wet area, climbs over the ridge top and descends along the SE side of the ridge. At 2.2 mi is the jct. with the Second Ridge Spur Trail to the Erebus Mt. Trail (trail 90 to 88). The snowmobile trail cuts to the R here, along with the blue-marked horse trail.

Head L for the Ridge Trail and up the rocky section that leads into a small ravine, now following yellow horse trail markers. At the head of the ravine is a sign for the trail to make a sharp L. From here the trail is mostly downhill to the lake along the NW side of the ridge. The trail descends gradually at first, and then at 2.5 mi begins a moderately steep descent with The Narrows of Lake George visible through the trees on the L.

At 2.8 mi, the trail goes down around a rocky ledge where there's a sign for a vista to the L. A spur trail leads to a small cliff in about 250 ft, with superb views of The Narrows with all the islands, the Bolton Landing area, Shelving Rock Mt. and the ridge the trail has been following, Tongue Mt., and numerous mountains in the distance. The trail rolls up and down a bit, then continues its descent on gradual to moderately steep grades, with a couple of steep sections.

Soon the trail follows and crosses a couple of small streams (these may be dry in late summer). At 3.6 mi, it crosses a larger stream, levels through evergreens for a short distance, and then swings L down around a rocky outcrop. There's a sign at 3.8 mi with an arrow pointing to the R. Before long the trail comes into a section of open hardwoods, with a few huge old oak trees towering overhead. The lake is visible through the trees, and the trail descends to the Lakeside Trail (trail 95) at 3.9 mi. Just beyond to the L are a tent platform and campsite (reservations required) on a small rocky point. This is a great place to enjoy the panorama up and down Lake George.

❋ Trail in winter: Not recommended as a ski trail, but a great snowshoe trail. With the leaves off the trees there are some better views, but not many. Instep crampons should be taken along for possible icy sections.

❊ Distances: Shelving Rock Mt. Trail (trail 92) to First Ridge Spur Trail (trail

89), 0.8 mi; to Red Rock Bay Trail (trail 96), 1.7 mi; to Second Ridge Spur trail (90), 2.2 mi; to Lakeside Trail, 3.9 mi (6.2 km). Highest elevation along the trail, approx. 1550 ft (472 m).

95 Lakeside Trail to Black Mt. Point
Trails Illustrated Map 743: L–M30

There is no public access through the Knapp Estate (see chapter introduction). The rather involved and strenuous access to the S end of this trail is via the Shortway Trail (trail 84) from its Shelving Rock Rd. Trailhead, up the Shelving Rock Mt. Trail (trail 92), and down the Shelving Rock Mt. to Lakeside Trail (trail 93). It is also accessible by boat at one of 20 campsites along Lake George or two picnic areas, all of which have docks. Other trails also connect to this old road, providing options for hikes of various lengths: from Erebus Mt. (trails 94 and 96), from Fishbrook Pond (trail 97), and from the Pike Brook Rd. trailhead (trails 98 and 99). But it is worth the effort, as this old roadway is a magnificent lakeside amble!

Reservations are required for the state campsites along the lake, and there's a nightly fee. In winter there is good skiing along the road and perhaps on the lake under optimal conditions. Shelving Rock Rd. is plowed in winter as far as the gate to the Knapp Estate.

This description begins at the SW end of the trail, 0.6 mi SW of its intersection with the Shelving Rock Mt. to Lakeside Trail (trail 93), which provides access from Shelving Rock Rd. as explained above, and proceeds ENE and then NE along the shoreline. Even with all these caveats, this is a wonderful lakeside hike!

From the private land boundary (0.0 mi), the trail mostly hugs the lakeshore as it heads ENE. At 0.1 mi, there is a point on the L, and at 0.2 mi a spring by the shore on the L with a dock for boaters to obtain spring water. At 0.4 mi, the road traverses a bluff by a point looking down into a lovely cove. The jct. with the Shelving Rock Mt. to Lakeside Trail (trail 93) is at 0.6 mi. Watch Island is offshore on the L. Red trail markers are infrequent here, but that is no problem since the trail, following an old roadway, is easy to follow.

Now the road goes uphill, levels off, and then goes downhill. At 1 mi, it passes a lovely low point that would be a good picnic spot. Now the road is level again, passing a point that forms the S boundary of Red Rock Bay. The road descends again a short distance, coming almost level with the bay.

The road reaches Commission Point at 1.2 mi, with hemlocks, a stone picnic pavilion, grills, and picnic tables spread along the S shore with six docks on the N shore. Overnight mooring from dusk to 9 AM has a fee (although boats may dock here overnight only if the campsites are full). Dogs are prohibited. There is a view S to Shelving Rock Mt., Pearl Point, and several islands, and directly W to Fork Island and Tongue Mt. In spring and fall this is a peaceful spot with the lake empty of motorboats and the tourists absent.

The road goes uphill from Red Rock Bay, rolls up and down, then at 1.5 mi levels out by the lake. To the L there is a dock on the N side of a point. This is the first of 20 state campsites along the way. A stream goes through a culvert under the old road. To the R is a dock on the S side of a point.

At 1.6 mi the road passes a springhouse in the woods to the R. A pipe from the springhouse goes under the road, then ends in mid-air, providing a source of water.

David Hough

Soon the road arrives above the second dock. There are two picnic tables, two grills, a stone fireplace, and two privies here. At 1.7 mi, there is another dock with several picnic tables, grills, a fireplace, and four privies, then two more docks.

At 1.8 mi, the road bends L. The Red Rock Bay Trail (trail 96) with yellow horse trail markers goes uphill to the R to the Ridge Trail (trail 94). Red horse trail markers indicate a little-used trail to the R. Keep on the road, which still bends L.

The road passes a R turn, then arrives at a T jct. It bears R onto a rocky bluff with a rope on a cable between two white pines above the water of Paradise Bay at 1.9 mi. The water has a green-blue tint here.

At 2 mi, the road meets another T jct. to complete a short loop. Turning L, at 2.1 mi the route passes an abandoned road on the R.

At 2.3 mi, the road arrives at the lake again, after an inland swing, at a tent platform, picnic table, fireplace, dock, and privy. At 2.4 mi, there is a similar campsite, also with a tent platform. After a third campsite, the road goes gently uphill, passing another campsite almost out of sight on a point at 2.5 mi. At 2.6 mi, the road passes another tent platform, another campsite without a platform, a dock in a cove within 50 ft of the road, then another tent platform campsite. At 2.7 mi, the Ridge Trail (trail 94) goes R up the W side of Erebus Mt. almost directly opposite a path lined with stones to a point with a tent platform campsite. At 2.8 mi, there are two more campsites on another point, with another campsite a short way beyond.

At 3.1 mi, the trail R leads to Fishbrook Pond (trail 97). There is yet another campsite on the R, and at 3.2 mi a campsite on the lake, followed by two more campsites. At 3.3 mi, the road crosses a rock streambed (sometimes dry) and arrives at Black Mt. Point with a stone picnic shelter, many picnic tables, and privies in a grassy area. At 3.4 mi there is another picnic area on a more northern point. On the N side are five docks. The Lakeside Trail ends at 3.5 mi, where the Black Mt. Trail (trail 98) heads uphill R.

❆ Trail in winter: Excellent lake-level skiing and snowshoeing, best accessed across the lake itself, only under amenable hard-frozen conditions.

🐾 Distances: Private land boundary at SW end to Shelving Rock Mt. to Lakeside Trail (trail 93), 0.6 mi; to Commission Point picnic area, 1.2 mi; to Red Rock Bay Trail (trail 96), 1.8 mi; to Ridge Trail (trail 94), 2.7 mi; to trail to Fishbrook Pond (trail 97), 3.1 mi; to Black Mt. Point picnic area, 3.3 mi; to trail up Black Mt. (trail 98), 3.5 mi (5.6 km).

96 Red Rock Bay Trail

Trails Illustrated Map 743: L–M29

This trail is marked as a horse trail, but is a fine hiking trail as it switchbacks up the rugged W flank of Erebus Mt. to meet the Ridge Trail (trail 94). A nice outlook at the top of a small cliff part way up looks over the central Lake George region. The trail is sparsely marked, but not too difficult to follow. At its terminus with the Ridge Trail a DEC sign states the distance to the lake to be 0.8 mi. ADK's measurement found this instead to be 1.4 mi.

▶Trailheads: On the N, this trail begins on the Lakeside Trail (trail 95) 1.3 mi NE of its jct. with the Shelving Rock Mt. to Lakeside Trail (trail 93), and 1.5 mi S of Black Mt. Point. The S terminus is on the Ridge Trail (trail 94), 1.7 mi from the Shelving Rock Mt. Trail (trail 92) and 3.1 mi from the Shelving Rock Mt. trailhead. The trail is marked with yellow horse trail markers.◀

From the jct. with the Lakeside Trail (trail 95), the trail heads uphill in a SE direction, and soon switchbacks up the hillside at a gradual to moderately steep angle. At 0.2 mi, the rocky trail heads up, over and around some rocky ledges, then, after using a small streambed, heads up and L across the hill. The sparsely marked trail soon turns L and then R up through a rocky gully and then winds across a level area to the side of the hill. This is quite a rugged horse trail, parts of it being more reminiscent of High Peaks foot trails than gentle horse trails.

The trail soon begins a gradual ascent, heading S along the hillside. It becomes moderately steep along some ledges on the L, then begins a series of switchbacks, some of them fairly steep. At 0.5 mi, the trail follows along a cliff, first with views through the trees, and then with a fine panorama from a rocky ledge (50 ft from the trail) of The Narrows, Tongue Mt., and the Shelving Rock Mt. area. Just beyond this lookout is a rock knoll about 100 ft off the trail with even more expansive views.

After climbing briefly, the trail levels among some hemlocks and then wanders around and across a small stream. At a R turn the trail begins climbing up on a moderate grade. It ascends a rocky area at 0.8 mi and continues a gradual ascent, heading SW along the hillside.

The trail soon turns L at a sharp switchback, now heading NE. After more switchbacks, the trail once again heads SW on a gradual to moderate grade.

At 1.1 mi, the trail follows along a ledge on the L, on a gradual grade through a deep hemlock forest. After leveling off at 1.3 mi, the trail begins a very gradual descent to its jct. with the Ridge Trail (trail 94) at a wet area at 1.4 mi, having ascended approx. 900 ft from Lake George.

❄ Trail in winter: This is not recommended as a ski route, but would be good for snowshoeing. It would be wise to carry instep or full crampons for the potentially icy sections.

🥾 Distances: Lakeside Trail (trail 95) to lookout, 0.5 mi; to jct. with the Ridge Trail, (trail 94) 1.4 mi (2.2 km).

97 Fishbrook Pond from Lake George
Trails Illustrated Map 743: M29–30

This is a nice connector trail, tying the Lakeside Trail (trail 95) with the midpoint of the trail system that runs up the E side from Hogtown to Pike Brook Rd. (principally trails 78 and 100). It climbs steadily at a fairly steep grade up along a brook that drains the N side of Erebus Mt., and contributes to several loop possibilities from both the N and the S. The trail gains about 1600 ft in elevation from the lake shore to the pond, so it's not to be taken lightly, but it adds some real diversity to the possibilities in the region.

▶Trailhead: The W terminus is at a jct. with the Lakeside Trail (trail 95) 2.5 mi N of the Shelving Rock Mt. Trail jct. (trail 93). This is 0.2 mi S of the Black Mt. Point picnic area and 0.4 mi S of the jct. with the Black Mt. Trail (trail 95). The E end is at a jct. at the NE corner of Fishbrook Pond, 4.6 mi N of the Hogtown trailhead via trail 78 and 4 mi S of the Pike Brook trailhead via trails 99 and 100. The trail follows red markers and yellow horse trail markers.◀

There are two beginnings to this trail where it intersects with the Lakeside Trail (trail 95) (0.0 mi). A short distance apart, these spurs join at 0.1 mi; the N leg is the official trail. The trail soon reaches switchbacks and an outlook at 0.4 mi and continues up the ravine with the stream and a steep drop-off on the L. At 0.5 mi, bear L where it looks like an old logging road might lead off to the R.

After climbing steeply along the ravine, the trail begins to moderate somewhat as it swings away from the stream. The woods are a mix of hardwood saplings interspersed with huge old trees.

At 1.6 mi, the Erebus Mt. Trail (trail 88) comes in from the R. Go straight ahead for Fishbrook Pond. The trail is now level with occasional wet spots. It passes a beautiful white ash just before reaching a ridge on the L that rises up from the N end of Fishbrook Pond. Elevation at the height of land here is approx. 1940 ft, about 1620 ft above Lake George. The trail descends moderately through an open hardwood forest, passing by a considerable amount of beaver handiwork, and at 2.2 mi meets the West Fishbrook Pond Trail (trail 79) on the R. Continue straight ahead following the red markers.

At 2.6 mi, the trail reaches the N lean-to on Fishbrook Pond. This lean-to is a great place to camp or just view the pond and the wildlife from the ledge that slopes into the water in front of it. The trail continues E and at 2.8 mi connects with the Hogtown Trail on the E side of Fishbrook Pond (trail 78) and the Lapland Pond Trail (100). The Greenland Pond trail (trail 102) is about 250 ft to the N on trail 100.

❊ Trail in winter: This is a steep trail and can be icy in spots; a great snowshoeing trail, but not a recommended ski route.

🦶 Distances: Lakeside Trail (trail 95) to Erebus Mt. Trail (trail 88), 1.6 mi; to West Fishbrook Pond Trail (trail 79), 2.2 mi; to lean-to, 2.6 mi; to end at trails 78 and 100, 2.8 mi (4.5 km).

98 Black Mt. Point to Black Mt.

Trails Illustrated Map 743: M30

Black Mt., on the E side of Lake George, is the highest mountain in the Lake George area. From the top of Black Mt. are some of the finest views in the Lake George region, and this trail from the shoreline of Lake George is the most spectacular way to climb to the top. It is the lesser used of the two trails up Black Mt. (the other is trail 99), but definitely the more interesting of the two. Leaving the shoreline at one of the wildest remaining areas of the lake, and then climbing past waterfalls and over open rock ledges on the way to the summit, the trail gives a feel of what it may have been like when this region was a summer home for Native Americans hundreds of years ago.

▶Trailhead: This trail begins at the N end of the Lakeside Trail (trail 95) at Black Mt. Point, which is accessible by boat, or by one of the many trails that come from S in the Shelving Rock area. This trail is also accessible from the summit of Black Mt. via the trail from Pike Brook Rd. (trail 99). It is marked with red markers.◀

At the jct. with the Lakeside Trail (trail 95) (0.0 mi) at Black Mt. Point, the trail heads steeply uphill E. At 0.3 mi, it crosses an expanse of bedrock, moderating as it meanders through a forest of tall hemlocks. A brook down to the L comes from the Black Mt. Ponds. The trail soon crosses the brook and climbs again until at 0.6 mi it levels off briefly and bends L.

At 0.7 mi, climbing begins again, past a small gorge on the L. Then the trail bends R away from the gorge and to the E. A short detour to the gorge will bring you to a number of pretty cascades and flumes just out of sight of the trail.

At 0.8 mi, the route makes a switchback L, not far from some more rushing water. Soon the trail is back along another gorge on the stream on the L, and at 1.1 mi the cascades in the stream are once again visible from the trail.

The trail soon bends R away from the stream, heading up over bare rock. At 1.3 mi, the trail climbs steeply along a huge rock filled with moss, lichens, and ferns on the L. It soon crosses a stream, then briefly levels off. At 1.6 mi, it crosses a stream on a wooden bridge, just below a small waterfall. The jct. with the Black Mt. Ponds Trail (trail 101) is at 1.8 mi; to the R are the Black Mt. Ponds and Lapland Pond.

From Black Mountain summit. Carl Heilman II

Heading L, the trail climbs to 2 mi, where it passes a huge rock wall on the R and then comes to a rocky outcrop with a nice view. Just off the trail there's a rock ledge that overlooks the twin Black Mt. Ponds. The trail levels off briefly, then climbs up several switchbacks with some nice views, reaching a spur trail on the R at 2.6 mi. This trail leads to a grassy clearing and ledges with a great view to the S of Lake George and many of the islands. Below are the Black Mt. Ponds, with Lapland Pond farther E.

The main trail soon passes a slanting rock wall, then heads over bare rock and reaches the NY State Police communications tower at the summit at 2.8 mi. Here it meets the trail from Pike Brook Rd. (trail 99).

❄ Trail in winter: A great snowshoe trip with a good snowfall, or an advanced-level ski from trail 99 down to Lake George. Access is a challenge. Be sure to have instep crampons for icy conditions.

🥾 Distances: Black Mt. Point to Black Mt. Ponds Trail (trail 101), 1.8 mi; to summit, 2.8 mi (4.5 km). Elevation, 2646 ft (807 m). Ascent from Lake George, 2326 ft (709 m).

99 Black Mt. from the East

Trails Illustrated Map 743: M30

Black Mt., on the E side of Lake George, is the highest mountain in the Lake George area. Since this trail, from Pike Brook Rd., starts at 1600 ft, it is a climb of only 1046 ft to the summit at 2646 ft. The ascent from the shoreline of Lake

Black Mt. view. John Kettlewell

George on the W trail is much greater (see trail 98).

▶ Trailhead: From NY 22, approx. 18 mi S of the Fort Ticonderoga entrance road, turn W at the sign for Huletts Landing and drive 2.7 mi to a L turn onto Pike Brook Rd. At 0.8 mi is the trailhead parking lot and register for Black Mt. ◀

Following red trail markers, at 0.5 mi the road reaches an old farmhouse and barn. It turns R here and goes up behind the farm. At 0.7 mi, the road crosses a wet place and ascends gently.

At 1 mi, the road reaches a jct. The Lapland Pond Trail (trail 100) to Lapland, Millman Pond, and Fishbrook Ponds (each with lean-tos) goes L; Black Mt. is straight ahead.

At 1.3 mi, the road divides; the L branch is recommended. At 1.4 mi, the trail crosses a wet place. It soon crosses a lovely brook tumbling across shelving rocks and at 1.6 mi crosses the brook at another jct., where a snowmobile trail joins the trail and veers off again. The trail goes L along the stream. It becomes steep, going up a small rock staircase. At 1.7 mi, it goes up bare rock next to the stream. Now the trail is washed out. At 2 mi, it follows a small streambed, then cuts R away from the stream.

At 2.1 mi, the trail becomes very steep in a fern-filled glen. At 2.2 mi, avoid a R turn for a snowmobile trail.

The trail divides again. These forks rejoin; the L fork enters a clearing with huge open rock. Ahead are the closed ranger's cabin, toolshed, and woodshed. At 2.5 mi, the trail reaches the NY State Police communications tower. There is a view the length of Lake George, except for The Narrows, which is obstructed by the W shoulder of the mountain.

Sugarloaf Mt., directly NE, has a transmitter tower on top. Elephant Mt. to the N obstructs the view of Huletts Landing; Bluff Point is the first point in view on the E shore, with Sabbath Day Point across on the W shore. The High Peaks stretch out to the NW.

❄ Trail in winter: A good snowshoe trail with some fairly steep climbing near the top. Instep crampons are recommended for icy sections.

🏃 Distances: Pike Brook Rd. trailhead to Lapland Pond trail (trail 100), 1 mi; to summit, 2.5 mi (4.3 km). Elevation, 2646 ft (807 m). Ascent, 1046 ft (337 m).

100 Lapland Pond Trail

Trails Illustrated Map 743: M30

This is a great hiking trail that connects the Pike Brook Rd. trailhead (via the start of trail 99) and the Black Mt. area with the NE corner of the Shelving Rock trails SW of Fishbrook Pond. It also takes in three ponds (Lapland, Millman, and Fishbrook), and connects with the trails to the others in this quadrant (Black Mt. Ponds and Greenland Pond). Within this embrace are a half-dozen lean-tos, all on ponds; some great hiking potential; and some great fishing, too.

▶ Trailheads: The N end of this trail is at the jct 1 mi SW of the Pike Brook trailhead on the Black Mt. from the East trail (99). S access is from the NE corner of Fishbrook Pond at the jct. with the trail from the Hogtown trailhead (trail 78) and the Fishbrook Pond from Lake George trail (97).◄

From the jct. with the Black Mt. from the East Trail (99) (0.0 mi), the trail heads S following blue markers. The trail goes along a wetland on the R until crossing a wooden bridge next to a beaver dam at 0.2 mi. Because of backwaters caused by industrious beavers, the routes in this area may change somewhat from time to time. At 0.5 mi, the trail passes a tiny pond, and soon crosses a stream. This section can be wet.

At 0.8 mi, the trail starts heading downhill and at 0.9 mi reaches a blue-marked spur for the Lapland Pond lean-to on the N shore. (This spur heads L over the stream and along the pond about 250 yd to a nice lean-to on a point above the pond. From the point, a giant rock slopes into the water. Ducks and herons feed in the shallows around the pond. This would be a great pond to paddle in a small ultralight canoe.)

The main trail proceeds from the jct. and at 1 mi crosses an inlet to Lapland Pond. After emerging from a grove of hemlocks, at 1.1 mi there is a sign for the trail R to "Black Mt. Ponds" (trail 101). An informal path goes sharp L to the shore of Lapland Pond.

The trail heads L toward Millman Pond, now following yellow markers. It soon becomes a narrow, little-used footpath, crosses a couple of inlet streams, and then heads uphill at 1.2 mi, arriving at the end of a marshy section of Lapland Pond at 1.4 mi. Here the trail turns L, following the marsh, and soon crosses a brook on stones. It crosses a wet area and then heads uphill to a T jct. with a wide snowmobile trail at 1.6 mi. (The snowmobile trail L heads E and eventually comes out on lower Pike Brook Rd.) It would be good to look behind you here to note this turnoff to pass on your return trip. Look for the trail markers, and listen for the rushing of the stream.

After turning R, the trail heads uphill with the stream on the R. It crosses the stream below a nice 4 ft waterfall. Here a snowmobile trail goes straight and the foot trail turns L.

Continuing uphill, with the stream on the R, the trail soon re-crosses the stream and goes up along the side of a hill. It comes to a flume on the outlet of Millman Pond at 1.8 mi. Soon the trail goes uphill, reaching a crest at 1.9 mi, then heads down toward Millman Pond. At 2 mi, the trail crosses an inlet stream on a bridge, with a bog on the L. It turns abruptly R and shortly comes to a lean-to on the E side of the pond at 2.1 mi. This is situated on a bluff that overlooks the pond. It has been very well taken care of by its adopter.

Heading S, the trail reaches the end of the pond at 2.2 mi, then turns L and uphill, following a stream and snowmobile markers. At a wet place, the snowmobile trail and the hiking trail divide. They soon rejoin after crossing a stream at 2.4 mi, and then make a sharp L.

The trail heads downhill with the stream on the L, flanked by a steep hillside.

It rolls up and down a little, then climbs again and reaches the top of a pass at 2.8 mi. Now the trail heads downhill to Fishbrook Pond, crosses a stream, then turns L and keeps heading downhill, first coming to the Greenland Pond trail (102) on the L, and then, in approx. 250 ft, a jct. with the Fishbrook Pond from Lake George Trail (97) to the R (W) and the trail to Hogtown trailhead via Bumps Pond and Dacy Clearing (trail 78) straight ahead. An unmaintained trail heads L (E) from this jct. There's a lean-to to the R at the N end of Fishbrook Pond, another along trail 78 at the S end of Fishbrook Pond (both of which are too close to the water, according to state regulations), and yet another 1.2 mi away on the E shore of Greenland Pond.

❄ Trail in winter: A good, challenging showshoe or intermediate-level ski trip.

🥾 Distances: Black Mt. Trail to lean-to spur on Lapland Pond, 0.9 mi; to Black Mt. Ponds Trail (trail 101), 1.1 mi; to Millman Pond lean-to, 2.1 mi; to jct. with trails 78 and 97, 3 mi (4.8 km).

101 Black Mt. Ponds Trail

Trails Illustrated Map 743: M30

This is a short connector trail between the Black Mt. Point to Black Mt. Trail (98) and the Lapland Pond Trail (trail 100) that not only helps form some interesting loops, but is also a good trail to hike in its own right. There's a lean-to on the westerly of the two Black Mt. Ponds, and the trail passes through some nice woods and beaver work. For those who walk slowly and take the time to observe all the signs, there's the possibility of seeing a good bit of wildlife in the area.

▶ Trailheads: This is an interior trail. The W end is 1.8 mi E of Black Mt. Point and 1 mi S of Black Mt. summit on trail 98. The E end is at Lapland Pond on trail 100, 2.2 mi SW of the Pike Brook Rd. trailhead. The trail is marked with yellow markers. It is described from W to E. ◀

Black Mt. Pond. James Appleyard

Heading E from the Black Mt. Point to Black Mt. trail (98) (0.0 mi), at 0.2 mi the trail follows a rise with the first Black Mt. Pond below to the R, and soon reaches the edge of the pond. Across a stream and up a short, steep hill is the lean-to just off the trail at 0.3 mi. There's a nice view of the pond from the lean-to.

The trail follows along the edge of the pond, then at 0.4 mi heads up a hill and back into a hemlock woods. At 0.6 mi, it goes down a short, steep hill to an inlet to the second of the Black Mt. Ponds. It crosses another inlet at 0.7 mi and provides a view of this pond and the beaver activity there at 0.8 mi. The trail continues back in the woods, reaching the jct. with the Lapland Pond Trail (trail 100) at 1 mi.

✣ Trail in winter: An easy winding and nearly level ski or snowshoe to two ponds.

❀ Distances: Black Mt. Point to Black Mt. trail (98) to lean-to, 0.3 mi; to second Black Mt. Pond, 0.8 mi; to Lapland Pond Trail (trail 100), 1 mi (1.6 km).

102 Greenland Pond

Trails Illustrated Map 743: L–M30

While this trail is short but sweet, any public route to get to it is at least 4 mi long. Greenland Pond, though, is well worth the visit. It's a pretty little isolated pond, with a lean-to situated on the E shore, a nice place to camp and fish.

▶Trailhead: The trail begins on the Lapland Pond Trail (trail 100) 250 ft N of the intersection of trails 78, 97, and 100 at the NE corner of Fishbrook Pond. The Hogtown trailhead is 4.6 mi to the S on trail 78, and the Pike Brook Rd. trailhead is 4 mi to the N via trails 99 and 100. Black Mt. Point, reachable by boat on Lake George, is 3 mi to the W via trails 97 and 95. The trail is marked with red markers.◀

From the Lapland Pond Trail (trail 100) (0.0 mi), the trail passes E over some potentially wet areas. At 0.3 mi, it crosses a stream on stones and begins heading downhill. It soon crosses the stream again, and then turns L and continues downhill. After passing a pretty set of falls at 0.5 mi, at 0.7 mi the trail crosses another stream and then comes to Greenland Pond.

The trail follows the SW shore of the pond, crosses a couple of inlets, and then at 1 mi crosses a larger inlet. It continues around the S end of the pond, and crosses the outlet on a bridge. There is a jct. here; an unmarked trail S leads to private land in a short distance. The red-marked trail heads N (L) a short distance up the E shore of the pond, reaching the lean-to at 1.2 mi.

✣ Trail in winter: Good snowshoeing and intermediate-level skiing, but remote.

❀ Distances: Lapland Pond Trail (trail 100) to falls, 0.5 mi; to Greenland Pond Lean-to, 1.2 mi (1.9 km).

GULL BAY PRESERVE

Trails Illustrated Map 743: P31

This preserve is a recent project by the very active Lake George Land Conservancy (LGLC), and it is located just back from the NE shore of Lake George. The preserve encompasses three trails, a lookout over the lake, and three wetlands, one of which houses a great blue heron rookery.

Richard Nowicki

▶Trailhead: From Ticonderoga, at the intersection of Montcalm St. and NY 22, head R (S) on Rt. 22 for 9.5 mi to Gull Bay Rd. Turn R. At 1.8 mi, turn R (W) on to Sagamore Rd., and at 0.6 mi turn R into the parking area, which may be muddy. Park in the first clearing and then walk to the preserve kiosk 0.1 mi up the dirt road. Please do not park in the sand pit by the kiosk; that area is being reseeded. There are numerous woods roads in the area so keep a careful eye out for trail markers.◀

103 Blue Trail

See Gull Bay Preserve above

This short trail leaves the sand pit behind the kiosk (0.0 mi), heading up along a rocky road. It flattens out in the woods, at 0.2 mi passes a jct. to the L with the Orange Trail (trail 104), and arrives at a lookout with wonderful views S over Lake George at 0.3 mi.

❄ Trail in winter: Very suitable for snowshoeing; the first hill could be challenging to skiers.

🚶 Distances: Kiosk to Orange Trail (trail 104), 0.2 mi; to lookout, 0.3 mi (0.5 km).

104 Orange Trail

See Gull Bay Preserve above

Leaving the Blue Trail (trail 103), the trail descends a steep, rocky road to a jct. with double orange markers in a small clearing at 0.1 mi. Turn L and follow the road over bare rocks and past vernal pools. The trail goes over a rise with a large rock face on the L at 0.5 mi and swings R past a swamp. It bears L at an unmarked fork at 0.9 mi and downhill to openings with good views of the heron rookery on the L.

The trail crosses the outlet of a pond, bearing R at a jct. at a tree with eight orange markers. It goes through a long and lovely stand of ferns to another fork. Follow the trail L at the two orange markers as it loops over a hill, down along the shore of the pond, and back to the jct. by the outlet at 1 mi.

✽ Trail in winter: Excellent for snowshoes; only the first hill would be problematic for skiers.

🐾 Distances: Blue Trail (trail 103) to first fork, 0.1 mi; to rock face, 0.5 mi; to unmarked fork L, 0.9 mi; to jct. at outlet of pond, 0.8 mi; loop back to outlet, 1 mi (1.6 km).

David Hough

105 Yellow Trail

See Gull Bay Preserve, p. 129

This new trail, on both path and woods roadway, runs along the W and N edges of the beaver and heron rookery pond. It is described from its start on the Blue Trail (trail 103), near the trail register at the Gull Bay Preserve.

At 0.1 mi along the Blue Trail (trail 103), turn L at yellow markers along a woods road. The roadway ascends gradually and becomes a footpath above the pond. There are occasional glimpses through the trees to the water. The route then climbs more steeply and winds along a side-hill before reaching a fork; either direction makes a loop back to this spot. The fork R heads downhill to the shore of the pond and several good vistas of beaver and heron activity. (This trail section is closed during the nesting season between April and July.) After reaching the foot of the pond at an overgrown beaver dam, the route bears L away from the water and avoids a woods roadway to the R. Head gently uphill past numerous clumps of ferns to a fork. Stay L to complete the loop as it circles back to the rest of the Yellow Trail and the route back to the parking lot.

✽ Trail in winter: This trail makes for good snowshoeing and intermediate-level skiing.

🐾 Distances: From Blue Trail (103) to beginning of loop intersection, 0.6 mi; around loop to same intersection, 1 mi (0.6 km).

LAST GREAT SHORELINE PRESERVE

Trails Illustrated Map 743: P31

This new (2008) Lake George Land Conservancy (LGLC) preserve protects the final significant stretch of undeveloped shore along Lake George. It is on the northeastern part of the lake, near the northern end of the LGLC's Gull Bay Preserve. There are two trails here. The terrain is rolling, with some steep drops both to the swamp on the E and to Lake George on the W. Dark hemlock glades mix with oak and pine and small meadow gaps in the forest. Bobcats were photographed here in 2010, and the preserve will become the first managed wildlife refuge along Lake George.

▶Trailhead: From the intersection of NY 22 and Montcalm Street in Ticonderoga, drive 5.8 mi S to Glenburnie Rd., CR 1. Turn R or W and travel 1.5 mi, and turn L on Warrick Rd. Follow this dirt road another 0.8 mi across a wetland and up a hill to the preserve parking area on the L (or along the shoulder until parking lot is completed).◀

106 Lake George View Trail

See Last Great Shoreline Preserve, p. 130

This trail, marked blue, begins at the trail register and heads S both on and alongside an old logging road. This land was logged in the 1960s, so there are skidder scars on some of the trees along the trail as well as second growth in some of the forest gaps.

It starts gradually uphill over rolling woods and intersects with the red-marked Ticonderoga and Green Mountain Overlook Trail (trail 106A) at 0.1 mi. The blue trail continues its slight climb on the old roadway until it again intersects with the far end of the same Overlook Trail at 0.4 mi. The Lake George View Trail heads W on the level before descending to cross a small scree field in a forest clearing. This up-down character continues by a fern-covered cliff on the R and through open and dark forest until it reaches two mossy hummocks, ending at four blue markers and an overlook above Lake George, at 1.3 mi.

❅ Trail in winter: Suitable for snowshoeing and intermediate-level skiing, with plenty of snow cover.

🐾 Distances: To first intersection with red-marked Overlook Trail (106A), 0.1 mi; to second intersection with red trail, 0.4 mi; to start of Gull Bay Extension Trail (105), 0.5 mi; to Lake George View, 1.3 mi (2.1 km).

106A Green Mountain and Ticonderoga Overlook Trail

See Last Great Shoreline Preserve, p. 130

This is a short spur trail, marked red, off of the Lake George View Trail (trail 106), which it leaves at 0.1mi past the trail register. The trail goes L uphill onto a plateau which drops steeply to a wetland on the E. The brink of this drop-off affords several good vistas toward the Green Mountains of Vermont. After 0.4 mi, the route returns to the main Lake George View Trail (106).

View from Crane Mountain. James Appleyard

Hoffman Notch Wilderness, Wilcox Lake Wild Forest,
and Other Areas West of the Northway

This is the most westerly section of the eastern region. The Hoffman Notch Wilderness is bordered by the Northway (I-87) to the E, and CR 2, the Boreas Rd., to the N. The Wilcox Lake Wild Forest encompasses a large area E of NY 30 N of Northville, and E of NY 8 N of Wells. It is bordered to the N by NY 8 and NY 28. In addition, this section includes various interesting hikes like Spruce Mt., the Pack Demonstration Forest, the Hudson River Recreation Area, and Moreau Lake State Park that are not associated with a wild forest or wilderness area. The major roads and highways surrounding the region grant relatively easy access to some of the most attractive, seldom visited mountains in the Park.

Although much of the land in this section is privately owned, many of the mountains are accessible using state trails or bushwhacking through unposted land. They are well-worth climbing for their rugged scenery and windswept, bare summits, a legacy of the forest fires at the turn of the century. Lumber companies had stripped most of the trees, and the dry slash they left burned fiercely when ignited by lightning or the sparks from a passing railroad engine. Rains and melting snows subsequently washed much of the thin soil from the rocky mountaintops. Today lichens, mosses and mountain berries grow there in undisturbed carpets of jewel-like green, red and yellow.

The forested slopes have largely recovered, and provide attractive routes for the hiker. Four of the loveliest mountains in this section are trailless and must be climbed with caution—and always with a topographic map and compass. (See Introduction for more information on bushwhacking.)

The Wilcox Lake Wild Forest and Baldwin Springs areas can be accessed by a number of trails and from several highways, including NY 30 and NY 8. The land is rugged, with a variety of terrain, including several small lakes and swamps. Although small wooded mountains dot the landscape, the only mountain worthy of climbing for its incredible views is Mt. Blue (trailless).

The Wilcox Lake Wild Forest and Baldwin Springs section contains the most lengthy hikes in the eastern region, and they are sometimes muddy and difficult due to use of many trails by ATVs and other off-road vehicles. Baldwin Springs, once the hub of several old roads, which led into a tiny settlement and surrounding farms during the heyday of the lumber and tanning industries, is an attractive and interesting pine barrens. The spring that gives the clearing its name can still be found to the R of the trail register, welling up through the center of an ancient hollow log.

Suggested hikes in the region include:

SHORT HIKES:
Hadley Mt.—1.8 mi (2.9 km). A short but rewarding climb to a bare summit with outstanding vistas.

Cod Pond—1.2 mi (1.9 km). A hike on varied terrain to an attractive pond with good wildlife viewing.

MODERATE HIKES:
Crane Mt.—1.4 mi (2.2 km). This spectacular mountain can be hiked up one side and descended on the other, with a visit to Crane Mt. Pond along the way, to make an adventure-filled loop back to the parking lot. (Loop distance 4.1 mi.)

Round Pond from Garnet Lake—2.3 mi (3.7 km). A pleasant walk along a snowmobile trail to a seldom-visited little pond offering privacy and superb scenery.

Tenant Creek Falls—2.1 mi (3.4 km). Follow a woodland path upstream and visit three beautiful waterfalls.

HARDER HIKES:
Baldhead Mt. and Moose Mt.—3.6 mi (approx.) (5.8 km). Bushwhack to a pristine pair of neighbors, each offering super views from bare, rocky summits.

Wilcox Lake from Brownell Camp—5.2 mi (8.3 km). A pleasant walk mostly along picturesque East Stony Creek to the shores of attractive Wilcox Lake.

Mt. Blue—2 mi (approx.) (3.2 km). If you can obtain a small boat to cross the lake, bushwhack up this marvelous mountain for a super view you have to see to believe (on a clear day!).

	Trail Described	Total Miles (one way)		Page
107	Hoffman Notch	7.4	(11.8 km)	136
107A	Big Pond	5.7	(9.1 km)	137
108	Bailey Pond	1.0	(1.6 km)	138
109	Severance Mt.	1.2	(1.9 km)	139
110	Charles Lathrop Pack Forest Demonstration Forest Nature Trail	1.1	(1.8 km)	139
111	Warren County Parks and Recreation Nature Trail	various		140
112	Palmer Pond	2.0	(3.2 km)	141
113	Moreau Lake State Park	various		142
114	Spruce Mt.	1.2	(1.9 km)	143

115	Hadley Mt.	1.8	(2.9 km)	144
116	Crane Mt.	1.4	(2.3 km)	146
117	Crane Mt. Cut-off Trail	0.5	(0.8 km)	147
118	Crane Mt. Pond and Northwest Ridge	2.7	(4.4 km)	148
119	Round and Mud Ponds	0.6	(1.0 km)	152
120	Round Pond from Garnet Lake	2.3	(3.7 km)	153
121	Baldwin Springs and West Stony Creek Road	7.0	(11.3 km)	155
122	Baldwin Springs from Harrisburg Lake on the Arrow Trail	7.9	(12.7 km)	156
123	Baldwin Springs via Fish Ponds on the Bartman Trail	6.3	(10.2 km)	158
124	Lizard Pond and Baldwin Springs Canoe/Hike from Garnet Lake	4.5	(7.2 km)	160
125	Indian Pond	1.8	(2.9 km)	163
126	Tenant Creek Falls	2.1	(3.1 km)	164
127	Wilcox Lake via East Stony Creek Trail	5.2	(8.4 km)	165
128	Wilcox Lake from Willis Lake	6.3	(10.1 km)	168
129	Kibby Pond	1.9	(3.0 km)	172
130	Cod Pond	1.0	(1.6 km)	173
131	Stewart Creek Flow and North Bend via the Oregon Trail	5.0	(8 km)	174
132	Girard "Sugarbush" Maple Plantation	0.9	(1.4 km)	176
133	Pine Orchard from Flater's	3.0	(4.8 km)	178
134	Pine Orchard from Pumpkin Hollow Rd.	6.6	(10.6 km)	180
135	Murphy Lake from Pumpkin Hollow Rd.	3.8	(6.1 km)	181
136	Murphy, Bennett, and Middle Lakes from Creek Rd.	3.8	(6.2 km)	184

Bushwhacks:

Trail Described	Total Miles (one way, approximate)		Page
Baldhead Mt. and Moose Mt.	3.6	(5.8 km)	150
Mt. Blue	2.0	(3.2 km)	170

107 Hoffman Notch Trail

Trails Illustrated Map 743: U25-S25

The Hoffman Notch Trail is a wilderness walk through a magnificent forest of huge trees. The route today varies little from that shown on the 1908 Adirondack Forest Map of the Forest, Fish, and Game Commission. The woods have been Forest Preserve land since that period of rampant forest fires, and it is quite likely that the area is wilder now than it was then. Certainly, there are fewer visitors now than in the earlier time of hotels and guides. For all the wildness, the walking is rather gentle, particularly on the southern side of the notch.

Those planning a point-to-point hike will need a car at each trailhead. The trail is described from S to N.

▶Trailheads: Trail access from the N end of the notch is off the S side of Blue Ridge Rd., approximately 5.7 mi W of I-87 Exit 29. This is 1.4 mi beyond the Elk Lake Rd. sign and immediately past the bridge over The Branch stream. If approaching from Newcomb on Blue Ridge Rd., it is 13.1 mi from the intersection of NY 28N and the Tahawus Rd. The trailhead is marked by a DEC sign and a green metal signpost and a small sandy pullout. The trail drops down a small grade.

The S trailhead is at Loch Muller. Turn W off NY 9 onto Hoffman Rd. in the village of Schroon Lake. Drive 6.4 mi to the jct. of Loch Muller Rd. Turn R. Continue 2.4 mi to a building above Warrens Pond with a delightful sign commemorating a tall tree at the road's edge. From this point onward the dirt road narrows. After 0.1 mi turn R at a fork and proceed another 0.1 mi to a large turnabout where the trailhead is located. A DEC trail sign marks the trailhead (0.0 mi).◀

The trail heads generally NE following yellow trail markers down a gradual slope. It crosses the W branch of Trout Brook (Bailey Pond Outlet) on a bridge at 0.4 mi. The trail now gradually ascends, trending ENE from 0.8 mi. It reaches the N branch of Trout Brook at 1.2 mi, abruptly veers to the N, and comes to a jct. (The blue-marked trail R crosses the N branch and heads SE to Big Pond and then out to Hoffman Rd.) Continue straight. The level course generally follows the N branch's W bank, sometimes close by and farther away at times.

The first of many large glacial erratics appears at 1.6 mi in a lush fern meadow. Then, at 2 mi, the trail clings to the W bank of the stream for quite some time, creating a musical interlude amidst the beauty of nature.

Glimpses of a large beaver marsh can be seen through the trees to the E at 2.7 mi. The trail is overgrown in places from here to Big Marsh. Watch for the yellow trail markers.

The trail comes to the W shore of Big Marsh at 3.8 mi. Excellent views of Texas Ridge, Hoffman Mt., and Blue Ridge Mt. are found here. Big Marsh is actually a very pretty large pond that makes an ideal lunch spot.

Returning to open woods, the trail makes an abrupt R at 4 mi. The grade is so moderate you may be through the notch and not realize it until you notice that the trail is following the R bank of a tributary stream downstream.

The trail becomes a wide, old wagon route. At a jct. at 4.4 mi, avoid the L turn, which crosses the stream. At 4.6 mi the rushing sounds of water indicate Hoffman Notch Brook. Rock-hop across. (This idyllic spot is worthy of exploration. Hike the short distance upstream around the bend to see the cascading waters cutting through ancient rock. Indistinct anglers' paths lead up to the small pond at the entrance to Hornet Notch. Hoffman Notch Brook makes a good bushwhack route to Hoffman Mt. and the Blue Ridge.)

From this spot to Blue Ridge Rd. the trail descends 500 ft. The valley closes perceptibly, creating an air of eerie wildness. The stream must again be rock-hopped to the L bank at 4.8 mi.

At 5 mi the alert hiker will note splendid high cliffs about 100 yd L of the trail. Here, remnants of a glacial meltwater overflow standout. Even today, spring snowmelts pour over this opening in Washburn Ridge, creating an awesome display of nature's power. Water falls nearly 200 ft to the base of the cliffs.

The route continues its descent amidst rugged boulders that give evidence of a violent past. At 5.8 mi, the chassis of an old Army half-track sits beside the trail, which re-crosses Hoffman Notch Brook to the R bank at 6 mi. At 6.3 mi, the trail passes under power lines. (USGS maps show the trail heading E near here and then turning N through a marshy area. By owner permission, the trail has been relocated through posted property. Please stay on the trail and do not camp in this section.) Continue N.

Hoffman Notch Brook is re-crossed yet again on a wide bridge at 6.5 mi, followed by a crossing of Sand Pond Brook on another wide bridge at 6.6 mi. Four small bridges cross low areas and streams in the next 0.3 mi and the trail turns E up a gradual slope. Traffic on the Blue Ridge Rd. may be heard.

At 7.1 mi, the trail passes through a large grove of white cedar, and at 7.3 mi it turns L on a woods road. A side path leads around a barrier gate at 7.4 mi, and then a roadway leads up a short grade to the trailhead on Blue Ridge Rd.

✻ Trail in winter: This is an excellent snowshoe or backwoods skiing trail. Through-trips are possible in winter. The N side of the notch requires good control.

❀ Distances: To W branch of Trout Brook, 0.4 mi; to N branch of Trout Brook, 1.2 mi; to Big Marsh, 3.8 mi; to Hoffman Notch Brook, 4.6 mi; to Washburn Ridge cliffs, 5 mi; to Sand Pond Brook, 6.6 mi; to Blue Ridge Rd., 7.4 mi. (11.9 km).

107A Big Pond Trail

Trails Illustrated Map 743: S25-26

This relatively gentle cross-country trail enters the Hoffman Notch Wilderness from the SE and follows a former logging road much of its length of five miles. There are two interesting and quite different bodies of water along the trail, and the route has an increasingly remote feel as it approaches the Hoffman Notch Trail (107).

▶ Trailhead: From the center of Schroon Lake, drive S to the edge of downtown to the Hoffman Rd. on the W side of US 9. There is also a sign here for the town highway department. Drive 2.2 mi uphill to a small, unmarked parking area on the R. A trail sign is visible 50 yd into the woods, and a bit farther on is a trail register. The trail is marked with blue disks. ◀

The route passes cleared blowdown from Hurricane Irene before it reaches a beaver flow at 0.4 mi. Cross the outlet bridge next to a beaver dam, pass a glacial erratic on the L, and continue winding up and down until there are glimpses of Big Pond on the L at 1 mi. This large body of water could qualify as a lake and has a varied shoreline worthy of exploration by bushwhack. A short spur down to the N shore is flagged at 1.2 mi, but not built, as of early 2012. The trail loses its character as a woods road as it narrows and passes Big Pond. It climbs over hummocks and down into swampy woods before starting the gradual climb over and beyond the S end of the Hoffman ridge, reaching the Hoffman Notch Trail (107), at 5.7 mi.

❄ Trail in winter: Excellent for snowshoeing and good for skiing, with a few twisty fast stretches.

🥾 Distances: To beaver flow outlet, 0.4 mi; to first glimpses of Big Pond, 1 mi.; to proposed shoreline spur, 1.2 mi; to Hoffman Notch Trail (107), 5 mi (8 km).

108 Bailey Pond Trail

Trails Illustrated Map 743: S24

Bailey Pond is a pretty little body of water that makes a good destination for a short walk. The trip can be extended to make a full day's outing.

▶ Trailhead: Access to the trailhead is the same as for the S trailhead for the Hoffman Notch Trail (trail 107). ◀

The trail leaves the rear of the parking area, following blue DEC trail markers to the NW. Passing behind a camp, it joins a woods road at 0.1 mi and continues with minor grades to 0.9 mi, where a side trail L, just before the outlet of Bailey Pond (W branch of Trout Brook), leads 0.1 mi W to Bailey Pond. There are a few rocks along the shore; they make pleasant places to sit and observe the water.

The hike can be extended for an enjoyable walk through open woods. The woods road continues as an unmarked trail beyond the outlet. Broad and easy to follow for the next mile beyond the outlet, it generally parallels Bailey Pond Inlet, which comes out of the pass between Bailey Hill and Washburn Ridge. The route once turned L at 2 mi and wound up the ridge to the summit of Bailey Hill. However, this section of the road has become overgrown and any attempt to climb the hill must be considered a bushwhack.

❄ Trail in winter: This is a little-used but relatively easy trail for skiing.

🥾 Distances: To woods road, 0.2 mi; to Bailey Pond outlet, 0.9 mi; to Bailey Pond, 1 mi (1.6 km).

109 Severance Mt.

Trails Illustrated Map 743: S26–27

▶Trailhead: From I-87 exit 28, drive 0.6 mi S on US 9. Turn R into a large parking lot on two levels—with a hitching post for each car. The lot is clearly marked with a large sign for Severance Mt. by the road.◀

Immediately beyond the parking lot (0.0 mi), two long culverts carry the trail under the N and S lanes of the Northway (I-87). The trail ducks into the woods at 0.1 mi, following yellow trail markers. The path is wide and starts to go up at 0.2 mi. The grade becomes steeper at 0.3 mi. The trail climbs steadily through mixed woods of maple, white pine, birch, hemlock, and white cedar. Unfortunately, the noise of traffic on the Northway is quite loud. Soon the trail takes a sharp turn R, avoiding an old logging road to the S side of the trail.

At 0.5 mi, the trail levels off. At 0.6 mi it crosses two plank bridges and then at 0.7 mi another plank bridge over the same small stream. Now the sound of traffic is faint. The trail begins to climb again, at 0.8 mi, winding on the level through a lovely hemlock grove. Then after a large boulder on the L at 0.9 mi, the trail climbs again. At 1 mi, it winds uphill through beech and hemlock woods.

At 1.2 mi, the trail reaches an overlook with a view of Schroon Lake and Pharaoh Mt. to the E. A second overlook about 100 ft farther overlooks Paradox Lake. The rest of the summit is covered with trees. Curious ravens with beady eyes often swoop over the treetops, then perform their feats of skydiving skill in front of the cliff directly below.

A DEC sign says the ascent is 813 ft, but the USGS map shows about 700 ft of ascent from the parking lot to the summit.

❈ Trail in winter: This is a pleasant snowshoe in winter and a nice trip for good skiers (intermediate and better).

❦ Distance: Trailhead to plank bridges, 0.6 mi; to summit, 1.2 mi (2 km). Ascent, 700 ft (213 m). Summit elevation, 1638 ft.

110 Charles Lathrop Pack Demonstration Forest Nature Trail

Trails Illustrated Map 743: L26

This handicapped-accessible nature trail is maintained by the State University of New York College of Environmental Science and Forestry. It offers a very appealing walk of a little over a mile through one of the greatest assemblages of truly huge hemlock trees in the Adirondacks. Its most striking attraction, however, is Grandmother's Tree. Grandmother's Tree is more than 315 years old and, with a height of approximately 175 ft, is the tallest white pine tree on record in the state.

▶Trailhead: Access is off the W side of US 9, 0.7 mi N of the US 9 and NY 28 intersection N of Warrensburg. A large sign marks the spot. Turn onto the macadam road and follow the directional signs for the nature trail parking lot. At 0.6 mi, a sign points R to parking in an unpaved open area. Returning to the

James Appleyard

main road, turn R and walk 150 yd along the road until you see the sign at L labeled "Grandmother's Tree Nature Trail." Printed trail guides are available at the trailhead. ◄

The trail enters an oak-hemlock forest from the trailhead (0.0 mi). It crosses a gurgling brook on a bridge at 150 ft and the valley widens. White pine and yellow birch are now found. The trail gradually circles a glacial hill on the R. Various ferns, mosses, and lycopodia keep your interest, as the trail swings N among huge hemlocks.

The trail crosses two more bridges at 0.4 mi and 0.5 mi before reaching Grandmother's Tree at 0.6 mi. Its top soars out of sight in the forest canopy. Less than 50 yd from the tree, the trail passes the last interpretive marker and turns R on a woods road. It turns R again at a T-intersection at 0.8 mi. The winding dirt road then skirts a small pond with lily pads to a third R turn at 0.9 mi. Passing through a set of buildings on a paved road, the trail ends at the parking lot on the L at 1.1 mi.

✤ Trail in winter: This trail is very short for a winter trip, but several of the roads in this facility can be walked or skied in winter.

🐾 Distances: To Grandmother's Tree, 0.6 mi; to T-intersection, 0.8 mi; to parking lot, 1.1 mi (1.9 km).

111 Warren County Parks and Recreation Nature Trail
Trails Illustrated Map 743: K26

A joint venture of DEC and Warren County, the Hudson River Recreation Area provides canoe access to the Hudson River, a picnic area, and hiking/cross-country skiing trails. Users can enjoy a stay of a few hours or a day in an attractive setting of towering pines adjacent to the Hudson River. This park also provides access to the Hudson River Ice Meadows, a preserve without trail, of the Adirondack Nature Conservancy.

▶Trailhead: Access to the trailhead is off the W side of Hudson St., 2.5 mi NW of the Floyd Bennett Park stoplight in Warrensburg. The N end of Hudson St. intersects NY 28, 1.7 mi N of the NY 28 and US 9 intersection. The nature trail is 2.2 mi S from NY 28. A large nature trail–canoe access sign points the way to a parking area. There is a large wooden map at the trailhead; printed trail guides were once available, but have not been for several years. The trail once had interpretive signs along it, but many of these have disappeared and have not been replaced. ◄

The map at the trailhead displays a number of interconnected trails that can be combined in a variety of loops ranging from 0.2 mi to 1 mi. The trail heading straight (W) from the trailhead reaches the Hudson River in 0.2 mi. Although most of the trails are easy to hike, a couple of short, moderate to steep pitches are encountered on the outermost loop (marked yellow on the trailhead map). The northernmost red loop (on the far R on the trailhead map) can be used to access the Hudson River, but the loop itself is overgrown in recent years.

❆ Trail in winter: Many cross-country trails, some requiring considerable skill, weave through this area. While none are very long, when combined they provide a nice circuit.

112 Palmer Pond

Trails Illustrated Map 743: N24-25

Palmer Pond is a large pond that can be reached by an easy walk along a woods road. Side trails provide a variety of attractive vistas.

▶Trailhead: Access to the trailhead is at the end of Palmer Pond Rd., off NY 8. Palmer Pond Rd. is 1 mi E of the Hudson River at Riparius and 1 mi W of the intersection of NY 8 and US 9, W of Chestertown. A barrier gate at 0.8 mi blocks Palmer Pond Rd. Parking is available for several vehicles at the barrier gate; additional parking spots can be found in the woods before the gate.◀

From the trailhead at the barrier gate (0.0 mi), a woods road heads S. After passing a flooded area on the R at 0.1 mi, the road ascends a minor knoll. At a jct. just over the crest of the knoll at 0.3 mi, continue straight. (The wide trail L makes a nice side trip. It skirts a marshy cove and reaches the E shore of the pond 0.4 mi from the road.)

The trail levels at a 150 ft beaver dam at 0.4 mi. This very large dam has totally flooded a small valley. Avoid the side trail L at the beginning of the dam. Continue on, across the solid, wide dam.

The road then ascends a gradual grade to Palmer Pond. Short side trails leading to the pond shore branch L at 0.5 mi and 0.6 mi. The road continues to a jct. in a clearing at 0.7 mi. Bear L. (The road straight ahead continues another 0.9 mi to private land. Although hikers must turn back at the boundary, the round trip offers a nice woods walk and occasional glimpses of old stone walls and foundations.) Skirting the pond, the trail terminates at a wide opening on its SW shore at 1 mi. The broad expanse of the pond can be seen from this vantage point. (The road continues beyond the opening, but the land is posted and should not be entered.)

❆ Trail in winter: The trail is suitable for skiing and snowshoeing, although it must be shared with snowmobilers.

🥾 Distances: To beaver dam, 0.4 mi; to clearing jct., 0.7 mi; to SW corner of pond, 1 mi (1.6 km).

Moreau Lake State Park. John Kettlewell

113 Moreau Lake State Park

Trails Illustrated Map 743: E27

Though located just outside the Adirondack Park "blue line," Moreau Lake State Park offers a wealth of short trails within easy reach of I-87. Hikers may or may not be interested in the public swimming beach with lifeguards and concession stands (in season), the picnic tables, the extensive playground, or the popular camp ground. Despite these more developed areas, a network of trails can soon take you around the pond and into the forest and up the Palmerton Range, where views of the nearby Hudson River can be found. To avoid getting lost be sure to pick up a copy of the trail map at the entrance booth ($2 in 2012). A compass can be very useful in determining which way to go at the many trail intersections. After a hot hike it is great to cool off with a dip in the lake.

From May 26 through September 3 (2012) the entrance fee is $8 per car, with lesser fees applying only on weekends earlier in May and through Columbus Day in October. However, in the off season the park is still accessible, though you might have to park your car near the entrance gate as the road is closed and/or covered with snow in the winter.

▶Trailhead: Take I-87 to Exit 17 for US 9 southbound. Just W of I-87 take the first R turn onto Old Saratoga Rd. and travel for about 0.7 mi to the entrance to Moreau Lake State Park on the R.◀

❅ Trails in winter: The entire park is a delight in the winter, and all trails are suitable for snow shoes. Most of the trails are skiable, though some of the routes up Palmerton can be steep and difficult, depending on snow conditions.

114 Spruce Mt.

Trails Illustrated Map 743: D24

Spruce Mt. is a good choice for those who like a wide trail over easy terrain. The summit can be reached by a trail mostly along the route of old logging roads that are intersected by numerous other logging roads. There is also a gated service road that is closed to the driving public, but could be walked, although the distance is about twice that of the trail. Some attention to the most heavily used path is required in order to avoid wandering onto a side trail. A currently (2012) abandoned fire tower that is in disrepair is on the summit. Trail and environmental interest groups are working toward restoring the tower and opening it to the public.

▶Trailhead: Take NY 9N S from Corinth and turn sharp R (W) on Wells Rd. 1 mi S of the second RR crossing.◀

The trail begins at the far end of the circle (0.0 mi) by crossing a fast-flowing stream that runs through a large culvert. Bearing R, it proceeds as a continuation of that road, which is now an old washed-out logging trail, although it shows evidence of a substantial amount of use in days gone by.

In about 70 yd the trail bears L up a second abandoned road. The trail up this old road leads N almost continuously uphill until at 0.2 mi an old logging road enters from the R. At 0.24 mi, a posted sign and orange and yellow paint blazes mark the boundary with private land. The trail continues straight ahead onto the improved logging road on the private land.

The trail climbs steadily, but moderately, through an area that was extensively logged in 2011. At 0.4 mi it curves R and is lined by boulders for the convenience of the hiker. At 0.57 mi the trail leaves the logged area and enters land owned by Saratoga PLAN (Preserving Land and Nature). This boundary is again marked by orange and yellow paint blazes and a Saratoga PLAN sign. The Saratoga PLAN section of the trail is marked by white, square trail markers.

Just 23 yd beyond, another old road crosses the trail from L uphill to R, but the trail continues straight ahead through on open forest of birch, beech, oak, and other hardwoods, with groves of moderately sized hemlocks adding to the pleasantness of this section. The road/trail exits the hemlock section and arrives at an abandoned shortcut to the L, which still has an old Saratoga PLAN marker. The approved trail continues straight ahead for about 150 ft and then curves L to arrive at the other end of the shortcut.

The trail leaves the old road at the other end of the abandoned shortcut, and the route continues N as a footpath ascending a bank beside an enormous ash tree. The route continues steadily up toward the summit ridge. It is occasionally marked with informal cairns. Another logging road crosses the trail, but again, the trail continues up a short steeper section. In another 150 yd the trail crosses a logging road at the upper extent of the Saratoga PLAN land at a muddy place in the trail. This boundary is marked by orange paint blazes. Beyond this point the trail ascends to the summit ridge, angling generally to the L (W) passing one more Saratoga PLAN trail marker.

The summit ridge is reached at 0.95 mi. The trail continues to ascend through generally open woods and fields the final 0.25 mi required to arrive at the summit. The trail winds up the summit knoll until the fire tower at last is visible through the final section of woods. The summit area around the tower is open and is visited in the winter by snowmobiles, which come up the road.

Until the day when the tower has been restored and reopened to the public, the hiker may enjoy the view N from the ledge to the R of the tower, where Crane Mt. is most prominent.

❋ Trail in winter: Good for snowshoes.

❀ Distances: Gravel parking lot to state boundary, 0.24 mi; to summit ridge 0.95 mi; to summit 1.2 mi (1.9 km). Ascent, 1048 ft (319 m). Elevation, 2009 ft (612 m).

115 Hadley Mt.

Trails Illustrated Map 743: H23

Hadley Mt. is the tallest of the three peaks that form West Mt. Ridge. The bare summit, which offers views in three directions, offers some of the most spectacular vistas in the southern Adirondacks. A fire tower still graces the summit, and it is staffed in the summer with volunteers who can provide information on what you are seeing.

▶Trailhead: From I-87 Exit 21 take NY 9N to the village of Lake Luzerne, then turn R (W) on Mill St., just past the school. Follow Mill St. to the bottom of the hill and bear left onto Main St., go through the business district, and then turn right on Rockwell St. to cross the Hudson River into Hadley. Shortly, there is a R turn to go N on Stony Creek Rd. (which is CR 1) for approximately 3 mi to Hadley Hill Rd. Turn L (W) and drive up Hadley Hill Rd. 4.6 mi to Tower Rd. on the R, which is marked with a small sign on a tree. Turn R (N) onto hard-packed dirt Tower Rd. and drive for another 1.5 mi. to the trailhead on the L where a rocky clearing will accommodate several cars. (Tower Rd. is usually in very good driving condition for normal passenger cars, although in early spring there may be some muddy areas and rocky washouts.)◀

The entire West Mt. Ridge and much of the surrounding forest was burned over in 1903, 1908, 1911, and 1915, but today it is covered with lush growth.

The trail begins to the W of the parking area and immediately climbs a moderate grade, traversing a washed-out old jeep trail. There is a trail register and the trail is marked with red DEC trail markers. It is easy to follow because of erosion and a good deal of use by hikers. Several sections have been worn down to bedrock, including an attractive area at 0.3 mi that resembles a slanted city sidewalk. In other areas large rocks and boulders have been revealed to create an obstacle course for the climber.

Climbing continues through predominantly hardwood forest for the first mile, except for the very beginning where the trail passes through a mature stand of hemlocks. The general direction is W, and the trail climbs steadily upward at a moderate pitch. There is a brief flat section where a small stream is crossed at 0.5 mi. Here, an attractive, large boulder makes a good resting place.

After crossing the stream, the trail bends slightly R and continues to climb. At 0.6 mi rock formations can be seen on the R. These are 10 to 15 ft high; while attractive in summer, they are noted in winter for their colorful blue-green ice formations.

Finally, a much steeper section of the trail culminates at the top of a ridge at 1 mi. A turn to the R begins a gentle section across the top of this rib of West Mt. Ridge. This is a lovely part of the trail, open and most welcome after the moderately steep but relentless climb.

Napping on Hadley Mt. David Hough

At 1.2 mi, after a brief upward grade, a swing L occurs and the trail passes through a grove of stunted, picturesque trees consisting of oak, mountain ash, maple, and birch, among others. Now headed in a NW direction, at 1.3 mi the trail jogs R and begins a moderate climb up the next ridge.

Cliffs rise on either side as the trail continues upward through the col. A clearing is reached at 1.3 mi. Here the trail branches to the L. Climbing continues at a moderate rate of ascent until at 1.4 mi the trail reaches the first of a series of lookouts—a spectacular view of Great Sacandaga Lake. For the remaining 0.3 mi the trail circles the SW side of Hadley, traversing several open areas that provide the hiker with marvelous vistas. At 1.7 mi, after the last rocky outlook, the trail levels briefly, then splits again with the R fork going 200 ft to the observer's cabin and the L making a slight climb to the summit and tower at 1.8 mi.

Here, on a clear day, the successful climber enjoys a brilliant panorama, an ample reward for the effort expended. In addition to Great Sacandaga Lake to the S and nearby Spruce Mt. to the W, one can see from the summit Crane, Mount Blue, Moose, Baldhead and Pharaoh mountains, as well as Lake Champlain—and on a very clear day (especially in winter) several of the High Peaks. A second Spruce Mt. can be seen far to the S and is described in this guide (trail 114).

Roundtop Mt. to the N on private land can be sighted from Hadley's tower. It is a small mountain with a bare summit and a pristine quality of peaceful isolation and unspoiled natural beauty.

✼ Trail in winter: A super snowshoe hike. Distances are not as daunting as those required to climb many other mountains, and the climbing will not require special equipment (like crampons) under normal winter conditions.

👣 Distances: To rock formations, 0.6 mi; to West Mt. Ridge, 1 mi; to clearing, 1.3 mi; to summit, 1.8 mi (2.9 km). Ascent 1525 ft (466 m). Elevation 2675 ft (818 m).

116 Crane Mt.

Trails Illustrated Map 743: L23

The most interesting, most used, yet one of the prettiest mountains in the southern Adirondacks is undoubtedly Crane Mt. It is unsurpassed for views and scenic side trails to explore. Unfortunately, in recent years it is becoming overused, with illegal camping areas trampled and trashed, and trees cut by careless campers without regard to esthetics or common sense. Ignorant campers have occasionally constructed large lean-tos of fresh green hemlocks, stripping the lower branches from nearby trees.

Hadley Mt. firetower. ADK Archives

Two approaches to the summit make it possible to do a loop trip up, across the summit, and down the other side, exploring Crane Mt. Pond and the E ridge as well as the summit. The old fire tower was removed long ago.

▶Trailhead: To reach the trailhead take Garnet Lake Rd. from the hamlet of Thurman (off South Johnsburg Rd.). Proceed 1.4 mi to a R turn onto Ski Hi Rd. This road is dirt and may be rough going, especially in spring. It is maintained, however, and a 4WD vehicle is not needed—just caution.◀

Continue to the top of a long hill for 2 mi to where a smaller dirt road cuts off to the R. Bear R here. For the next 0.6 mi this road is extremely rough going and sometimes partially flooded. High ground clearance is desirable.

The parking area can accommodate at least 10 cars. Walk L 20 ft from the N end of the lot to locate the trail register and the beginning of both trails (3 and 4) to the summit. The trail sign indicates 1.8 mi to the summit to the R (about 0.4 mi. more than it really is); 1.4 mi to Crane Mt. Pond; 1 mi to Putnam Junction; and 1.9 mi to the pond taking the L route.

Taking the shortest route to the summit, the R fork, the trail goes through pleasant hardwoods and begins a moderate ascent at 0.1 mi. At 0.2 mi one must negotiate a group of large boulders. The first cliff face appears on the R at 0.3 mi, after which the trail levels off.

Following the contour of the side of the mountain only briefly, the trail now becomes steeper. A very steep section commences at 0.4 mi. On the R are more sheer rock faces and perhaps a small cave can be seen, but the cliff is too steep to attempt an investigation without rock climbing experience and proper equipment.

A level section occurs at 0.5 mi. A path goes L to bare rock and a lookout. At 0.6 mi the trail hooks around a few pine trees and goes a bit R, then up and L over a bare rock expanse. The general direction here is NE. Cross the rock face N to the pines to find the continuation of the trail.

At a junction at 0.7 mi, a sign pointing R indicates 0.8 mi to the summit. Take the R fork. The L fork is the Crane Mt. Cut-off Trail (117), which goes through a cool ravine to reach the pond in another 0.4 mi. At 0.8 mi climb a short, steep rock extrusion. The trail now turns L and continues through a flat area and a stand of fragrant balsam trees. Hemlocks, too, are in abundance as the trail continues along the ridge.

At 1.1 mi the climbing begins again, and at 1.2 mi a long ladder provides a means to ascend a very rugged cliff face. Those hiking with large dogs may have some difficulty negotiating this ladder. Reaching the top of the cliff, the trail bends R and the hiker scrambles over some large boulders to reach the bare rocks of the summit at 1.4 mi.

Views to the S and SW are magnificent. To the S are Mount Blue, Hadley, Moose, and Baldhead. Looking NW, on a clear day, Snowy Mt. and Indian Lake can be seen.

Continuing NW across the summit, the trail meanders in and out of the stubby, wind-bent evergreens, descending gently. At 1.7 mi there is a fork L to a lookout with a great view of Crane Mt. Pond. Just after this wonderful lookout, the descent begins W and down a very steep section that tends to stay icy late into the spring. At 2.3 mi the trail levels off for about 500 yd and then begins a more gentle descent to the pond. At 2.4 mi a marshy spot must be negotiated shortly before a junction is reached. The path to the R leads to a popular camping area near the pond, while the L fork reaches the pond at 2.6 mi. This trail continues around the pond and to the W trail and NW ridge.

The pond is popular with campers and fishermen. There are several overused camping areas along the shore. Despite this it is a lovely jewel of a lake with super scenery, although in recent years the resident beaver have left. Also it was recently poisoned by the DEC and now contains stocked trout only. Fishermen are warned not to bring bait fish with them.

❉ Trail in winter: Snowshoes are the recommended footwear for winter climbs. Skiing the old Putnam Farm road (trail 118) is delightful, but the mountain is too steep for backcountry skiers.

🐾 Distances: To first lookout, 0.5 mi; to junction with Cut-off Trail (117), 0.7 mi; to summit and tower, 1.4 mi (2.3 km); down to pond, 2.6 mi (4.2 km). Ascent, 1154 ft (353 m); Elevation, 3254 ft (995 m).

117 Crane Mt. Cut-off Trail

Trails Illustrated Map 743: L23

This trail is located at the S end of the pond where there is a sign. The hiker can continue around the pond and descend along the marked W trail (see trail 118), or take the Cut-off Trail E through a long draw on the mountain's W shoulder to a junction with trail 116.

During wet seasons a small inlet stream runs into the S end of the lake at the beginning of the trail. Heading S away from the pond (mileage 0.0 at the pond), the trail begins a steady but moderate ascent through a long natural cleft in the rocks. It is rocky and wet in many places. Hemlocks and small maples lead into a lovely stand of gray paper birch. The trail levels off at 0.3 mi briefly, but continues to climb through mossy rocks where ferns and asters can be seen in the fall. A beautiful grove of large hemlocks is entered at 0.4 mi at the height of land.

The junction with the E trail (trail 116) is reached at 0.5 mi. Here the hiker can turn R and retrace part of the route used for the ascent. All the trails are well marked and well used.

118 Crane Mt. Pond and NW Ridge

Trails Illustrated Map 743: L23

There is a second route from the parking area up the SW side of Crane Mt. It leads first to Crane Mt. Pond, then around it to the E, and up again to the summit. Hikers who want to explore a little-visited section with bare rock faces and good views to the N and W can bushwhack across the NW rib of the mountain. The climb can be combined with a loop to the main summit and back down the E trail (trail 116).

▶Trailhead: See trail 116.◀

The trail register is approximately 100 ft N of the parking area. From the register the main trail (116) goes R and up the mountain, but for trail 118 take the L branch. The path parallels the road and is a short connector that returns to the yellow disk-marked ski/hiking trail that is the old Putnam Farm Rd. This L connector path is only 0.2 mi and leads through attractive young maples and old apple trees, obviously once a farm field and orchard.

Turn R at the intersection with the old farm road. The trail leads downhill in a very gentle incline. It is very attractive, wide and easy walking through tall hardwoods. At 0.4 mi a small brook is crossed and the old road follows the brook on the L until the trail forks at 0.9 mi. Turn R onto the trail to the pond and summit (the old farm road shortly ends at a private property sign and barrier). Here a sign pointing to the R indicates Crane Mt. Pond 0.9 mi and Crane Mt. Summit 1.9 mi.

 The trail begins to climb moderately and then levels off at 1.1 mi and crosses a natural rock bridge over a rushing brook. A careful check to the L and R of this reveals that the brook has carved a tunnel-like cavern through the rock. Be careful while exploring, as the sides are steep and slippery.

Hikers may also wish to walk another 500 yd to the R and look over an impressive beaver dam that has been reestablished in recent years.

After crossing the rock bridge, the trail swings slightly R, and the steeper climb

Crane Mt. Pond. James Appleyard

up the ridge commences. At 1.2 mi the trail begins to be very steep, with numerous large boulders for the hiker to negotiate.

The next 0.7 mi of trail is very steep and zig-zags over and across numerous ledges and large boulders. There are several lookouts with wonderful views into the valley. Finally, at 1.7 mi an extensive bare rock area is encountered, offering more views to the SW. The trail is poorly marked here (2011), but continues up the gently sloping wide rock face, or alongside it. Cross the outlet of the pond to find the path and continue to Crane Mt. Pond itself at 1.9 mi. The beaver dam that raised the water level two feet in years past is no longer operational, the beaver having left or been trapped out in recent years. Observe the shoreline of dead standing trees, a legacy of the beaver, although many of these are mere sawed-off trunks, thanks to wood-hungry campers.

To visit the NW ridge, which has no marked trail, turn L when trail 118 reaches the pond and begin a gentle climb in a general NNW direction. Two or three faint herd paths lead to several rocky outlooks on the ridge line to the L. It is an easy and pleasant bushwhack through attractive red pines for approximately 0.8 mi to the bare rocks of the summit of the NW ridge of Crane Mt. Because there is not a marked trail, explorations might require a compass, although the hiker should have no difficulty as long as he or she continues up and not down! Dramatic cliffs drop off to the SW. There are super views and exquisite scenery in this little-visited area.

To make a loop, return to the pond and continue the trip around it and up the main NW summit trail (see trail 116). Or hikers may take the Cut-off Trail (117) at the S end of the pond and do a figure-8 loop.

❄ Trail in winter: Cross-country skiing is very enjoyable along the old farm road, but a switch to snowshoes becomes necessary if an attempt to climb to the pond or summit is planned. Instep crampons may also be helpful, as some of the rocks will no doubt be ice-covered.

🐾 Distances: To trail fork on old farm road, 0.9 mi; to rock bridge, 1.1 mi; to Crane Mt. Pond, 1.9 mi; to NW ridge rocks, 2.7 mi (4.4 km). Elevation of NW ridge, 2876 ft (880 m).

Baldhead and Moose Mts. *(unmarked footpaths)*

Trails Illustrated Map 743: J-K23

Baldhead and Moose Mts. are two of the most interesting, attractive mountains in the southern Adirondacks. Open views and dazzling rocky cliffs and ledges provide the adventurous hiker with magnificent rewards for the risk. And the risk is minimal, since each mountain is easy to locate and climb. As these two wonderful small mountains are quite close together, a loop trip is possible, and recommended. Climbing Baldhead first and then going across the ridge connecting to Moose takes advantage of the elevation already gained.

▶ Trailhead: Drive N on Harrisburg Rd. from the village of Stony Creek, turn

R on Tucker Rd. and continue to the height of land where there is a parking turnout on the R. Park here and begin the climb on the L (N) side of the road, bushwhacking through a stand of beech trees where numerous young beech saplings make the going somewhat difficult.◀

Travel over a small knoll that tops out at approximately 0.6 mi and then descends quickly into a col. Now begin climbing a much larger knoll. Note on the R very bright yellow paint slashes on various trees, which mark the boundary line between state and private land. The E side of this boundary shows signs of logging in the past few years, so staying to the W of the yellow boundary markers will make the walking much easier. The hiker can follow the paint blazes to the top of this knoll.

Continue heading due N to reach the crest at 1 mi. The top is flat and has some attractive rock slabs decorated with lichen, mosses and blueberries. Limited views are available to the S and N where Baldhead Mt. can now be seen.

Continue N and descend a steep grade approximately 250 ft to cross a small stream at the bottom and begin the actual climb up the flank of Baldhead. A series of open rock terraces provides easy walking and various views to the S and W.

At l.9 mi a larger open rock area begins. The terrain becomes steeper, yet affords ample rocky resting places. Sandstone boulders can be found here, among blueberries and small mountain ash trees. Several varieties of green and gray mosses and lichens crackle and crunch underfoot.

The last quarter mile to the summit is quite steep, but there are plenty of grassy sections, interspersed with shrubs and slabs of flat rock, lending a special beauty to this untrammeled place.

At approximately 2.2 mi the summit is reached. There are several bald areas and beautiful thickets of spruce and hemlock, stunted white birch and twisted cherry and mountain ash. Views to the N are excellent and show the S cliffs of Crane Mt. in their rocky splendor. To the E, and seemingly very near, is Moose Mt. with its dramatic bare rock expanses.

To continue on to Moose Mt., head NE and descend to the flat ridge, which is covered with scrubby spruce and balsam and numerous small white paper birch trees. At the end of the ridge, descend into the col briefly, then begin the climb up Moose Mt. The ascent of Moose also provides numerous rocky outlooks and bare stretches of rock slabs that are easily climbed. The summit of Moose Mt. is approximately l.4 mi from the summit of Baldhead.

The large, bare summit is outstanding, with a balancing rock, spruce and colorful mountain ash, and many open rock areas upon which to sit and enjoy the scenery.

To return, retrace your route back to Baldhead and reverse your compass bar.

❋ Trail in winter: A snowshoe trek up either or both mountains is recommended for superb scenery. With care and good winter snow conditions the experienced group should have minimal difficulty. Like any other bushwhack, a map and compass are a must, as well as adequate winter emergency equipment.

🚶 Distances: To top of knoll, 1 mi; to Baldhead Mt. summit, 2.2 mi (3.6 km); to Moose Mt. summit from Baldhead, 1.4 mi; (from road, 3.6 mi [5.8 km]).

119 Round and Mud Ponds

Trails Illustrated Map 743: K23

Both ponds may be reached from a seasonal road off of Garnet Lake Rd. It is short walk from the road to aptly named Mud Pond and an only slightly longer walk to a Round Pond that is not really round. Neither trail is marked but both are easy to follow. Hikers may also walk a longer DEC-marked trail to Round Pond via the snowmobile trail that begins from the trailhead along the shore of Garnet Lake (see trail 120).

Mud Pond is an extremely popular name for small bodies of water in the Adirondacks. Folklore has it that many attractive fishing lakes were so named by the old-time guides who thought people wouldn't be so likely to travel to them and spoil a good thing. This Mud Pond, however, is well on its way to becoming yet another swamp, although beaver seem to be regulating the water level to their own advantage, thus reestablishing the pond's water level for a few years, only to have it shrink again when they depart.

▶Trailhead: To reach the trailhead, drive W on Garnet Lake Rd. from the hamlet of Thurman. At 1 mi past Little Pond, a small dirt road on the L (SW) is seen. The road is marked by a "Seasonal Limited Use Highway" sign. If coming from the N turn S off NY 8 onto Garnet Lake Rd. in the village of Johnsburg and drive a total of 8.3 mi to the trailhead on the R. (This point is 2 mi past the R turnoff to Garnet Lake.)

If you miss this intersection, Garnet Lake Rd. continues up a hill 0.8 mi to run along the edge of picturesque Little Pond. In another 0.1 mi you can find a place to turn around just past a big pine tree and boulder next to the lake. Return the 0.9 mi to the first one-lane road on the L.◀

The one-lane seasonal road crosses a small stream in the first 100 ft and then climbs gently through attractive open hardwoods before leveling off at 0.45 mi. At about 0.6 mi there is a pulloff L large enough for two cars.

At the R corner of this parking lot is the start of a trail down to Mud Pond marked only by the yellow "Motorized Vehicles Prohibited" sign. After a short 0.15 mi descent the trail reaches the shore of Mud Pond. This pond is aptly named as there is no approach to the water that does not require negotiating dark muck. Nevertheless, it is an attractive little pond surrounded by water loving plants that will help create a swamp years from now.

The road ends at 0.95 mi at a clearing which was the site of a cabin at one time but has now been converted into a parking area large enough for 8-10 cars. The trail to Round Pond starts at the far L (SW) corner of the parking area and is marked by a yellow "Motorized Vehicles Prohibited Except Snowmobiles" sign. The trail enters the woods between a fat spruce tree and an old apple tree. At

0.1 mi the trail crosses a small stream and continues on the flat through a brief muddy stretch. It leaves the flat at 0.2 mi to ascend gently over the shoulder of a hill, and then descends and skirts a small beaver pond to reach the shore of Round Pond at 0.6 mi. The trail ends at the marshy shoreline of Round Pond.

It is possible to cross the beaver dam 100 ft back up the trail and follow a herd path around the N shore 150 yd to an excellent vantage point next to the lake where its beauty and charm can be appreciated. Beyond this point the herd path becomes much less distinct and even intermittent; however, it is possible to bushwhack through the open woods along this N shore to link up with the trail coming in from Garnet Lake.

❄ Trail in winter: Skiing the marsh between Mud and Round ponds might be more interesting than the snowmobile trail, but with good snow conditions skiing will be enjoyable. Take care to watch and listen for approaching snowmobiles.

🐾 Distances: To Mud Pond, 0.15 mi; to Round Pond, 0.6 mi (1 km).

120 Round Pond from Garnet Lake

Trails Illustrated Map 743: K23

There are two routes into this extremely pretty, little-visited pond. (See also trail 119.) The most direct is to take this snowmobile trail that begins from the parking area on the E side of Garnet Lake.

▶ Trailhead: To reach Garnet Lake take Garnet Lake Rd. W from Thurman. If coming from NY 8 in the village of Johnsburg, turn S onto Garnet Lake Rd. and go 6.2 mi to a road on the R called Garnet Lake Rd. Extension. A R turn (SW) leads 1 mi to the lake and then another 0.9 mi L to the parking area. ◀

The parking area will hold four to six vehicles; in summer it is heavily used by fishermen and canoeists because a very small boat access area is opposite. The trail sign is easy to spot among the foliage; it points the way to Round Pond, indicating that the hike is 2.3 mi, which is accurate.

The trail begins on the L (N) side of the parking area. It immediately begins a brief ascent of the ridge as it parallels the road heading in a NE direction for a short distance. The trail is sporadically marked with orange snowmobile signs. The forest is mostly mixed hardwoods—beech, maple, and birch, with an occasional fragrant balsam.

A small wet area can be rock-hopped at 0.2 mi. The general direction is now S, and the trail here is very level and pleasant. Another wet area occurs at 0.3 mi. Very soon after, a large collection of attractive mossy boulders is seen on the L, many 30 to 35 ft high. The trail continues along a flat plateau and enters, at 0.5 mi, a handsome stand of hardwoods. It is even and easy going through the open woods.

Now begins a brief descent at 0.6 mi; the general direction is still S. The trail bends to the R past several enormous yellow birches at 0.9 mi. One tree is at

Mark Bowie

least 8 ft in circumference. At 0.8 mi a very faint path forks off to the R, but the main trail is marked with a sign pointing L. The trail bends slightly R and passes over several little undulations, between which are tiny wet areas. The woods are still open as the trail parallels a stream for about 250 yd; it then makes a slight bend to the L and begins to climb a long ridge.

A leveling off occurs at 1.1 mi, and the general direction is now SE. Steady climbing commences again as the trail becomes steeper at 1.2 mi and reaches the height of land at 1.3 mi. It begins a bit of descent to cross a swift small stream at 1.4 mi, and then briefly turns R to parallel this stream for a short time. Then a gentle bend R occurs, signaling the beginning of the ascent of yet another ridge.

At 1.6 mi a brief level area is traversed. The trail enters a rock-strewn area and proceeds through a dry gully, climbing again, although moderately. After a series of brief undulations, at 1.8 mi the descent to Round Pond begins. Notice a large, attractive, 15 ft high erratic boulder on the R at 2.1 mi. At 2.3 mi the trail reaches the shore of this most attractive little pond. There may be beaver activity.

Although this W side of Round Pond is marshy, one can bushwhack L (N) to reach higher land and a few possible camping areas. Although none appear to be used frequently, there is evidence of previous campfires.

Round Pond has several rocky outcroppings and a wide variety of trees and colorful plants lining its shores. If one is quiet for several minutes, it may be possible to see beaver, and sometimes loons.

❋ Trail in winter: As with most trails in the southern Adirondacks, this one must be shared with snowmobiles. However, with proper snow conditions, it can be an invigorating trip for the backcountry skier, with its many small ups and downs, then a challenging run down to the pond.

🐾 Distances: To large boulders, 0.3 mi; to height of land, 1.3 mi; to Round Pond, 2.3 mi (3.7 km).

121 Baldwin Springs and West Stony Creek Road
Trails Illustrated Map 743: J-K22

Baldwin Springs was one of several short-lived, tiny settlements that sprang up in response to farming and lumbering in the north country. Today it is an interesting, sprawling area of sand barrens with numerous overgrown clearings, interspersed with several species of pines. Exploration will reveal several stone foundations, although they are becoming more and more difficult to find as the shrubs sprout and grow to trees within them. It is also an interesting destination, or starting point, for the hiker since four trails begin or end here.

▶Trailhead: To reach Baldwin Springs by the road, drive from Stony Creek on Harrisburg Rd., turn R (N) on Wolf Pond Rd. and drive 0.9 mi to an unsigned road on the L. This is West Stony Creek Rd. Turn here and continue W 6.5 mi to the T intersection at Baldwin Springs.

Be advised that driving this road is sometimes very dicey for regular two-wheel-drive, low-slung vehicles, a few sections are still subject to flooding and wash-outs. With caution, most vehicles should now be able to drive the entire road as water run-outs have recently been created, and the road has been graded and rebuilt in several areas.◀

Reaching the T, a turn to the R (N) brings one to a pine grove and fireplace with two picnic tables that see extensive use. After another 0.1 mi is the traditional fording place for 4WD or offroad vehicles. There is also a wooden plank bridge to the L. Crossing here is one way to enter Baldwin Springs main clearing where the spring is located.

Back at the T, a turn to the L (S) leads to a second wooden footbridge (this one with handrails) at 0.2 mi, just over a small knoll on the R. A DEC trail sign worded "Baldwin Springs 0.3 mi" marks the spot. Parking is very limited.

Continuing, the narrow dirt road reaches the Dog and Pup Club at 0.7 mi. This is a private in-holding, and although there have been "posted" signs, hiking across the land is permitted. Driving this road SW to the Arrow Trail is not recommended. It might be more suitable as a mountain bike ride.

Enter the main clearing of Baldwin Springs using either the footbridge or by fording the stream in a vehicle. The name Baldwin Springs comes from a cool spring that wells up from the earth here. It can be located about 20 ft to the R of the trail register, next to a hummock of shrubs. Look for a mossy, old hollow log set into the ground. The current prevalence of giardiasis should make the hiker cautious about this and any water source, so although it looks clean, one should not indulge. All drinking water should be carried in or boiled at least three minutes.

This is a popular camping area; in winter, deer-watching is the local attraction for snowmobilers, as in recent years deer have yarded in the immediate vicinity. Explore the maze of vehicle trails tangled through the pines. The forests in this area are mainly used by the motorized set of campers and forest lovers. Hikers may find the mud and motors distracting.

❋ Trail in winter: West Stony Creek Rd. is plowed only to the last year-round resident's dwelling, leaving approximately 5 mi of rugged road to travel before one can access any trails. Moreover, these routes must be shared with numerous snowmobiles. There are many quiet, pleasant backcountry ski trails to choose from in other locations. This one is not recommended.

🐾 Distances: Wolf Pond Rd. to T intersection, 6.5 mi; to footbridge across East Stony Creek, 6.7 mi; to Baldwin Springs trail register, 7 mi (11.3 km).

122 Baldwin Springs from Harrisburg Lake on the Arrow Trail

Trails Illustrated Map 743: I-K21

The Arrow Trail is long and arduous, made more so by the location of the trailhead, which requires walking over 2 mi on a very badly rutted and muddy dirt road unsuitable for normal vehicular use. The approach to Baldwin Springs from the N (trail 121) is not quite as difficult, since there is a 6.5 mi driveable road most of the way, though it too can be very rough and subject to wash-outs. This trip makes a challenging backpacking trip with an overnight at Hill Creek or Baldwin Springs. The trail is frequently travelled by off-road vehicles, and is not very attractive. It might be a more interesting mountain bike route. I don't recommend it as a hiking or backpacking route any longer.

▶ Trailhead: To reach the Arrow Trailhead to Baldwin Springs, take Harrisburg Rd. W out of Stony Creek and pass through Knowelhurst, then on to Harrisburg, which is a hamlet of summer homes and a small resort. Drive past the resort to a parking area on the R just before Harrisburg Lake. Here is a trail register; brown and yellow DEC signs point to the blue-marked trail which is a continuation of the road, now changed to dirt. A walk from here to the beginning of the trail into the forest is approximately 2.3 mi over this woods road, passable only to 4WD vehicles or ATVs. ◀

The Arrow Trail originally started from this clearing at the top of the big ridge about 1.3 mi E of the current state trailhead. This cleared section once served as a roundout area where logs were gathered and loaded for the trip out of the woods. For many years an old wagon axle marked with a big arrow stood in the clearing, pointing the way to the trail. The axle has rusted away, although signs of the original trail are still in evidence here. The land is now privately owned, so the hiker must travel an additional 1.5 mi to state lands and the newer "Arrow Trail."

The trail begins on the R at the bottom of a dip in the road approximately 1 mi from the clearing described above. A DEC sign indicates that Baldwin Springs is 7.5 mi via the Arrow Trail. (This mileage is short by 0.4 mi to the trail register at Baldwin Springs.) The sign also points W to indicate that a continuation along the road leads to Wilcox Lake.

The trail begins (0.0 mi.) by heading NE and slightly uphill. The trail is in good condition, with a few wet areas, and for the next mile goes gradually uphill. At 0.5 mi the trail makes a sharp bend R and continues due E. This is the backtracking detour necessary to avoid the old Arrow Trail's original, more direct route. At 1.1 mi it bends R again and then continues steeply uphill to the top of a ridge at 1.3 mi.

After another slight curve to the R, the trail becomes rocky and wet for the next tenth of a mile and then begins to climb moderately. The forest is open, mature hardwoods: yellow birch, maple, and beech trees with occasional clumps of dark green hemlocks. At 1.4 mi the trail passes through a grove of attractive, mature hemlocks. It then crosses a small brook which has no bridge at 1.5 mi, and continues uphill and swings slightly to the R. The top of a ridge is reached at 1.6 mi and the trail bears to the R again. The trail is mostly flat at this point, the general direction being NNE.

At 1.7 mi the trail reaches an old road, which is rutted and torn by the passage of ATVs. The R turn leads along the original Arrow Trail back through private land. Take the L turn to continue toward Baldwin Springs.

The trail reaches a brook at 2.2 mi and now becomes rocky and wet, continuing downhill. It crosses another creek at 2.3 mi and a flat area after climbing another small ridge. At 2.9 mi there is a benchmark on a rock to the R at the top of a knoll, next to an enormous hemlock tree. The trail crosses a larger stream at 3.1 mi. The woods are lush and open. It begins climbing away from the stream bed and at 3.4 mi crosses another small stream. At 4 mi the large wooden bridge over Hill Creek, one of the major tributaries of East Stony Creek, is reached. Here is a good place to camp, or just rest and picnic.

After crossing the bridge the trail makes a sharp R and then heads NE to begin to ascend a small ridge. It is wide and easy walking along the old road through young hardwoods, probably lumbered within the last 10 or 15 years. Now the trail goes up more steeply and levels off at 4.4 mi. At 5 mi a branch L leads to a beaver dam. Between 5.4 mi and 5.6 mi, four wet areas are encountered in quick succession. The trail shows more evidence of frequent use by off-road vehicles.

At 6 mi the trail is overgrown and brushy, but very easy to follow due to its width. The pine barrens and open areas of Baldwin Springs begin to be encountered at 6.4 mi as the trail curves W and approaches Madison Creek. Paper birch, balsam, and spruce are abundant. If you continue another 150 ft on the trail you will have to wade across Madison Creek to continue. After the trail crosses this swift-running section, it passes through the private inholding of the Dog and Pup Club. Travel N past the clubhouse to the main dirt road at 7.3 mi. The road reaches a cutoff L to a footbridge at 7.6 mi and, after crossing the bridge and traversing a lovely grassy path filled with seasonal wildflowers, reaches the hub of Baldwin Springs at 7.9 mi.

❄ Trail in winter: Distances are too long for backcountry skiers to do in a day, although as a ski-camping route it has possibilities. Bear in mind that snowmobilers travel this entire area in large numbers; there are no doubt much quieter choices for long-distance skiers.

🐾 Distances: Walk along the road to trail beginning, 2.3 mi; to junction of original Arrow Trail, 1.7 mi; to Hill Creek bridge, 4 mi; to Madison Creek bridge, 6.8 mi; to cutoff and bridge to Baldwin Springs, 7.6 mi; to Baldwin Springs trail register, 7.9 mi (12.7 km).

123 Baldwin Springs via Fish Ponds on the Bartman Trail
Trails Illustrated Map 743: I22-K21

This is a long and not particularly interesting walk along one of the many old routes to North Bend and Baldwin Springs from the N. The trail is an old road that passes two pretty ponds—now well on their way to becoming bogs—and it is surprisingly flat, dry, and easy going for the hiker. DEC is planning to designate this old road in 2012 as a community connector trail that will be groomed with Snocats. This trail also suffers from frequent illegal use by ATVs.

▶Trailhead: To reach Bartman Rd. drive SW on Rt. 8. At 1.1 mi from the Bakers Mills post office Bartman Rd. begins to the L (S). A brown and yellow DEC sign here indicates that the Bartman trailhead is in this direction. Drive 1.1 mi to a T-intersection and turn R, proceeding another 2.7 mi to the trailhead. A state parking area will be seen on the R at 2 mi. Continuing on the road past the parking area will be rough going for all but 4WD vehicles, especially in spring, so it may be necessary to walk the last 0.5 mi to the beginning of the trail.◀

Assuming one decides to drive the last section, parking is sporadically available on the sides of the road, which in approximately 1 mi dead ends at the site of an old hunting camp. A trail sign at 0.5 mi from the parking area says: "Fish Ponds North Bend and Baldwin Springs," with no mileage. Turn R onto a grassy trail, obviously an unused old road. It soon bends R and passes through a very overgrown apple orchard and past the cellar foundations of an old farmhouse on the R. A stream must be crossed right after the old farm clearing; it can be crossed carefully on several strategically placed rocks.

At 0.3 mi the general direction is S and the old road passes through scrubby thickets of hemlock and other young trees and shrubs, obviously an old field rapidly returning to a mature forest state. At 0.4 mi the route bends R through a mucky area and a draw, crisscrossing from one side to the other. The forest is now more open, but the young hardwood trees are not large, indicating lumbering within the past 30 years.

At 0.5 mi the trail crosses a rocky and flat area with some wet spots. A descent and bend to the L begins at 0.6 mi. The trail is very rocky, rough, and washed out—still heading down at 0.8 mi, bearing L. It follows a tiny stream on the R, attractively decorated with mosses and small rocks, and soon crosses it.

At 0.9 mi the trail continues to descend moderately through the draw and recrosses the creek. Continuing down the draw, it reaches the bottom at 1.1 mi after passing through a beautiful stand of young balsam trees. A log bridge is used to cross the small stream again, and at 1.2 mi a substantial wooden snowmobile bridge crosses one of the major inlets to Fish Ponds. After crossing the inlet and curving L, the trail begins to climb moderately, then levels off and follows the contours and the ridge around the ponds, avoiding the swampy shoreline.

The first Fish Pond comes into view at 1.3 mi. The partial views of the pond from various sections of the ridge indicate that the pond is very pretty, although it is located in the center of a large swamp.

There appears to be only one camping spot, with reasonable access to the water, at 1.5 mi. It is, however, worth the walk to the pond to enjoy the quiet beauty.

The trail in this section is even and fairly easy walking, undulating on occasion and crossing small inlets from time to time. The general direction is W as the trail hugs the ridge along the pond. Shortly, however, it turns S again.

At 1.8 mi the trail approaches a creek that has recently changed its course due to heavy flooding. The continuation of the old road can be discerned straight across the brook approximately 50 yd, even though the snowmobile markers show a route to the R (W) to avoid the swift but shallow stream directly ahead. The hiker can cross with no difficulty.

At 2 mi a large mucky spot is passed on the L, and another again at 2.3 mi. The beautiful cinnamon fern can be seen in this wet area. The second Fish Pond comes into view at 2.5 mi, and the trail continues along the old roadbed several ft above the very wet and swampy shoreline. The pond is subject to frequent beaver flooding.

At 3.1 mi the trail reaches a poorly marked fork to the R that is a trail to North Bend. This trail runs SW along the Fish Ponds swamp extension and is not recommended for hiking. The 4.2 mi to North Bend is overgrown and difficult to follow. Snowmobile disks are spaced too far apart, are too high, and cannot be depended upon to mark the way for the foot traveler. Moreover, the trail is extremely rough, with numerous slippery rocks hidden in the leaves and undergrowth, and swampy and boggy areas that present major problems. The main trail continues via the L fork (S). Continue on this trail and cross a tiny brook. At 3.2 mi a larger brook flows with vigor through large moss-covered rocks, which are easy to hop across on.

A sharp division occurs in the forest composition at 4 mi, immediately after the trail crosses a medium-sized creek. Here the hardwoods end abruptly and the trail enters a large stand of good-sized hemlocks. The sharp-eyed hiker may find evidence of bear, coyote, and deer.

Soon the trail enters a ravine between two small mountains. It crisscrosses from one side to the other several times, seeking the best passage. Although the old roadbed appears at times to have been scarred badly by rampaging waters, by and large it is still very flat, dry, and easy to walk. At 4.8 mi, the trail leaves the ravine and hugs the ridge on the R (W) going in a S direction.

At 5.1 mi it leads through a rocky, wet, and mucky area and then across a small stream. There is a clearing at 5.2 mi, and here the evidence of wheeled vehicles begins. The trail becomes increasingly rutted and muddy, until at 5.8 mi a junction and large clearing is reached. Brown and yellow DEC signs point the way to Baldwin Springs, NE to Lizard Pond in 3.1 mi, and to Garnet Lake in 4.1 mi.

Continuing straight for another 0.5 mi to Baldwin Springs, the trail crosses a large stream on a sturdy plank snowmobile bridge and ends in the large, grassy clearing of Baldwin Springs. Here there is a trail register and several campsites scattered among the pines and maze of dirt trails.

The old Baldwin Spring can still be found to the R of the trail register. It is partially hidden in the grasses in front of a clump of shrubs. Long ago an ancient upended hollow log was set into the spring, creating a small log well. Since there are a few resident frogs, and probably other water creatures living in the log, it is best to get spring water to the L, down the incline, where it runs out of the hillside. But, one is cautioned against drinking any water without treatment due to the prevalence of giardiasis or "beaver fever." This area was once dammed by man to create a small lake, and then by beaver several years ago. Most recently it has become a very shallow grassy pond.

To continue to North Bend walk NW for 1.8 mi on a well-used jeep trail, which is part of the old Oregon Trail.

A loop trip from Baldwin Springs to North Bend and back to Fish Ponds is possible, using the North Bend end of the snowmobile trail that began at the Bartman Trail junction at 3.1 mi. However, as previously stated, this is not recommended for hiking.

❋ Trail in winter: A long trek for expert, well-conditioned, experienced backcountry skiers only. Trails will very likely be shared with many snowmobiles.

𝕸 Distances: To first Fish Pond, 1.4 mi; to second Fish Pond, 2.5 mi; to junction of North Bend snowmobile trail, 3.1 mi; to junction with trail to Lizard Pond and Garnet Lake, 5.8 mi; to Baldwin Springs, 6.3 mi (10.2 km).

124 Lizard Pond and Baldwin Springs Canoe/Hike from Garnet Lake

Trails Illustrated Map 743: K22

This trail is long and very attractive. It traverses mostly flat areas and goes through some beautiful and unusual old white pine groves enroute from Lizard Pond (sometimes spelled Lixard, thought to be a misspelling that remains on many maps) to Baldwin Springs. To reach the trailhead on the W shore of Garnet Lake one needs to use a canoe (or another type of boat) to cross the lake.

▶ Trailhead: (See trail 120 for directions to Garnet Lake and the E shore parking area.) A popular put-in point along Garnet Lake is located across from a small DEC parking area that accommodates 6 to 8 cars. Canoe SW from the parking area; the hiking trail begins on the W shore directly across from the narrowest section at the S end of the lake opposite the peninsula that juts out on the E shore. ◄

The landing and take-out area at the trailhead is sandy, flat, and very pretty, a grassy clearing shaded by several large maples. It is large enough to store several canoes and still leave space for picnickers. In the past, the DEC trail sign pointing to Lizard Pond has been missing. It is, however, 1.3 mi from this take-out clearing to the lean-to on Lizard Pond.

The trail leads W away from the lake and immediately begins a moderate uphill climb. At 0.2 mi it levels briefly, and at 0.3 mi, after a short dip, continues climbing. Yellow or red snowmobile signs occasionally mark the way. A wet area is encountered at 0.4 mi and then the trail levels briefly, leading around or over a blowdown.

The trail continues to climb, making a tiny dip at 0.5 mi where a small ravine is to the L. The top of the ridge at 0.6 mi is also the beginning of the marsh that has gradually filled in the E end of Lizard Pond.

Jogging L, the trail rises about 2 ft, paralleling the edge of the marsh and continuing through a stand of hemlocks. The marsh can be seen intermittently through the trees. It deserves a closer look as it is a very interesting and beautiful area filled with a large variety of flowers in season and groves of young tamaracks.

Some small ups and downs are traversed until, at 0.9 mi, a side trail cuts R for 50 yd to provide an unrestricted first view of the pond. The main trail crosses a small brook at 1 mi. This is the outlet of the pond.

After a short rise and curve L, the trail turns away from the pond to climb a small ridge. The ridge crest is reached at 1.1 mi, where the pond can be seen through the trees. After traversing an attractive grove of hemlock and paper birch, the trail reaches at 1.3 mi a lean-to that sits on a small knoll overlooking the W end of the pond. The stark cliffs of Mt. Blue are directly across the pond, and looking NE the dramatic crags of Crane Mt. can be seen.

Continuing W to Baldwin Springs, at 1.4 mi, the trail is pleasant and sometimes hard to follow, with occasional rocky and rough areas. Beaver activity can force you to make detours to regain the trail on dryer ground—bring your map and compass. The end of Lizard Pond is reached at 1.5 mi. The trail now turns L through a marshy area in a SW direction. The trail bends R at 1.7 mi and spans a wet area on a primitive log corduroy that is extremely slippery when wet.

Descending slightly at 1.8 mi, a flooded section of trail must be crossed. The conditions here vary according to season and beaver activity. Traverse the N side of the pond if water is backed up. It is a considerable distance around the flooded area to the S. The trail turns SW and passes through a ravine. Here the trail, wildly overgrown with ferns and witch hobble, is difficult to discern.

Traversing the side of a small ridge, the trail is still hard to follow. At 1.9 mi a bridge crosses a brook and then in another 10 yd a second bridge crosses another stream. The trail turns L and goes quite close to the bank of the stream for the next 0.3 mi, still traveling W.

At 2 mi, still paralleling the stream, the trail bends to the R through a level valley and once more is easy to follow. After a slight bend L the direction becomes more SW. At 2.3 mi another stream is crossed on yet another wood-plank bridge.

A thicket of tall hemlocks at 2.5 mi provides very pleasant and cool walking. The trail varies from easy to rough and wet, but the wetter sections have plenty of rocks on which to walk. At 2.8 mi large white pines predominate. A larger wet area begins at 3.1 mi, testing your balance on the rocks. At 3.4 mi a vly comes into view on the L. The trail ascends into a stand of scrubby spruce at 3.5 mi.

The trail reaches a junction at 3.7 mi. To the L is Indian Pond, actually a large marsh, and the trail leading to it is an overgrown snowmobile trail. The sign says: "Indian Pond 0.8 mi; Lizard Pond 2.4 mi; Garnet Lake 3.4 mi; W Stony Creek Road 1.6 mi." These distances all appear to be short by 0.3 mi.

At 3.8 mi another new snowmobile bridge spans a small stream. Watch for the showy, purple-fringed orchis, which blooms here in June and July. The trail now enters a grove of hemlocks and very soon passes two enormous glacial erratics on the R.

The character of the trail begins to change as the sandy pine barrens of Baldwin Springs are approached. As the trail enters the scrubby pines and sedge grasses, there are also numerous sun-loving plants, such as the beautiful orange hawkweed, wild strawberries, and, everywhere, blueberries. At 4.2 mi the junction of the Fish Pond trail is reached. Continue L to cross the bridge over Stony Creek and into the main clearing of Baldwin Springs at 4.5 mi.

❋ Trail in winter: This trail provides a lovely, long backcountry ski trek, begun by skiing across the lake. The trail may be shared with snowmobiles. You may not wish to attempt the entire trip to Baldwin Springs, but instead angle SW (L) in the vicinity of the lean-to and bushwhack approximately a mile to reach Madison Creek Vly, where beautiful upturned trees create an extraordinary winter landscape. This could be a long day, so plan accordingly. For experienced backcountry skiers only. Map and compass a must.

David Hough

🐾 Distances: To end of Lizard Pond marsh, 0.6 mi; to Lizard Pond Lean-to, 1.3 mi; to white pine forest, 2.8 mi; to Indian Pond junction, 3.7 mi; to Fish Ponds trail junction, 4.2 mi; to Baldwin Springs, 4.5 mi (7.2 km).

125 Indian Pond

Trails Illustrated Map 743: K22

This hike is a short, beautiful walk through an old pine forest to the banks of a small pond and remains of an old stone dam on Madison Creek. At one time this shallow pond, created at the turn of the century by the damming of Madison Creek, was a mile or more in length. With the destruction of the dam, the area has returned to boggy swampland. The narrow, mile-long pond still shows on the topographic map, but all that remains now is the memory.

Occasionally beaver will enlarge sections of the swamp, recreating a pond for a few years, but recently the flow is once more rather narrow, meandering through wet marshlands. The walk to the site of the old dam is mostly flat, very open, and beautiful. The trail is often cushioned with soft pine needles, bordered by ferns and bunchberry. The walk will be remembered for the many very old white pines and the murmur of the wind through their branches.

▶Trailhead: The trail into Indian Pond from West Stony Creek Rd. is located 4.9 mi from the beginning of the road, or 1.6 mi E of the T-junction at Baldwin Springs. The trail is on the N side, marked occasionally with orange snowmobile disks and a brown and yellow DEC trail sign prominently mounted near its beginning. The trail is very seldom used by snowmobiles. The trail is in good shape from West Stony Creek Rd. N to Madison Creek. Past the creek it is less brushed out and defined N to the Lizard Pond trail (124).◀

Parking along the shoulder of the dirt road in front of the trailhead is not recommended as it is on a narrow bend and the shoulders are soft and sandy, but a small cleared area about 50 yd to the E on the N side is large enough for two vehicles. Since West Stony Creek Rd. has been much improved in recent years, other parking space can be found at several places in the vicinity.

As the trail begins, note the enormous white pine to the R. This is just the first of many ancient pines found growing in the forest traversed by this trail. At 0.1 mi a second marked snowmobile trail is encountered; the L (N) branch leads toward Indian Pond and the marshlands. The right branch returns to the road in a short distance at the old Barber place.

Turn L (N) here. The trail very shortly, at 0.2 mi, encounters a new beaver pond and dam. Cross to the L below the dam without difficulty. Interrupted ferns and many other lush green plants fight for growing space among the brown pine needles underfoot. At 0.3 mi the trail ascends a small knoll with a few undulations. At 0.5 mi it crosses a minor wet area, and a curve L occurs at 0.6 mi. On the L the marsh comes into sight. The shore of Indian Pond comes into view at 0.9 mi.

Several large boulders that formed the base of the manmade dam are now visible, and many can be used as points of interest for photos and/or picnic rocks. The tiny pond is hardly worthy of the name at present, but it is a very picturesque area, with its rocks and tall pine borders. It is quite possible to walk along the foot of the dam at the W edge of the pond.

After crossing the dam, the trail makes a sharp L to the S. It then turns R (W) and climbs a draw, proceeding through a hemlock forest. At 1.2 mi a mucky area is encountered. The trail climbs a small ridge and then descends to the outlet of Lizard Pond. The trail is quite nice, but is recommended only for those adventurous hikers willing to risk a wet walk along the edge of an old, overgrown beaver dam to cross a small pond at Lizard Pond outlet, which is encountered at 1.6 mi. Box elders and other edge vegetation have utilized the old dam, and are now grown to the point where they have created impenetrable brush all along it. One can, however, in low water pick a way across along the edge, and climb the ridge on the other side to the trail junction at 1.8 mi. A circle trip to Baldwin Springs (and your vehicle on West Stony Creek Rd.) can be made by turning L here. A R turn will lead to Lizard Pond and Garnet Lake (see trail 124).

❋ Trail in winter: Distances required to reach the trailhead along unplowed West Stony Creek Rd. prohibit backcountry skiing for all but those able to winter camp.

🐾 Distances: To snowmobile trail, 0.1 mi; to beaver dam, 0.2 mi; to Indian Pond, 1 mi (1.6 km). Continuing to beaver dam at Lizard Pond outlet, 1.6 mi; to Lizard Pond trail junction, 1.8 mi (2.9 km).

126 Tenant Creek Falls

Trails Illustrated Map 743: G-H20

The state trails to Tenant Creek Falls and the East Stony Creek to Wilcox Lake (trail 127) begin at the end of the Hope Falls Rd. and cross private property. While DEC does have a trail easement for the East Stony Creek trail to Wilcox Lake, there is no formal agreement with the landowner for access to the to the Tenant Falls Trail. DEC is working on a resolution to this issue by constructing a new section of trail that will be routed around the southern edge of the private property. In the meantime, hikers must respect the private driveway at the trailhead for both trails and do not block that private driveway under any circumstances. Stay on the two trails as you walk through the private property and do not stray off the marked trail.

Three lovely waterfalls are the reward for this short walk which, in the beginning, follows an old overgrown logging road, but after reaching the first falls becomes a less-distinct herd path upstream to the even more rewarding second and third falls.

▶ Trailhead: To reach the trailhead at Old Brownell Camp, turn R (E) off NY 30 onto Old Northville Rd. at a point 0.5 mi N of a bridge over the Sacandaga River N of Great Sacandaga Lake. Or, from the town hall in Wells take NY 30 S for 11 mi, and turn L onto Old Northville Rd. Drive along Old Northville Rd. 1.4 mi. Turn L on Hope Falls Rd., marked by a large carved and painted sign. Proceed along Hope Falls Rd. winding up East Stony Creek for 7.4 mi, the last 1.3 mi of which is unpaved. At 7.4 mi, find a small parking area on the L and a barrier blocking further motorized travel. ◀

The well-worn footpath is an old logging road leading upstream along Tenant Creek. It is flat and enjoyable hiking through mixed open woods above the creek. At about 0.7 mi it descends and crosses a wet area, then rises again above the creek. Continuing along the creek bank, the trail crosses a small brook and then on the R can be seen an open knoll dotted with several mature hemlocks. Beyond a dip in the trail, the first of the three waterfalls appears at 0.9 mi. The clear waters and large rocks that form a natural amphitheater invite a stop for rest and exploration.

The path continues along the S side of Tenant Falls above the falls and is shaded by large hemlocks. Gradually it becomes rougher and harder to follow, but the creek remains in sight on the L. At 1.2 mi there are several enormous yellow birches that were spared during the last lumbering of this section.

At 1.3 mi the path crosses a second small creek and veers briefly away from Tenant Creek to avoid a large marshy area. The easy footpath has now become a small rocky trail. At 1.8 mi a large hemlock-covered ridge rises to the R. After climbing this, the faint foot trail descends the ridge and continues along the creek again.

At 2 mi the second waterfall is reached. The third waterfall is another 250 yd upstream. Each is uniquely attractive, and although small (30-50 ft) as waterfalls are measured, the wild, scenic glen is filled with beauty and appears to be seldom visited.

✵ Trail in winter: Not suitable until DEC builds the new trail to avoid the private property.

✽ Distances: To first waterfall, 0.9 mi; to second waterfall, 2 mi; to third waterfall, 2.1 mi (3.1 km).

127 Wilcox Lake via East Stony Creek Trail
Trails Illustrated Map 743: G-H20

Wilcox Lake is one of the most attractive and most popular bodies of water in the southern Adirondacks. Somewhat overused, but much appreciated, this small lake is a worthwhile destination for the day hiker.

The walk to Wilcox Lake from the old Brownell Camp along the East Stony Creek Trail is very attractive yet only moderately strenuous. It traverses, for the most part, an old road through an open forest of mixed hardwoods and evergreens. This hike is recommended for those who enjoy walking more level areas, as the uphill sections are invigorating, but not difficult. Walking along the banks of picturesque East Stony Creek for three-quarters of the way displays the lowlands of the southern Adirondacks at their best. Furthermore, Wilcox Lake is a worthy destination, despite sections of trail erosion that seem to have recovered in recent years.

▶ Trailhead: To reach the trailhead at Old Brownell Camp, turn R (E) off NY 30 onto Old Northville Rd. at a point 0.5 mi N of a bridge over the Sacandaga River N of Great Sacandaga Lake. Or, from the town hall in Wells take NY 30 S for 11 mi, and turn L onto Old Northville Rd. Drive along Old Northville Rd. 1.4 mi. Turn L on Hope Falls Rd., marked by a large carved and painted sign. Proceed along Hope Falls Rd. winding up East Stony Creek for 7.4 mi, the last 1.3 mi of which is unpaved. At 7.4 mi, find a small parking area on the L and a barrier blocking further motorized travel. ◄

Beyond the barrier, the road leads to the site of Old Brownell lumber camp. "No Trespassing" signs are posted here. The present owners graciously permit access around their property but request that hikers respect their privacy and walk the marked trail only.

Brown and yellow DEC signs point to the trail, which begins to the L, going N, and follows the banks of East Stony Creek. A trail register is on the R, approximately 50 yd from the trailhead. Although the land is posted against everything except hiking, skiing, and snowmobiles, there is evidence of repeated use as a camping area for the first 0.2 mi. There is an unmarked cutoff to the R at 0.2 mi, just before an impressive wooden snowmobile and foot bridge. The cutoff leads to the blue-marked trail 126 to Tenant Creek Falls. (Trails here are going to be re-routed by DEC to avoid crossing private land. Please stay on the marked trails.) Crossing the bridge, the trail proceeds straight ahead through a stand of white pine. An unmarked trail that turns R immediately after the bridge is an old fishermen's path that runs briefly upstream along Tenant Creek.

At 0.4 mi a gentle climb begins and the trail bends R away from the creek. The climb avoids wet areas and takes the hiker part way up the shoulder of the small unnamed mountain on the L. The trail is well marked by blue DEC trail markers as well as shiny, bright-orange snowmobile disks, and occasional faded yellow ones.

At 0.6 mi the first of several boardwalks spanning wet areas is encountered, but soon the trail becomes pleasantly flat and free of debris and blowdown, due in part to illegal use by ATV riders. In this section the forest is quite open, composed of mixed hardwoods with a scattering of hemlocks. The trail traverses the contour of a ridge in a gentle series of ups and downs and at 0.7 mi finally levels off.

At 1 mi, the descent of the ridge commences. A second small, wooden boardwalk is reached at 1.1 mi and a rougher trail section at 1.2 mi. Two additional small wooden bridges cross wet areas at 1.3 mi and then the trail drops gently and enters a swampy clearing. Directly ahead is East Stony Creek again, which the trail now parallels for most of the next two miles. There is a fishermen's path off to the L, but the main trail crosses a muddy inlet (no bridge) and turns R (NE) in the upstream direction.

This is a very attractive section. The boulder-strewn creek displays a variety of flowers along its banks during the warm seasons. Pink joe-pye weed and bright red cardinal flowers, among others, can be found in riotous profusion in midsummer.

The trail passes through a hemlock grove at 1.5 mi, turns briefly R, and then at 1.6 mi returns quite close to the creek bank. It becomes wet and rocky at 1.7

mi, then rises slightly, and at 2 mi begins to pull away from the stream again. The trail crosses a large inlet at 2.1 mi, turns R briefly again, climbs a short incline, and becomes level again along the bank.

Once more, at 2.7 mi, after a gentle series of ups and downs, the trail bears R (E) and up. At 2.9 mi a larger wet area is encountered, but paths lead around it to the R and L. A large blowdown of four or five large pines occurs at 3 mi, but the trail itself has been cleared. The stream can occasionally be seen and heard on the L as the trail continues up, climbing a ridge, and passing through majestic hemlocks. At 3.1 mi it reaches the crest of the ridge.

For a short time the trail is flat and easy to walk. Descending the ridge, it encounters another mucky spot at 3.2 mi and turns R and crosses a brook at 3.3 mi. After a moderate up-and-down section another small stream is crossed at 3.4 mi after a sharp L. At 3.6 mi the trail descends to a lovely clearing where an attractive wooden bridge used to span Dayton Creek just before it flows into East Stony. In the spring of 1993, this bridge was washed out. Until it is replaced, crossing can be achieved using several large boulders, except in very high water. Since the stream here races downhill and is very swift, high-water crossings could be difficult.

The trail now becomes rougher, with areas of blowdown and rocky, wet sections at 3.8 mi. At 4 mi another swampy area and tiny pond are negotiated on large rocks to the L. Finally, the Bakertown Bridge, which crosses East Stony Creek, is reached at 4.2 mi. The Bakertown Bridge is a suspension bridge barely wide enough to accommodate a snowmobile and will, unfortunately, also accommodate illegal ATVs and dirt bikes, permitting them another access route into this area.

After crossing the bridge, the trail swings L then almost immediately sharp R where it begins climbing the ridge, gradually circling around and up. It flattens out briefly at 4.7 mi, going through an attractive stand of mature hardwoods consisting mostly of ash, beech, and birch.

At 4.9 mi the top of the ridge and a trail junction are reached. According to the sign, Bakertown Bridge was 0.5 mi. It is actually 0.7 mi. Willis Lake is to the W 4.5 mi. The third sign declares Wilcox Lake to be to the R and another 0.2 mi.

Turning R, the trail joins the jeep road from Harrisburg Lake at 5 mi. Here another DEC sign directs the hiker L along the road, which officially ends before the short descent to the lake. The jeep trail ends at the barrier. Although "Motorized Vehicles Prohibited" signs are posted and a barrier periodically replaced, the "trail" down to the lakeshore has been used repeatedly and illegally by 4WD vehicles and ATVs, which legally come in on the jeep trail. The wide, eroded mud track leading down to the lakeshore and the lean-tos is sprouting vegetation again and is in much better condition than it has been in years, but also has massive permanent gouges.

Despite this, Wilcox Lake itself remains one of the prettiest jewels in the southern Adirondacks. Decorated with numerous large rocks along its shores and a small island with picturesque pines and pink azaleas in the spring, it often echoes with the cry of the loon. There are several camping areas along its S shore, and an attractive lean-to is to the R overlooking the lake. A second, newer lean-to is reached by walking L an additional 0.4 mi along the shore. Both lean-tos have been "adopted" by an ADKer and are kept in excellent condition.

❋ Trail in winter: This area is the winter playground of the motorized set, with cross-country skiers limited by the distances necessary to access the trails due to the unplowed road. However, after skiing the unplowed road for approximately 2 mi to reach the trailhead, one can continue as far as feasible, taking into consideration the time required to ski in and back out again. The road and trail will be shared with snowmobiles.

🐾 Distances: To East Stony Creek, 1.3 mi; to Dayton Creek, 3.6 mi; to Bakertown Suspension Bridge, 4.2 mi; to 4WD road from Harrisburg Lake, 5 mi; to Wilcox Lake shore, 5.2 mi (8.4 km).

128 Wilcox Lake from Willis Lake

Trails Illustrated Map 743: H19-20

A second approach to Wilcox Lake, in addition to the one from East Stony Creek Rd. (trail 127), can be made from the SE via the Willis Lake trail. This trail traverses rugged terrain in sections, traveling through some of the wildest areas of the Wilcox Lake Wild Forest.

▶Trailhead: Drive N on NY 30 along the Sacandaga River and turn R onto Pumpkin Hollow Rd., which is 0.3 mi after a sign that says "Town of Wells." Continue driving on Pumpkin Hollow Rd. for 1.6 mi—mostly uphill—until the DEC trail signs are seen on the L. Parking is available for several vehicles on both sides of the road, although in spring the shoulders are extremely soft. This is not the trailhead to Wilcox Lake, however.

It is suggested that hikers park here and walk the additional mile along the road to reach the trailhead. Although it is usually possible to drive a regular vehicle on the unpaved road past Willis Lake, passing several private camps en route, the road shoulders have no parking and the road rapidly deteriorates for the last half mile. Hikers who elect to drive this additional mile may find the road impassable in spring and summer due to floods and washouts. A careful driver can drive on the Pumpkin Hollow Rd. past Willis Lake to a parking area just W of Doig Creek.◀

Hiking or driving the dirt road leads up a long, gentle grade after leaving Willis Lake and the camps. The road is very pleasant to walk, and passes a hunting camp on the left at 0.9 mi. At the end of the road there is a small clearing with parking for only one or two vehicles, where at 1 mi an iron DEC barrier marks the trailhead.

Almost immediately after the barrier, the trail crosses a small stream on a sturdy plank snowmobile bridge. It begins climbing a long ridge, passing through mixed hardwoods and evergreens. This is a continuation of the road that once led all the way through to Harrisburg Lake. It is fairly easy walking at this point.

At 1.4 mi the trail levels off and soon begins climbing through a washed-out, rocky and difficult section. The top of the ridge is reached at 1.6 mi, after which the trail quickly jogs R and then L. Here the trail passes through a stand of very large, old white pines.

A fork in the trail occurs at 1.7 mi. Either branch may be chosen, as they rejoin in another 0.5 mi, although the L one has a red trailmarker. The general direction is E. The trail now makes a few snake-like turns, and at 1.9 mi begins to descend. Here it becomes rougher underfoot and wildly overgrown, but still discernible.

At 2.1 mi a slight jog to the R occurs. The surrounding forest is still predominantly hardwoods with hemlocks and large white pines randomly encountered. A stand of very large maple trees that measure at least 4 ft in circumference indicate that this is obviously an area that escaped the most recent logging.

At 2.2 mi a steep downhill section begins. At the bottom of this ridge is a brook; after crossing it the trail bears L briefly. At 2.5 mi there is a wet area, and then the trail bends L slightly.

A very pretty but small clearing, surrounded by hemlocks, is passed at 2.6 mi. Another small stream must be crossed at 2.7 mi, and then the trail makes a series of twists and turns until at 3.1 mi it straightens out again, passing through a valley containing a large stand of hemlocks.

The trail now makes a series of rollercoaster ups and downs across a ridge until reaching and crossing a brook at 3.5 mi. A swift-running, small stream is encountered at 3.6 mi and a swamp can be seen on the R. The trail now passes through very wild and seldom-travelled country heading NE through a ravine, twisting L and R through mostly flat terrain. At 4.3 mi it reaches an unusually old grove of hemlocks with trees measuring 6 to 8 ft in circumference.

At 4.8 mi you reach Wilcox Lake Outlet—a larger, fast-running stream with a bridge that is frequently washed out. In the spring during high water, and in winter, if the bridge is gone, it may not be feasible to continue; however, in fair weather hikers can probably wade, as it is not very deep. Look up and downstream for fallen logs on which to cross, too. In times of low water, the hiker can cross on the rocks.

After the crossing, the trail goes L along the outlet for about 60 yd, then bears R and continues up a ridge, climbing moderately to reach the top at 5 mi. Here an enormous white pine stands majestically at the side of the trail. The trail begins to descend, and at 5.1 mi reaches a dry watercourse, then a small stream at 5.3 mi. The trail flattens out and turns R to climb another ridge in a SE direction.

Now the forest becomes lush and overgrown with small beech saplings. Many of the larger beech trees have died, but smaller ones are growing in great numbers. An impressive pine, with a trunk of more than 7 ft in circumference, lies across the trail at 5.7 mi. At 5.8 mi the trail descends through a very open and attractive beech, ash, and maple forest.

Finally, a junction with the East Stony Creek trail (trail 127) is reached at 6.1 mi. A guideboard pointing the way back says that Willis Lake is 4.5 mi, but this is short by 1.7 mi. Take the L fork to Wilcox Lake; the sign says 0.2 mi farther, which is correct. Lovely Wilcox Lake is reached at 6.3 mi.

Wilcox Lake is popular and very picturesque, with a small island off shore and several rocks and boulders offering fishing and picnic spots. There are two lean-tos, one to the R (E) approximately 0.2 mi, and the other to the L (W) 0.6 mi. In the past, ATVs and other off-road vehicles have destroyed the path to the lake shore, but in recent years it has been recovering, although it is still a large man-made gully. One reason for the recovery is that the Jeep road into the area has become so impassible in spots that fewer and fewer vehicles can make it at all.

❄ Trail in winter: Snowmobiles are the primary users of this long trail and skiers will find the distances daunting. Some of the small but steep ridges in the interior may also be covered with brush, depending upon the snowmobilers, trail maintenance, and thus not readily skiable, making this a long, arduous trip. Not recommended.

🐾 Distances: From parking area to trailhead, 0.9 mi; to trail fork, 1.7 mi; to Wilcox Lake Outlet, 4.8 mi; to junction of East Stony Creek Trail, 6.1 mi; to Wilcox Lake shore, 6.3 mi (10.1 km).

Mt. Blue (bushwhack)

Pristine and incredibly attractive, Mt. Blue offers an adventurous bushwhack up a relatively easy, trailless mountain that rewards the successful hiker with outstanding views. To reach the foot of the mountain, the hiker must canoe across Garnet Lake.

The quickest and most scenic route to the trailhead to Lizard Pond and the cutoff point at the foot of Mt. Blue is to launch a canoe, or other small boat, and paddle across Garnet Lake. Small boats can be launched across from the parking turnout on Garnet Lake's shore road. Since Garnet Lake's shores are either privately owned, or surrounded by swampland, it is not possible to walk around the lake to the trailhead from either direction.

After launching the canoe, paddle SW, or directly across to the W shore, and then turn S (L) to follow the lake shore approximately one mile to the trailhead, which is directly across from the tip of the E peninsula's point. Paddle close to the W shore to an obviously well-used large, grassy clearing. Leave the canoe or boat here in order to walk the trail to Lizard Pond and/or to bushwhack up Mt. Blue. There is no herd path up Mt. Blue, so map and compass are a must, especially for the first half of the climb after one leaves the trail.

Marked for snowmobiles and hikers, the trail begins climbing almost immediately, and is rough and rocky underfoot. There is a brief level section at 0.2 mi, after which it continues to climb the ridge at a moderate incline, with a slight bend to the R at 0.25 mi.

The forest is mixed evergreens and hardwoods, with several mature specimens

Mt. Blue from Crane Mountain. Jack Freeman

intermingled, making an attractive, high and open canopy of greenery. At 0.3 mi the trail crosses a very small brook, after which a wet area must be negotiated. Continuing to climb at 0.5 mi, the trail passes through a heavy understory of witch hobble. At 0.7 mi the end of the Lizard Pond vly is seen through the trees. Here, too, the trail levels off. The hiker who wishes to climb Mt. Blue should cut off to the R (N) at this height of land and begin bushwhacking up the shoulder of a small ridge in order to begin the climb up Mt. Blue.

Two small knolls will be traversed in the beginning, with quick descents into tiny valleys before the climb up Mt. Blue begins in earnest. Consult the compass frequently, and travel in a general NNW direction. Hikers should watch the contours of the land, and stay to the high ground, traveling along the SE shoulder of the mountain.

At approximately 1.5 mi the hiker will begin to encounter bare rock stretches. Lookouts will afford stunning views as more elevation is gained. Mt. Blue was burned during the early 1900s and the bare rock slopes are a direct result. However, they do provide the hiker with outstanding vistas at many points in addition to the summit.

The summit is reached at approximately 2 mi. Because it is flat and contains extensive stretches of bare rock, there are several viewing locations. To the E and NE are the craggy cliffs of Crane Mt. and the jewel-like waters of Garnet Lake. To the S are Lizard Pond, Bearpen Peak, Baldhead, and Moose mts. Hikers should spend time exploring to discover small, cleared overlooks offering a magnificent variety of spectacular scenes—especially on a crisp, clear day.

❄ Trail in winter: A wonderful winter trip for a combination snowshoe and ski trek. Ski across the lake and as far up the trail as feasible, depending upon snow conditions. Snowmobiles may pack the trail section. Stash the skis and snowshoe up Mt. Blue for a stunning winter panorama of the surrounding countryside.

🥾 Distances: To beginning of vlei, 0.7 mi; to summit of Mt. Blue, 2 mi (3.2 km). Ascent, 1400 ft (427 m); Summit elevation, 2925 ft (892 m).

129 Kibby Pond

Trails Illustrated Map 743: M-L21

Kibby Pond is a short hike up a long ridge (a climb of 600 ft) and then down to the shores of a lovely little pond that is a favorite with trout fishermen. There are at least three camping areas with fire rings and relatively level tent sites.

▶Trailhead: To reach the trailhead, drive SW on NY 8, 5.1 mi past the post office in Bakers Mills. A brown and yellow DEC sign, very obvious on the E side of the road, says: "Kibby Pond 1.8 mi" (It's actually 0.1 mi more.) There is parking for two cars in the turnaround road at the beginning of the trail, but it is better to park on NY 8. There is ample space on the flat, dry road shoulders to accommodate several cars.◀

The trail begins behind the hemlocks and immediately descends to cross a medium-sized stream, which shortly will join the East Branch of the Sacandaga River. In spring and times of high water, this stream may present a problem for the hiker as there is no bridge. Flat exposed rocks normally form a series of stepping stones to the opposite side.

After crossing the stream, the trail begins an immediate ascent heading S and up a moderately steep grade that is very rocky and rough underfoot. Hemlocks predominate, with several mature maple trees. The trail snakes to the L and R several times as it ascends the ridge, picking the easiest way up the rock-strewn hillside. At 0.2 mi the trail still climbs moderately; the direction is more SSE. The trail leaves the rocky areas behind and enters a mature hardwood forest with numerous wildflowers. Canada lilies carpet the ground, with mosses and ferns in abundance. The trail now becomes level and very easy to walk.

A mucky area is encountered at 0.3 mi. Traverse it to the R or L. At 0.5 mi the trail crosses a creek. Green mossy rocks along its banks create a very attractive section. The trail becomes steeper and at 0.8 mi turns L through a wet area and then R again. Still climbing, it curves R. The forest here is open although the underbrush is more dense, and at 0.9 mi a short descent occurs.

The trail crosses a tiny brook at 1 mi and continues to meander R and L as it picks a way up the ridge. It begins to climb more steeply after crossing a wet area at 1.1 mi. At 1.2 mi the trail still climbs and continues its switchbacking from R to L to moderate the pitch for the hiker. After a short level section a steep descent begins at 1.3 mi and the trail hugs the contours of the small mountain to the L (N). At 1.6 mi it flattens out again on the plateau. Beautiful rock formations can be seen to the L and up the hillside.

Kibby Pond is sighted through the trees at 1.8 mi. After a short but steep drop, the shore of this lovely little pond is reached at 1.9 mi.

❉ Trail in winter: Not the ideal backcountry ski trail due to an almost constant climb going in, and rather steep descents on a return. The trip in to Kibby, however, is a nice, easy snowshoe hike.

🐾 Distances: To top of large ridge, 1.2 mi; to Kibby Pond, 1.9 mi (3 km).

130 Cod Pond

Trails Illustrated Map 743: K20-21

Cod Pond is small, very attractive, and such a short distance from the road that it is a favorite of anglers, children, and short-distance hikers. Its location near a large vlei fed by Stewart Creek makes it home to numerous animals and birds. For nature lovers it is a never-ending series of surprises. Carry binoculars and a camera.

▶Trailhead: To reach the trailhead from the S, take NY 30 to Wells. Then about 3 mi N of Wells turn NE on NY 8. Proceed 8.3 mi to the parking area on the R (E) just before the bridge over Stewart Creek. You may see a DEC trail sign at the trailhead. The parking area is large enough for 10–12 vehicles. If you are coming S on NY 8 from Wevertown, there is a sign on the R side of the road announcing Cod Pond. ◀

Take the trail out of the S end of the parking area where a DEC trail sign mentions distances to Cod Pond, Cod Pond Flow, North Bend, and Baldwin Springs. Head uphill (E) on a rocky path. A junction is reached at 0.15 mi. One sign indicates Cod Pond 0.8 mi, Cotter Brook Trail, and Route 8 at Georgia Bank are to the R. Another sign points straight ahead to North Bend and Baldwin Springs. There is also a trail register at this junction. Turn R to reach Cod Pond.

The trail ascends 80 ft to another trail junction at 0.35 mi. Here, one sign indicates Cotter Brook Trail, and Route 8 at Georgia Creek are straight ahead. Another sign shows that the Cod Pond trail forks to the L and indicates 0.7 mi. The trail is occasionally marked with orange snowmobile signs, and the direction is S. The trail surface is level and easy walking. It ascends another 60 ft before beginning a gentle downhill course through more open, mature hardwoods.

You may encounter annoying blowdown in the area where Cod Pond is visible through the trees. Since this is a snowmobile trail, the blowdown may also be cleared, but in any case it is easy to skirt it through open woods. Soon a large camping area is entered. Here, amid the beeches, are spots for several tents. Turn L and walk an additional 100 yd down to the rocky shores of sparkling Cod Pond. There is a picnic rock here, and although the area shows signs of much use, it is usually clean and in good order.

This is an area rich in wildlife, with ducks, otter, muskrat, beaver, deer, bear, coyote, and numerous species of birds and fish living in and around the waters of the pond and surrounding swamplands.

❊ Trail in winter: Snowmobilers will pack the snow for skiers, who must share the trails and be alert. The uphill sections are long but mostly moderate in steepness, and for backwoods skiers of intermediate to expert abilities, this trail should present few problems.

❀ Distances: To first trail junction, 0.15 mi; to second trail junction, 0.35 mi; to Cod Pond, 1 mi (1.6 km).

131 Stewart Creek Flow and North Bend via the Oregon Trail

Trails Illustrated Map 743: K21

This is an attractive, easy walk to a small waterfall and a bridge crossing at the picturesque site of an old dam. Adventurous hikers may continue on the E side of Stewart Creek Flow to walk through seldom-visited majestic pine forests to North Bend, and then on to Baldwin Springs. This is a well-marked and well-used snowmobile trail all the way to Baldwin Springs. The downside of this is that there are a few muddy stretches due to the fact that there is no penalty for a snowmobile trail to pass through what are wet areas in the spring and summer. The upside is that three bridges that cross what otherwise would be difficult and wet places along the route have been installed to assist snowmobile traffic, thus making the trip much more feasible for the hiker.

▶Trailhead: To reach the trailhead from the S, take NY 30 to Wells. Then about 3 mi N of Wells turn NE on NY 8. Proceed 8.3 mi to the parking area on the R (E) just before the bridge over Stewart Creek. You may see a DEC trail sign at the trailhead. The parking area is large enough for 10–12 vehicles. If you are coming S on NY 8 from Wevertown, there is a sign on the R side of the road announcing Cod Pond.◀

T*ake the trail out of the S end of the parking area* where a DEC trail sign mentions distances to Cod Pond, Cod Pond Flow, North Bend, and Baldwin Springs. Head uphill (E) on a rocky path. At 0.15 mi a junction is reached. One sign points to the R (see trail 130): Cod Pond, Cotter Brook Trail, and Route 8 at Georgia Bank. Another sign points straight ahead to North Bend 2.9 mi and Baldwin Springs 4.7 mi. There is also a trail register at this junction

Continue straight; the general direction is E. A small brook is reached and crossed at 0.3 mi. The old roadbed is flat here and passes through open stands of hemlock trees. At 0.6 mi it bends R; the direction is SSE. It now enters a shallow valley where hemlocks grow on the L and hardwoods on the R. The snowmobile signs in this area indicate the heavy snowmobile traffic in the winter. The orange diamond snowmobile trail signs will accompany you the rest of the way. Stewart Creek can be seen on the L at 0.8 mi, flowing slowly because of a beaver dam which comes into sight at 1 mi. Just past the dam, the creek rushes around and over a small but attractive waterfall and then around the bend. This is the longest stretch of intermittently muddy trail.

The trail reaches an open area beside the stream and ascends a little knoll, and then turns sharply L to cross a sturdy plank bridge at 1.2 mi at the outlet of Stewart Creek Flow. To the L a stone trough channels the waters to create a rushing flume. There is a picturesque swamp to the R. On the far side of the bridge a series of large boulders are the remains of a dam, providing a convenient resting and picnic place.

Hikers who choose to continue can do so by continuing on the trail, which stays to the L of the vlei until at 1.6 mi it begins its descent to the level of the vlei. At that point look for a small, white disk on a tree to the L that points L to the dry footpath around a 0.1 mi stretch through the wet vlei bottom. This lightly used trail passes through a much more rugged hill side than is encountered anywhere else on this route. It is marked with yellow disks. If you are prepared for an ankle- to calf-deep wet crossing, then following the snowmobile trail would be shorter and easier.

After skirting the vlei, and crossing and rejoining the snowmobile trail, the trail continues to the edge of the swamp at 2.2 mi where a snowmobile bridge is a welcome aid to the crossing. The approach on each side of the bridge may require the use of pine logs to keep your feet dry. The trail continues through some wonderful grassy areas with tall, attractive trees. The waters of Stewart Creek are on the R for about another mile, as the trail passes through a wonderful section of mature pines. At about 2.7 mi the trail passes close to a tumbling section of the creek at the bottom of a short ascent. This may be a good place to stop for a rest along the stream. After a final, short muddy stretch in the lowlands in the area of Stewart Creek, an attractive snowmobile bridge is crossed at 3.1 mi. Continuing beyond this bridge a short distance brings the hiker into North Bend, a popular camping area for hunters, but a quiet, attractive clearing at other times of year.

Another 1.9 mi must be hiked to reach Baldwin Springs. The trail is generally easy walking on a 4WD road; however, a number of muddy sections have been created by vehicles. (See trails 121-123 for other trails into Baldwin Springs.)

❄ Trail in winter: Aside from steep sections at the beginning, and some ups and downs after crossing the bridge over Stewart Flow, this is a picturesque and adventurous ski trip that offers the skier opportunities to explore the extensive marshes. It will be shared with snowmobiles.

🐾 Distances: To first junction, 0.15 mi; to flume and Stewart Creek bridge, 1.2 mi; to edge of Stewart Creek Flow crossing, 2.2 mi; to large wooden bridge and North Bend, 3.1 mi (5 km), to Baldwin Springs 5 mi (8 km).

132 Girard "Sugarbush" Maple Plantation
Trails Illustrated Map 743: J20

This hike holds interest for the history buff as well as those who just like a short hike in the woods. It was along this trail, then a road, that Henry Girard hauled his maple syrup and sugar out to market for a number of years in the early 1900s. It is said that he tapped 10,000 maple trees to produce up to 2000 gallons of syrup. The maples have been logged and many others have died, but there are still several very large trees left along the trail to give the hiker a bit of a flavor for what the forest must have looked like in those days.

▶Trailhead: Travel NY 8 to the tiny hamlet of Griffin, which is easily missed since the remaining buildings are well off the road, largely hidden by vegetation. The beginning of the trail will be found approximately 1.4 mi to the E of the hamlet, or 3.6 mi N from the junction of NY 30 and NY 8. The trail begins beside the large green sign that says: "1000 ft Ahead Parking." Parking is also available near the sign, along the road on either side, or park at the large parking area and walk the 1000 ft back to the trail on the same (E) side.◀

There is a barrier and sign advising "No Motorized Vehicles," but no other signs or markings at the entrance. The trail is clearly discernible, however.

The old road, now a path, begins an immediate uphill through a grassy section, and angles away from NY 8; the direction is SE. This is quite obviously an ancient road, wide, and still a bit rutted in places. It quickly levels off and at 0.1 mi a fork is reached. The trail R leads snowmobilers on a course which parallels NY 8 for another half mile. A sign tacked to a pine tree says "Girard Trail." Do continue straight ahead on the well-defined path. Bluets and butterflies will be seen in June, with a variety of other wildflowers taking advantage of a sunny clearing at 0.2 mi. The forest is mixed hardwoods with a scattering of hemlocks and balsams. Continuing through the clearing, the trail begins a brief uphill. After a wet section, the trail encounters another fork, this one to the L. This is unmarked, but it, too, is another old road to NY 8. Continue straight (or R). At 0.3 mi a stream enters the trail and runs down the middle for several feet, after which the path curves R.

Another brief uphill is traversed at 0.4 mi. Look for deer and coyote evidence in this area. A second small stream flows along the trail from L to R, and at 0.4 mi orange snowmobile disks mark a snowmobile bridge over another small brook. At 0.5 mi the trail begins to climb a small ridge. At 0.8 mi the top is reached. Here, amid a grove of hemlocks, the first evidence of the old sugar-making camp is seen. Look for an old vat to the R.

A small clearing is entered where the trail bears R—then it jogs L and enters a larger clearing. The trail continues past a large tub and a large, much-deteriorated metal platform. Stovepipes, buckets, and all manner of abandoned sugar-making equipment can be found. This clearing at 0.9 mi is all that is left of the substantial maple sugar operation. Notice that several old roads converge here. None, however, can be followed any distance, as they were created to serve as arms into the maple groves.

The trail continues past several old stumps and becomes more difficult to see. It climbs a steep hill, sporadically marked as a snowmobile trail. The trail then jogs L through hardwoods, crossing a small wooden bridge at 1.1 mi. Very large maples can now be seen in abundance. Perhaps this is what an old-growth maple forest was like.

At the height of land, the casual hiker may wish to turn around as the continuing snowmobile trail is poorly marked and unremarkable for another half-mile to a junction. Trails here lead, according to the signs, to Georgia Brook, 3 mi, Cod Pond another 6.6 mi, or Willis Lake at 8.5 mi more. All of these are built for, and suited to, the winter snowmobiler. They are long, wet, and next to impassible in some places for the average group of hikers. Therefore they are not described in this guide.

✤ Trail in Winter: As with most other trails in the southern Adirondacks this one must be shared with snowmobiles, but very good cross-country skiing is possible under the right snow conditions. Adventurous skiers could make a more challenging 5 mi loop using the Georgia

Brook connector trail and spotting a car at that trailhead on NY 8. However, caution is advised in crossing Georgia Brook and vlei, as the snowmobile bridge may not be in good condition.

❀ Distances: To first fork, 0.1 mi; to second fork, 0.25 mi; to sugar camp, 0.9 mi (1.4 km).

133 Pine Orchard from Flater's

Trails Illustrated Map 743: I19

Pine Orchard consists of several acres of enormous white pines reputed to be one of the few vestiges of virgin timber left in the Adirondacks. There is no sign to indicate when Pine Orchard has been reached, but the old tote road does pass through the orchard for about a mile. There are several huge pines along both sides of the trail, growing tall and stately, with trunk diameters exceeding 6 ft quite common.

At least three approaches can be used to reach Pine Orchard. The quickest and easiest walking, by far, is via the Windfall Road entrance near Wells. Here, the trail crosses private property, which at this writing is owned by the Flater family, who graciously permit access. A second walk to the orchard begins at the trailhead near Willis Lake on Pumpkin Hollow Rd. (trail 134). A third alternative is to enter the area via NY 8 where at least two snowmobile trails eventually join to lead into the Pines. However, because this third route traverses wet swamps and is so overgrown, it is not recommended for hiking and has not been included in this trail guide.

▶Trailhead: To reach Pine Orchard via the Flater family property, take NY 30 to Wells. Turn N on Griffin Rd., which is directly across from the town beach in Wells. If coming from the S, this is a R turn about 200 yd before the bridge that crosses Algonquin Lake. If the approach is from the N, make a L immediately after crossing the bridge.

At 0.8 mi turn R onto Windfall Rd. At 1.8 mi turn R again and continue another 2 mi to the end of this road where signs say "Visitor Parking" on the L and R and announce this to be the private property of the Flater family, where visitors "may need permission to proceed" (0.0 mi). If the Flaters are at home, ask permission; if they are not, leave a note with your destination and expected time of return on the car dashboard. Local residents are conscientious and may become concerned if a car remains overly long; therefore, backpackers who plan to spend a few days exploring should indicate this.◀

The trail is a continuation of the now overgrown road. A sturdy barrier bars motor vehicles at 0.2 mi where the road enters the Forest Preserve. Although the first 0.2 mi is muddy and rutted by vehicles, the barrier seems to be respected and the road section of the trail beyond is delightfully free of unsightly tracks and mud. A sign says that snowmobiles are permitted in winter.

Immediately after the barrier, a second trail forks R. A sign points the way S to Willis Lake, which is on Pumpkin Hollow Rd., but the 2.6 mi is most inaccurate. It is instead over 5 mi (trail 134).

The trail descends moderately to 0.6 mi, at which point the waters of a large vlei can be seen to the R (S). This is an extension of Taylor Vlei, fed by several small streams that eventually join Mill Creek to the E. A small path to the R leads down 0.1 mi to a small rock where the marsh can be viewed.

The main trail reaches the bottom of the ridge, bears R, then crosses a sturdy snowmobile bridge at 0.8 mi. The old road gradually climbs a small ridge until at 1 mi it enters a unique and beautiful corridor of green. In summer, this area is shaded and fringed with lacy greenery created by small spruce, hemlock, and taller white pines with ferns filling in gaps along the lower edges. The trail here is 3-4 ft wide, and carpeted with lovely, lush grasses.

A small stream, crossed at 1.4 mi, then joins a brook paralleling the trail on the R. The trail begins to rise moderately after passing through a clearing with evidence of an old camper's fire ring. Gradually the white pines have become larger and more numerous and now dominate the landscape. This is Pine Orchard, where local residents claim the pines have never been cut. These towering giants serve as reminders of what the forest may have looked like before the intervention of man. (A well-known botanist thought these trees were probably too small to bother with during the initial lumbering of the area, thanks to their natural reestablishment, more or less at the same time, after some natural disaster—perhaps a fire or wind storm. They have now grown to giant sizes under ideal conditions after an undisturbed 200 to 250 years.)

At 1.8 mi the trail bends L and then R again, climbing the ridge through open glades to enter a second clearing, which also has been used as a campsite. The trail turns L again at 2.2 mi and descends toward the marsh, which can be seen on the R. Although the trail still traverses an open pine forest, the trees here are younger and smaller. The giants of Pine Orchard have been passed.

The trail becomes narrower and less traveled as it skirts the edge of the vlei, becoming rough and much more difficult to walk. Although there are only a few small wet areas, at 2.6 mi a rather swampy section with wet, moss-covered rocks leads deceptively into wetter, grass-covered muck. The hiker should go to the R through some low brush to avoid this, rejoining the main path about 250 ft beyond. Continue N and cross a small brook at 2.8 mi.

The beautiful old road is now a small path that at times becomes a challenge to find, especially amid the lush growth of summer or in late fall after the leaves have fallen. Snowmobile signs are posted, but not frequently enough to reassure the novice hiker.

Hikers who continue should be familiar with, and use, a map and compass. Although this trail is occasionally brushed out and cleared by snowmobilers, there is no consistent trail maintenance from one year to the next. Because it has no interest except as a trail-finding exercise for hikers, it is not described as a through trail in this guide.

❈ Trail in winter: This is a super ski trip over a good trail with gentle ups and downs, and enough variety in scenery and terrain to make the trip interesting for everyone. Although shared with snowmobiles, for the most part the trail is wide enough to accommodate all. The average backcountry ski group should not attempt through trips to Willis Lake or NY 8 on the snowmobile trails. The distances and the rugged trail conditions make through trips foolhardy. Find a friend with a snowmobile.

🐾 Distances: To snowmobile bridge, 0.8 mi; to Pine Orchard, approximately 1.6 mi; to ridge and suggested turnaround, 3 mi (4.8 km).

134 Pine Orchard from Pumpkin Hollow Rd.
Trails Illustrated Map 743: H19

This is a long walk through seldom-visited wild forests. Though it follows a snowmobile trail, it is an adventure to be undertaken only by those who want practice in trail following and map and compass reading, for the trail fades in several areas.

▶Trailhead: To reach the trailhead from the S, take NY 30 and turn R (N) on Pumpkin Hollow Rd. (S of Wells) at 0.1 mi. Continue 1.6 mi up Pumpkin Hollow Rd. to the trailhead, which begins on the L (N) where large guideboards point the way. There is parking on the L and R shoulders of the road. This is also the beginning of the trail to Murphy, Middle, and Bennett lakes to the R (S) (trails 135 and 136).◀

The DEC sign obviously has been corrected to read 5 mi to Pine Orchard. However, it is 5 mi to the junction of an old tote road that leads another 1.6 mi into the Pine Orchard; a total of 6.6 mi (see trail 133).

The trail begins on a well-defined path from the Willis Lake/Pumpkin Hollow trailhead and proceeds through a young pine forest. The original trail was rerouted to avoid private property around Willis Lake; thus for the first 0.5 mi it leads NE, passing a small pond on the R, then crosses a footbridge and passes below two privately owned camps on the hill to the R. At 0.5 mi an intersection is well marked by a trail sign on the R and a big white pine on the L. The trail now joins the original old farm road and proceeds L (N) toward Coulombe Creek.

The trail provides easy walking through a mature forest of mixed pines. It is covered with pine needles, and the grades are gentle. A bend R (E) at 1.2 mi takes the hiker along the side of an openly wooded ridge, then down and across a small creek. A series of small grades is encountered and the old road becomes rocky and eroded in many places. Several fallen trees lie across the trail at 1.6 mi, after which it becomes more level and then makes a gradual turn N.

The impressive foundations of the barn of an old farmstead lie L and R of the trail at 1.9 mi. Descend through a wet area and up a small rise, and look to the R at 2 mi to observe the square foundation of the tiny farm house. Continue along this old road for another 0.4 mi until it crosses Coulombe Creek.

The old road the trail has been following apparently ended at the creek. From here to the junction of the trail into Pine Orchard the hiker should carry a compass and know how to read it. After crossing the creek this trail becomes a mere overgrown path, rough and very poorly defined and marked, although on occasion sections will be cleared by snowmobile enthusiasts—but don't count on this.

The trail now enters and crosses an overgrown clearing, and for the next 2 mi it climbs and descends numerous ridges, often becoming rock-strewn and difficult to walk and to find. Snowmobile signs are infrequent.

At 3.8 mi a turn R (E) and up a knoll is indicated by bright orange snowmobile disks. Although the trail is somewhat obscure, at the top of the knoll watch for a long, flat rocky ridge on the L that rises above this small valley. This is a picturesque section.

A flat rock clearing at 4.1 mi is shaded by trees and is high enough to catch a breeze in the heat of summer—a good spot to take a break. Leaving the clearing the path continues E through mixed hardwoods, then descends over more rocks, travels through an evergreen thicket, and finally, at 5 mi, intersects the old tote road leading to Pine Orchard. Turn R and follow this easy section mostly downhill for another 1.6 mi into the heart of Pine Orchard. (See trail 133.)

This is a long walk (12 to 14 mi round-trip) for the hiking group that does not leave a car at the trailhead near the Flater's off Windfall Road. (See trail 133.) Due to the poor condition of the trail and non-use by hikers of the section between the old farm ruins on Coulombe Creek and the old road through Pine Orchard, it is not recommended that anyone hike this section without a group of at least three persons and prior knowledge of, and experience in, the use of map and compass.

❋ Trail in winter: It is suggested that backcountry skiers go only to the farm ruins and return by the same route—unless they are very experienced, and prepared to traverse very difficult terrain—and to winter camp, if necessary. The trail may be shared by snowmobiles.

𝕸 Distances: To ruins of old farmstead, 1.9 mi; to Coulombe Creek crossing, 2.4 mi; to old road, 5 mi; to Pine Orchard, 6.6 mi (10.6 km).

135 Murphy Lake from Pumpkin Hollow Rd.
Trails Illustrated Map 743: G-H19

Murphy Lake is charming, surrounded by small foothills, with rocky cliffs to the N and W lending an air of unlimited adventures to the day's outing. A bushwhack up the ridge to either cliff top is feasible, with care. For most hikers, though, the moderate trail walk through attractive stretches of hardwoods and evergreens, along creeks and past beaver meadows and ponds, will more than satisfy. A through trip of 7.6 mi can be made around Murphy, then past Middle and Bennett lakes—making this one of the nicest day hikes in the southern Adirondacks. (See trail 136, Murphy Lake from Creek Road, for driving directions to the other end of the trail.)

State of New York, Forest, Fish & Game Commission, 1901

The trail, for the most part, follows an ancient road used by the early settlers of the region as a main N-S route. Farms once occupied the valleys and one can still find stone foundations, as well as old apple trees, on occasion.

▶Trailhead: To reach the trailhead, drive N on NY 30 along the Sacandaga River and turn R onto Pumpkin Hollow Rd., which is 0.3 mi after a sign that says "Town of Wells" near a large building. Continue driving mostly uphill on Pumpkin Hollow Rd. for 1.6 mi until the DEC trail markers are seen on the L. Parking is available for several vehicles on both sides of the road, although in the spring the shoulders are extremely soft.◀

The yellow-marked trail for Murphy Lake begins on the R through a pine plantation consisting of mature white pines and hemlocks. The trail register is encountered immediately as the hiker enters the forest. Heading S, the trail turns L at 0.1 mi. Now heading E, the trail begins to descend a short but steep ridge. At 0.2 mi a bend L occurs and the trail passes through a wet area at the bottom of the hill. This trail is well marked with snowmobile signs as well as yellow DEC hiking trail signs.

The trail continues through a thicket of hemlocks, scattered white pines, and spruce until at 0.3 mi it reaches a corduroy boardwalk of rounded logs spanning a swampy area for approximately 50 yd. At 0.5 mi the trail leaves the swamp and goes through an avenue lined with green pines, their needles making the trail surface soft and pleasant. This is a beautiful area, flat and easy walking. Note the yellow state-land boundary marks on the trees to the R.

The trail begins a descent at 0.65 mi and then passes through a rocky, wet area at 0.7 mi. At the bottom of this small ridge a little wooden bridge spans a marshy area. That is shortly followed by a section of densely laid rocks over more small wet sections.

A curve R leads shortly to a trail junction. Bear L. To the R is private land, the continuation of the original road back to Pumpkin Hollow.

At 0.9 mi the trail bends sharply L. The trail is now part of the remains of the historic old road that served the farms along the way. A barrier restricting access to motorized vehicles appears after the trail crosses another swampy area on a series of dual split-log bridges.

Now the trail is flat as the evergreens begin to give way to deciduous trees. A fairly steep descent begins, traversing a rocky, washed-out gully that once was the road. At the bottom at 1.3 mi, a wood-plank snowmobile bridge crosses a medium-sized stream.

Soon the trees change to a more open woods of ash, birch, and maple. Wildflowers are abundant here, especially in spring. At 1.4 mi another wet area is spanned by planks. A major wood bridge crosses over large Doig Creek at 1.5

mi. On the other side of the bridge the trail is usually wet and muddy, thanks to flooding by beaver upstream, which has changed part of the flow.

After the wet area, the trail climbs a ridge. It now passes through a very washed-out area. A check to the L in this vicinity will reveal the stone foundation ruins of an old building as well as an apple tree here and there, which are the remains of an old farm orchard.

At 1.9 mi another moderate uphill begins as the forest changes to more open hardwoods. Top a small rise at 2 mi and note to the L an old beaver meadow, which may be flooded anew by beaver from one year to the next. Another sturdy bridge at 2.1 mi has recently been flooded by beaver who built a dam against the bridge. Note that there are two dams, one abutting the bridge on the L and another about 50 yd into the pond.

The trail now begins to follow the creek upstream toward the outlet of Murphy Lake. Note the enormous pine at 2.2 mi. It is obviously a survivor of the original logging days, due, perhaps, to its position on the stream bank at the side of the road.

The trail continues up a small ridge. At 2.8 mi the outlet creek must be crossed. The bridge that spanned this shallow but swift-flowing section of creek has been washed out, and during spring and other high-water times the hiker may have to go upstream, or down, to find a suitable crossing spot.

After crossing the outlet stream, the trail goes through and up a small, very attractive ravine covered with moss and cascades of ferns. As the trail exits the ravine, notice the pink boulder on the R. The trail continues to follow the stream to the outlet of Murphy Lake at 3 mi.

The trail continues to circle Murphy Lake to the L (N) for another 0.8 mi. to the lean-to on its SE end. Just before the lean-to, however, it is necessary to turn L (E) again and circle around a wet section created by a beaver dam that has raised the lake level by at least a foot, backing up the water and flooding the original trail.

The lean-to is located on a knoll sheltered by large white pines and attractive boulders. This has been a favorite camping area for hunters, hikers, skiers, and snowmobilers for many years.

The trail continues from the lean-to E and up a ridge for another half-mile to Middle Lake. (See trail 136 for the continuing trail description.)

❊ Trail in winter: A wonderful ski trip, with only three or four steep ridges to negotiate. A through ski trip to Creek Rd. can be done on a typical winter day, after spotting a car there. It is recommended that skiers begin at the Pumpkin Hollow end, since the terrain is mostly downhill from Middle Lake to Creek Rd. The only problem area might be the outlet stream, but there is generally enough ice to cross in safety. Beware of the waters during spring runoff.

❊ Distances: To junction of old road and barrier, 0.9 mi; to Doig Creek bridge, 1.5 mi; to beaver dam and bridge, 2.1 mi; to Murphy Lake outlet, 3 mi; to lean-to on Murphy Lake, 3.8 mi (6.1 km).

136 Murphy, Bennett, and Middle Lakes from Creek Rd.
Trails Illustrated Map 743: F-G19

Murphy, Middle, and Bennett lakes lie along an ancient road that has been in use for well over 100 years. Perhaps it was even used by the Indians prior to the early farmers who attempted to till the area. Along sections of the trail you can still identify ancient apple trees and the stone foundations and cellar holes of homes and barns.

▶Trailhead: To reach the trailhead, take NY 30 N from Mayfield. After crossing the bridge over the Sacandaga River at Benson, drive another 4.1 mi and turn R onto Creek Rd. Proceed up Creek Rd. for 2.3 mi to the trailhead on the L (N), marked with DEC brown and yellow guideboards. Park on either side of the road; the shoulders are very wide.◀

The trail begins on the N side of the road, through a thick forest of mixed evergreens and hardwoods. A wood plank bridge spans a small stream and wet area at 0.1 mi and then the trail begins to climb a ridge—moderately, for the most part, with a few steeper sections, using the old washed-out roadbed. In places it is very rocky and rough underfoot.

At 0.6 mi, after passing through a lovely avenue of white pines, look to the L to see an ancient stone wall. There is a substantial iron barrier to discourage motorized traffic (except snowmobiles in winter) at the top of the ridge at 0.8 mi. The trail descends for about 75 yd, then jogs sharply R, although it appears at first glance to continue straight ahead.

At the top of the small rise at 1 mi the trail passes over an area of dark red soil. There is also a depression on the L. This is all that remains of a settlement and ferric oxide mine, which produced pigments used to make paint at the turn of the century. No readily visible evidence remains, although exploration will uncover cellar holes and occasional iron scraps of machinery and stoves—the forest has reclaimed the land.

The trail climbs moderately in a NNW direction through lovely open hardwoods and mixed evergreens. The old road is sometimes illegally used by ATVs and is wet and mucky in some sections as it continues a moderate uphill until, at 1.3 mi, a fork, marked by a large stone cairn, goes R. This unmarked path leads 0.4 mi down the ridge to the shore of Bennett Lake, which in fall and winter can be glimpsed through the trees. There are two or

Middle Lake. Linda Laing

three open camping areas, well-used, but attractive. The main trail, however, continues to follow the contours of the ridge, about a quarter-mile above the lakeshore.

At 1.6 mi a steeper and rocky section is reached. A faint cutoff to the R has been created by motorized vehicles to avoid the rocky ravine, but it is hardly necessary for the hiker.

At 1.7 mi the main trail reaches a stream with a sturdy plank, but somewhat twisted, snowmobile bridge across it. After crossing the bridge, the trail bends R and up, making a few snake-like turns. At 2.2 mi the trail passes through a picturesque ravine and at 2.3 mi reaches a small stream that does not have a bridge. It can, however, be crossed on rocks or a convenient log.

At 2.4 mi the trail traverses a level section, and then bends R. It is very smooth and easy to walk, and very attractive. A cutoff R at 2.6 mi goes to a camping area on the shore of Middle Lake and the lake itself comes into view shortly thereafter. The trail continues along the ridge approximately 200 ft from the lakeshore, until at 3 mi a path to the R leads to the water. From here, Middle Lake's island can be seen, as can the attractive rocks on the E shore.

Middle Lake, although shallow, is charming. If time permits, a bushwhack to the E shore will provide many attractive scenes and picnic spots.

At the N end of Middle Lake, the trail comes very close to the water, then leaves its shores to continue in a general NW direction toward Murphy Lake. A short but steep climb up a small hill occurs, and then the trail begins a moderate descent at 3.5 mi through a quiet, densely overgrown section of the forest. The trail itself, however, is grass-covered and smooth underfoot.

At 3.6 mi a large mucky area must be negotiated, and at 3.7 mi the shores of Murphy Lake come into view. The lean-to on its shore is reached at 3.8 mi.

Murphy Lake is situated in a bowl among three small mountains, with dramatic bare cliffs lending an air of ruggedness to the scene. Large boulders decorate its shoreline, and the knoll upon which the new lean-to sits is shaded by huge white pines.

The trail continues to circle the lake along its N shore, then turns NW for a loop return to civilization and the Pumpkin Rd. trailhead (trail 135).

❄ Trail in winter: This is a favorite ski trip, with skiers often spotting a car at either end. The suggested direction of travel is to ski in from the NW (see trail 135) as the group will gain a nice gradual downhill for most of the trip out to Creek Rd. This trail is open to snowmobiles, but it is not very long for them, so the traffic here is usually minimal. There are some steep sections, and as with all backcountry ski trips, recommended for experienced skiers only.

🐾 Distances: To iron barrier, 0.8 mi; to path to Bennett Lake shore, 1.3 mi; to Middle Lake, 2.6 mi; to Murphy Lake and lean-to, 3.8 mi (6.2 km).

Glossary of Terms

bushwhack: To make one's way through natural terrain without the aid of a formal trail.

cairn: A pile of stones to mark a summit or route.

chimney: A steep, narrow cleft or gully in the face of a mountain--usually by which the mountain may be ascended.

cobble: A small stony peak on the side of a mountain.

col: A pass between two adjacent peaks or between high points of a ridgeline.

corduroy: A road, trail, or bridge formed by logs laid side by side transversely to facilitate crossing swampy areas.

duff: Partly decayed plant matter on the forest floor. Duff's ability to burn easily has started many forest fires.

lean-to: A three-sided shelter with an overhanging roof on the open side.

logging or lumber road: A crude road used to haul logs after lumbering.

tote road: A road constructed in connection with logging operations and used for hauling supplies. Often built with corduroy, many of these roads are still evident after 100 years and are often used as the routes for present-day trails.

vernal (pool): Occurring in the spring, when snowmelt and rain create pools that disappear with drier weather.

Acknowledgments

In revising this book, I have used a number of Betsy Tisdale's and Carl Heilman's trail descriptions from the first and second editions, respectively, and want to thank them for all they did in putting together those editions. Carl, in particular, got me on my feet as I set about this project, which has wonderfully introduced me to new places and people. My huge thanks to those who have assisted with helpful information along the way—these include Elizabethtown and North Hudson Town Supervisors Maggie Bartley and Ron Moore; Mike Carr, Bill Brown, Sarah Hoffman, Chris Krahling, Lynn LaMontagne Schumann, of the Adirondack and Lake George Basin Conservancies; Chris Maron of the Champlain Valley Conservation Partnership; Paul Clickner, Will Geraud, Jaime Laczko, Dan Levy, Tom Martin, Tad Norton, Jim Papero, Charlie Platt, Ben Thomas, Ed Russell, and Werner Schwab of the New York State Department of Environmental Conservation (DEC); Dr. Bill Brown, Steven Engelhart, Roger Harwood, Elizabeth Lee, and Gary Randorf of their own accords; Ann Bailey of ADK's Algonquin Chapter; and of course, ADK staff and mentors in this process: Neal Burdick, Jack Freeman, Tony Goodwin, Bonnie Langdon, John Kettlewell, Andrea Masters, and John Million. David Lambert of National Geographic has been a great cohort on the mapping work.

—David Thomas-Train

About the Editor

David Thomas-Train, born in Washington, D.C., has lived in Keene Valley, New York, since 1981. He has a B.A. in English Literature from Kenyon College and an M.S. in Early Childhood Education from Wheelock College. He has been an educator for over thirty-five years, now tutoring students of all ages. He leads canoeing, hiking, and ski trips in the Adirondacks, incorporating environmental education into these activities for various organizations, including the Adirondack Nature Conservancy, Adirondack Mountain Club, Adirondack Ski Touring Council, Adirondack Trail Improvement Society, Champlain Area Trails, and Natural History Museum of the  Adirondacks. He is the Coordinator of The Friends of Poke-O-Moonshine, a grassroots organization dedicated to the restoration of the fire tower and trail on that mountain, and to its use as an environmental education site. He also directs the Adirondack Fire Tower Association, a Park-wide entity dedicated to strengthening private and public initiatives for state-owned fire towers. He has been chair and/or Conservation Coordinator of the Keene Valley Chapter of the Adirondack Mountain Club for over twenty years, and a mapping consultant for the Adirondack Mountain Club and National Geographic Society map series on the Adirondacks. A volunteer for numerous Adirondack scientific and advocacy groups, he contributes his time to fund-raising, invasive species, loon surveys, and mammal tracking.

Join us!

30,000 members count on us, and so can you:
- We produce the most-trusted, comprehensive trail maps and books
- Our outdoor activities take you all around the world
- Our advocacy team concentrates on issues that affect the wild lands and waters important to our members and chapters throughout the state
- Our professional and volunteer crews construct and maintain trails
- Our wilderness lodges and information centers give you shelter and direction

Benefits of Membership include:
- Fun outdoor recreation opportunities for all levels
- Adirondac magazine (bimonthly)
- Special rates for ADK education and skill-building programs, lodging, parking, publications, and logo merchandise
- Rewarding volunteer opportunities
- Supporting ADK's mission and thereby ensuring protection of the wild lands and waters of New York State

Lodges and campground
- **Adirondak Loj**, on the shores of Heart Lake, near Lake Placid, offers year-round accommodations in private and family rooms, a coed loft, and cabins. It is accessible by car, and parking is available.

- **The Adirondak Loj Wilderness Campground**, located on ADK's Heart Lake property, offers thirty-two campsites and sixteen Adirondack lean-tos.

- **Johns Brook Lodge (JBL)**, located near Keene Valley, is a backcountry facility accessible only on foot and open on a seasonal basis. Facilities include coed bunkrooms or small family rooms. Cabins near JBL are available year-round.

Both lodges offer home-cooked meals and trail lunches. Member discounts are available at all lodges and the campground.

Visit us!
ADK centers in Lake George and on our Heart Lake property near Lake Placid offer ADK publications and other merchandise for sale, as well as backcountry and general Adirondack information, educational displays, outdoor equipment, and snacks.

ADK Publications

FOREST PRESERVE SERIES
1 Adirondack Mountain Club High Peaks Trails
2 Adirondack Mountain Club Eastern Trails
3 Adirondack Mountain Club Central Trails
4 Adirondack Mountain Club Western Trails
5 Adirondack Mountain Club Northville–Placid Trail
6 Adirondack Mountain Club Catskill Trails

OTHER BOOKS
Adirondack Alpine Summits: An Ecological Field Guide
Adirondack Birding: 60 Great Places to Find Birds
Adirondack Canoe Waters: North Flow
Adirondack Mountain Club Canoe and Kayak Guide: East-Central New York State
Adirondack Mountain Club Canoe Guide to Western & Central New York State
Adirondack Paddling: 60 Great Flatwater Adventures
An Adirondack Sampler I: Day Hikes for All Seasons
Catskill Day Hikes for All Seasons
Forests and Trees of the Adirondack High Peaks Region
Kids on the Trail! Hiking with Children in the Adirondacks
No Place I'd Rather Be: Wit and Wisdom from Adirondack Lean-to Journals
Ski and Snowshoe Trails in the Adirondacks
The Adirondack Reader
The Catskill 67: A Hiker's Guide to the Catskill 100 Highest Peaks Under 3500'
Views from on High: Fire Tower Trails in the Adirondacks and Catskills
Winterwise: A Backpacker's Guide

MAPS
Trails of the Adirondack High Peaks Region
Northville-Placid Trail
Trails Illustrated Map 742: Lake Placid/High Peaks
Trails Illustrated Map 743: Lake George/Great Sacandaga
Trails Illustrated Map 744: Northville/Raquette Lake
Trails Illustrated Map 745: Old Forge/Oswegatchie
Trails Illustrated Map 746: Saranac/Paul Smiths
Trails Illustrated Map 755: Catskill Park

ADIRONDACK MOUNTAIN CLUB CALENDAR

Price list available upon request, or see www.adk.org.

Contact Us

ADK Member Services Center (Exit 21 off I-87, the Northway)
814 Goggins Road
Lake George, NY 12845-4117
Website: www.adk.org   Information: 518-668-4447
Membership, donations, publications, and merchandise: 800-395-8080

ADK Heart Lake Program Center (at Adirondak Loj on Heart Lake)
PO Box 867
1002 Adirondack Loj Road
Lake Placid, NY 12946-0867
Educational programs and facility reservations: 518-523-3441

ADK Public Affairs Office
301 Hamilton Street
Albany, NY 12210-1738
Public Affairs: 518-449-3870

The Adirondack Mountain Club (ADK) is dedicated to the protection and responsible recreational use of the New York State Forest Preserve, and other parks, wild lands, and waters vital to our members and chapters. The Club, founded in 1922, is a member-directed organization committed to public service and stewardship. ADK employs a balanced approach to outdoor recreation, advocacy, environmental education, and natural resource conservation.

ADK encourages the involvement of all people in its mission and activities; its goal is to be a community that is comfortable, inviting, and accessible.

The Adirondack Mountain Club is a charitable organization, 501(c)(3). Contributions are tax deductible to the extent the law allows.

Adirondack
ADK
Mountain Club

Index

Locations are indexed by proper name with Lake or Mt. following.

A

abbreviation keys, for guidebook and maps, 12–13
Adirondack Forest Preserve, 9, 10–11
Adirondack Mountain Club, 9, 189
Adirondack region, 9–11
Adirondack State Park, 11
  map, 6
Arnold Pond, 37
Arrow Trail, Baldwin Springs from Harrisburg Lake and, 156–158

B

Bailey Pond Trail, 138
Baldhead and Moose Mts., 150–152
Baldwin Springs
  from Harrisburg Lake on Arrow Trail, 156–158
  Lizard Pond Canoe/Hike
    from Garnet Lake and, 160–162
    via Fish Ponds on Bartman Trail, 158–160
  and West Stony Creek Road, 155–156
Bartman Trail, Baldwin Springs via Fish Ponds on, 158–160
Bass Lake Trail, 26–27
Bear Pond Trail, 48–49
bears, safety and, 21–22
"beaver fever," 20
Bennett Lake, from Creek Rd., 184–185
Berrymill Flow
  and Moose Mt. Pond, 27, 28–29
  from North and South, 53
Berry Pond Preserve, 89
  Loop Trail, 89–92
  Overlook Trail, 89–91
Big Bridges Trail, 113–114
Big Pond Trail, 137–138

Black Mt.
  Black Mt. Point to, 122, 124
  from East, 124–125
  Ponds Trail, 127–128
Black Mt. Point
  to Black Mt., 122, 124
  Lakeside Trail to, 118–120
Bloody and Hammond Ponds, 29–30
Blue Mt. bushwhack, 170, 172
"blue line," 11
boating access sites
  Black Mt. Point to Black Mt., 122
  Blue Mt. bushwhack canoe access, 170, 172
  Eagle Lake, 46
  Jape Pond, 72
  Lakeside Trail to Black Mt. Point, 118
  Peaked Hill and Peeked Hill Pond, 32
  Putnam Pond State Campground, 47, 50
  Rogers Rock, 62
  Round Pond from Garnet Lake, 153
  Tongue Mt. Range Trail, 76
Buck Mt.
  Connector Trail, 98–99
  from Hogtown to, 97–98
  from Pilot Knob to, 96–97
Bumps Pond
  Hogtown Trailhead to Fishbrook Pond via, 103–104
  Spur, 111
Buttermilk Pond
  Duck, Round Ponds and, 68–69
  Loop Trail to, 70
Butternut Brook Trail, 94–95

192 *Eastern Trails*

C

camping. *See also* lean-tos
  ADK facilities, 189
  Baldwin Springs and West Stony Creek Road, 155
  Bass Lake Trail, 27
  Berrymill Flow, 28
  Challis Pond, 28
  Crane Mt. Pond, 147
  Greenland Pond, 128
  group camping permit requirements, 16, 18
  Hogtown Trailhead to Fishbrook Pond, 104
  Lakeside Trail to Black Mt. Point, 118–119
  Lily Pond from Grassville Rd. to NY 8, 67
  Little Rock Pond, 49
  Lost Pond, 54
  Middle Lakes, 185
  Moreau Lake State Park, 142
  Pharaoh Lake via Mill Brook, 55
  Putnam Pond State Campground, 47, 50
  regulations, 15–17
  Rock Pond to Lilypad Pond, 50
  Thomas Mt. Trail, 80, 82
Cartier, Jacques, 10
Cat and Thomas Mountains Preserve, 80
Cat Mt. Trail, 81–82
  Thomas Mt. Blue Trail, 81
  Thomas Mt. Trail, 80–81
Cat Mt. Trail, 81–82
cell phones, 15, 17
Challis Pond, 27–28
Champlain, Samuel de, 10
Charles Lathrop Pack Demonstration Forest Nature Trail, 139–140
Clear Pond Trail, 47
Cod Pond, 173–174
Cook Mt., 61–62
Crab Pond, spur to Glidden Marsh Trail, 43–44
Crane Mt., 146–147
  Cut-off Trail, 147–148
Crane Mt. Pond and NW Ridge, 148, 150
Crane Pond
  Long Swing Trail to, 42
  to Pharaoh Lake, 44–45
Crane Pond Rd., 41
Creek Rd., Murphy, Bennett, and Middle Lakes from, 184–185
Crown Point section. *See* Hammond Pond Wild Forest/Crown Point/Moriah Section
Crown Point State Historic Site, 33–35

D

Dacy Clearing, Hogtown Trailhead to Fishbrook Pond via, 103–104
Deer Leap, 76–77
deer ticks, Lyme disease and, 22–23
DEET, 23
Department of Environmental Conservation (DEC), of New York State
  emergency contact information, 4, 23
  regulations, 15–17
  website, 15
Desolate Brook Trail, to Pharaoh Lake, 59–60
Dome Island bird sanctuary, 78
drinking water safety, 20
Duck, Round, and Buttermilk Ponds, 68–69

E

emergency procedures and contact information, 4, 23
Erebus Mt. Trail, 111–113
  Ridge Spurs, 113

F

fire regulations and restrictions, 16, 17
fire towers
  abandoned, at Spruce Mt., 143–144
  at Hadley Mt., 144, 145
  remains, at Prospect Mt., 89
Fishbrook Pond
  Hogtown Trailhead to, 103–104
  from Lake George, 121–122
  West Trail, 104–105
Fish Dam Trail, 31–32
fishing. *See also* boating access sites
  Crane Mt. Pond, 147
  Fish Dam Trail, 32
  Greenland Pond, 128
  Kibby Pond, 172–173
  Long and Island Ponds, 70
  Pharaoh Lake Wilderness, 39
  Round, Duck, and Buttermilk Ponds, 68
Fish Ponds, Baldwin Springs from, on Bartman Trail, 158–160
Five Mile Point, 78–79
Flater family land, 178–180
food storage and safety, animals and, 17, 21–22
From Then 'Til Now (Stiles), 85

G

Garnet Lake
  Lizard Pond and Baldwin Springs from, 160–162
  Mt. Blue bushwhack canoe access, 170, 172
  Round Pond from, 153–155
George, Lake. *See* Northwestern Lake George Wild Forest Section; Southeastern Lake George Wild Forest Section
Giardia lamblia, 20
Gill Pond, 61
Girard, Henry, 176

Girard "Sugarbush" Maple Plantation, 176–178
Glidden Marsh
  Crab Pond Spur to, 43–44
  to Pharaoh Lake, 46–47
Goose Pond, 41–42
GPS navigation system cautions, 17
Grandmother's Tree, 139–140
Greenland Pond, 128
Green Mountain and Ticonderoga Overlook Trail, 131
Grizzle Ocean Trail/Grizzle Ocean Circuit Trail, 51–52
group camping, permit requirements, 16, 18
Gull Bay Preserve, 129–130
  Blue, Orange, and Yellow Trails, 129–130

H

Hadley Mt., 144–146
Hammond Pond Wild Forest/Crown Point/Moriah Section, 25–26
  Arnold Pond, 37
  Bass Lake Trail, 26–27
  Berrymill Flow and Moose Mt. Pond, 27, 28–29
  Challis Pond, 27–28
  Crown Point State Historic Site, 33–35
  Fish Dam Trail, 31–32
  Hammond and Bloody Ponds, 29–30
  North Hudson Trail System, 30–31
  Old Ironville Rd., 36–37
  Peaked Hill and Peeked Hill Pond, 32–33
  Putts Creek Wildlife Management Area, 35–36
  Walker Brook Access, 26
handicapped-accessible nature trail, 139–140
Harrisburg Lake, Baldwin Springs from, on Arrow Trail, 156–158

heron rookery, 129–130
Hoffman Notch Wilderness, Wilcox Lake Wild Forest, 133–135
  Bailey Pond Trail, 138
  Baldhead and Moose Mts., 150–152
  Baldwin Springs and West Stony Creek Road, 155–156
  Baldwin Springs from Harrisburg Lake on Arrow Trail, 156–158
  Baldwin Springs via Fish Ponds on Bartman Trail, 158–160
  Big Pond Trail, 137–138
  Blue Mt. bushwhack, 170, 172
  Charles Lathrop Pack Demonstration Forest Nature Trail, 139–140
  Cod Pond, 173–174
  Crane Mt., 146–150
  Girard "Sugarbush" Maple Plantation, 176–178
  Hadley Mt., 144–146
  Hoffman Notch Trail, 136–137
  Indian Pond, 163–164
  Kibby Pond, 172–173
  Lizard Pond and Baldwin Springs Canoe/Hike from Garnet Lake, 160–162
  Moreau Lake State Park, 142
  Murphy, Bennett, and Middle Lakes from Creek Rd., 184–185
  Murphy Lake from Pumpkin Hollow Road, 181–183
  Palmer Pond, 141
  Pine Orchard from Flater's, 178–180
  Pine Orchard from Pumpkin Hollow Rd., 180–181
  Round and Mud Ponds, 152–153
  Round Pond from Garnet Lake, 153–155
  Severance Mt., 139
  Spruce Mt., 143–144
  Stewart Creek Flow and North Bend via Oregon Trail, 174–176
  Tenant Creek Falls, 164–165
  Warren County Parks and Recreation Nature Trail, 140–141
  Wilcox Lake from Willis Lake, 168–170
  Wilcox Lake via East Stony Creek Trail, 165–168
Hogtown
  Buck Mt. Trail from, 97–98
  to Fishbrook Pond via Dacy Clearing and Bumps Pond from, 103–104
Honey Pond, 43
horse trails
  Big Bridges Trail, 114
  Butternut Brook Trail, 95
  Erebus Mt. Trail, 111–113
  Inman Pond, 96
  Longway Trail, 109–110
  Ridge Trail, 116–117
hostel, at Prospect Mt., 88
Hudson, Henry, 10
Hudson River Ice Meadows, 140
human waste, disposing of, 16
hunting
  hunting season safety, 21
  Putts Creek Wildlife Management Area, 35–36

I
Indian Pond, 163–164
Inman Pond, 95–96
insect-borne diseases, 22–23
Island and Long Ponds, 70–71

J
Jabe Pond, 73

K
Kibby Pond, 172–173
Knapp Estate, 85

L

Lake George Land Conservancy, 60, 80, 88, 90, 92, 128, 130
Lapland Pond Trail, 125–127
Last Great Shoreline Preserve, 130–131
lean-tos, 15, 16, 17. *See also camping*
  Berrymill Flow, 53
  Black Mt. Ponds Trail, 127, 128
  Clear Pond Trail, 48
  Fishbrook Pond, 104, 115, 125
  Greenland Pond, 128
  Grizzle Ocean Trail, 52
  Lapland Pond Trail, 125, 126
  Lilypad Pond, 43, 49
  Lizard Pond, 161
  Millman Pond, 125
  Murphy Lake, 183, 185
  Northwest Bay Trail from Clay Meadow, 78
  Oxshoe Pond, 44
  Pharaoh Lake, 55, 56
  Pharaoh Mt. Trail, 45
  Rock Pond, 47
  Split Rick Bay, 52
  Tongue Mt. Range Trail, 74, 75
  Tubmill Marsh Trail, 43
  Wilcox Lake from Willis Lake, 170
  Wilcox Lake via East Stony Creek Trail, 168
Leave No Trace program, 16, 19
Lichen Ledge Preserve, 92
Lilypad Pond, Rock Pond to, 49–50
Lily Pond from Grassville Rd. to NY 8, 66–68
Lizard Pond and Baldwin Springs Canoe/Hike from Garnet Lake, 160–162
Long and Island Ponds, 70–71
Longway Trail, Shelving Rock area, 109–110
  Spur, 110–111
Lost Pond, 54
Lyme disease, 22–23

Lynn LaMontagne Schumann Preserve at Pilot Knob, 93–94

M

maple plantation, 176–178
maps
  abbreviation key for, 12
  of Adirondack Park, 6
  available from Adirondack Mountain Club, 12
  available for North Hudson Trail System, 30
markers and signs, on trails, 13–14
Mill Brook, Pharaoh Lake via, 54–55
mobile phones, 15, 17
Moose and Baldhead Mts., 150–152
Moose Mt. Pond and Berrymill Flow, 27, 28–29
Moreau Lake State Park, 142
Moriah section.
  See Hammond Pond Wild Forest/Crown Point/Moriah Section
mosquitoes, West Nile virus and, 22–23
mountain biking, 10
  Baldwin Springs and West Stony Creek Road, 154
  Baldwin Springs from Harrisburg Lake on Arrow Trail, 156
  Lily Pond from Grassville Rd. to NY 8, 67
  North Hudson Trail System, 30
  Northwestern Lake George Section, 64
  Southeastern Lake George Section, 84, 85
Mud and Round Ponds, 152–153
Murphy Lake
  from Creek Rd., 184–185
  from Pumpkin Hollow Road, 181–183
museums
  Crown Point State Historic Site, 34
  Penfield Museum, 36

Up Yonda Farm Environmental Education Center, 80

N
National Geographic Trails Illustrated maps, 12
Native American artifacts, 101
North Bend, and Stewart Creek Flow via Oregon Trail, 174–176
North Hudson Trail System, 30–31
Northwest Bay Brook, 79
Northwest Bay Trail from Clay Meadow, 77–78
Northwestern Lake George Wild Forest Section, 65–66
  Buttermilk Loop Trail, 70
  Cat and Thomas Mountains Preserve, 80
  Cat Mt. Trail, 81–82
  Deer Leap, 76–77
  Five Mile Point, 78–79
  Jabe Pond, 73
  Lily Pond from Grassville Rd. to NY 8, 66–68
  Long and Island Ponds, 70–71
  Northwest Bay Brook, 79
  Northwest Bay Trail from Clay Meadow, 77–78
  Richard Hayes Phillips Trail, 82
  Round, Duck, and Buttermilk Ponds, 68–69
  Thomas Mountain Blue Trail, 81
  Thomas Mt. Trail, 80–81
  Tongue Mt. Range Trail, 73–76
  Up Yonda Farm Environmental Education Center, 80
  Wardsboro Rd. from N to S/Wardsboro Side Trail, 71–73

O
Old Farm Rd., 106–107
  East and West legs, 107
Old Ironville Rd., 36–37
Oregon Trail, North Bend and Stewart Creek via, 174–176
Otter Pond, 46–47

P
Palmer Pond, 141
Paradox Lake State Campground, 32
Peaked Hill and Peeked Hill Pond, 32–33
Penfield Museum, 36
pets, on trails, 16
Pharaoh Lake Wilderness/SchroonLake/ Ticonderoga Section, 7–8, 39–41
  Bear Pond Trail, 48–49
  Berrymill Flow from North and South, 53
  Clear Pond Trail, 47
  Cook Mt., 61–62
  Crab Pond, spur to Glidden Marsh Trail, 43–44
  Crane Pond Rd., 41
  Gill Pond, 61
  Glidden Marsh to Pharaoh Lake, 46–47
  Goose Pond, 41–42
  Grizzle Ocean Trail, 51–52
  Long Swing Trail to Crane Pond Rd., 42
  Lost Pond, 54
  Otter Pond, 46–47
  Pharaoh Lake, East Shore, 55–56
  Pharaoh Lake via Mill Brook, 54–55
  Pharaoh Mt. Trail (Crane Pond to Pharaoh Lake), 44–45
  Putnam Pond to Clear Pond Trail, 48
  Rock Pond Spur, 47–48
  Rock Pond to Lilypad Pond, 48–50
  Rogers Rock, 62–63
  Spectacle Pond, 60–61
  Springhill Ponds, 56–58
  Sucker Brook and Desolate Brook Trail to Pharaoh Lake, 59–60
  Treadway Mt. Trail, 50–51

Index **197**

Tubmill Marsh Trail, 43
West Clear Pond Trail, 48
Whortleberry Pond, 58–59
picnic areas
   Baldwin Springs and West Stony Creek Road, 155
   Baldwin Springs from Harrisburg Lake on Arrow Trail, 157
   Cod Pond, 174
   Crown Point State Historic Site, 34
   Duck Pond, 69
   Grizzle Ocean Trail, 52
   Indian Pond, 163
   Lakeside Trail to Black Mt. Point, 118–119
   Lizard Pond, 161
   Longway Trail, 110
   Lost Pond, 54
   Middle Lake, 184
   Moreau Lake State Park, 142
   Northwest Bay Trail from Clay Meadow, 78
   Prospect Mt., 89
   Shortway Trail, 108
   Stewart Creek Flow and North Bend via Oregon Trail, 175
   Warren County Parks and Recreation Nature Trail, 140
   Wilcox Lake, 170
Pilot Knob
   Buck Mt. Trail from, 96–97
   Lynn LaMontagne Schumann Preserve at, 93
   Old Road on Shoulder of, 92–93
   Orange and Blue Trails, 94
Pine Orchard
   from Flater's, 178–180
   from Pumpkin Hollow Rd., 180–181
"posted" signs, 14
Primitive area, defined, 11
Prospect Mt., 88–89
Pumpkin Hollow Rd.
   Murphy Lake from, 181–183
   Pine Orchard from, 180–181

Putnam Pond State Campground, 47, 50
Putnam Pond to Clear Pond Trail, 48
Putts Creek Wildlife Management Area, 35–36

R
rabies, 22
rattlesnakes
   Deer Leap, 76
   Five Mile Point, 78
   Northwest Bay Trail from Clay Meadow, 77
   Tongue Mt. area, 65, 73, 75
Red Rock Bay Trail, 120–121
Richard Hayes Phillips Trail, 83
Ridge Trail, 116–118
Rock Pond
   to Lilypad Pond, 48–50
   Spur, 47–48
Rogers, Robert, 63
Rogers Rock, 62–63
Round Pond
   Duck and Buttermilk Ponds and, 68–69
   from Garnet Lake, 153–155
   and Mud Pond, 152–153

S
safety issues
   bears, 21–22
   compass use, 18
   drinking water, 20
   emergency telephone numbers, 4, 23
   food storage, 17, 21–22
   GPS use, 17
   hunting season, 21
   insect-borne diseases, 22–23
   rabies, 22
   weather, 18, 20
Sagamore Hotel, 78
Saratoga PLAN, 143–144
Schroon Lake.
   See Pharaoh Lake Wilderness/Schroon Lake/Ticonderoga Section

Severance Mt., 139
Shelving Rock
  East and West Connector Trails, 102–103
  Ridge Trail from, 116–118
  Shelving Rock Falls Lakeshore Loop/Shelving Rock Falls Trail, 99–102
  Shelving Rock Mt. to Lakeside Trail, 115
  Shelving Rock Mt. Trail, 114–115
signs and markers, on trails, 13–14
Sleeping Beauty, 105–106
snakes. *See* rattlesnakes
Southeastern Lake George Wild Forest Section, 85–88
  Berry Pond Loop Trail, 89–92
  Big Bridges Trail, 113–114
  Black Mt. from East, 124–125
  Black Mt. Point to Black Mt., 122–124
  Black Mt. Ponds Trail, 127–128
  Buck Mt. Connector Trail, 98–99
  Buck Mt. Trail from Hogtown, 97–98
  Buck Mt. Trail from Pilot Knob, 96–97
  Bumps Pond Spur, 111
  Butternut Brook Trail, 94–95
  East Shelving Rock Falls Connector Trails, 102–103
  Erebus Mt. Trail, 111–113
  Fishbrook Pond from Lake George, 121–122
  Greenland Pond, 128
  Green Mountain and Ticonderoga Overlook Trail, 131
  Gull Bay Preserve, 129–130
  Hogtown Trailhead to Fishbrook Pond via Dacy Clearing and Bumps Pond, 103–104
  Inman Pond, 95–96
  Lake George Recreation Area, 89
  Lake George View Trail, 131
  Lakeside Trail to Black Mt. Point, 118–120
  Lapland Pond Trail, 125–127
  Last Great Shoreline Preserve, 130–131
  Lichen Ledge Preserve, 92
  Longway Spur, 110–111
  Longway Trail, 109–110
  Lynn LaMontagne Schumann Preserve at Pilot Knob, 93–94
  Old Farm Rd., 106–107
  Old Road on Shoulder of Pilot Knob, 92–93
  Overlook Trail, 89–91
  Prospect Mt., 88–89
  Red Rock Bay Trail, 120–121
  Ridge Trail, 116–118
  Shelving Rock Falls Lakeshore Loop/Shelving Rock Falls Trail, 99–102
  Shelving Rock Mt. to Lakeside Trail, 115
  Shelving Rock Mt. Trail, 114–115
  Shortway Trail, 108–109
  Sleeping Beauty, 105–106
  West Fishbrook Pond Trail, 104–105
  West Shelving Rock Falls Connector Trails, 102
Spectacle Pond, 60–61
Springhill Ponds, 56–58
Spruce Mt., 143–144
Steinbeck, Elsa, 85
Stewart Creek Flow and North Bend via Oregon Trail, 174–176
Stiles, Fred, 85
Stony Creek Road, Baldwin Springs and West, 155–156
Stony Creek Trail, Wilcox Lake via East, 165–168
Sucker Brook and Desolate Brook Trail to Pharaoh Lake, 59–60
Sweet Peas and a White Bridge (Steinbeck), 85

swimming
  discouraged at Long Pond, 70
  Fish Dam Trail, 32
  Five Mile Point, 78–79
  Moreau Lake State Park, 142
  Northwest Bay Trail from Clay
    Meadow, 77–78
  Peeked Hill Pond, 32
  Pharaoh Lake, 56
  Shelving Rock, 101

T
telephones
  cautions about cellular, 15, 17
  emergency numbers, 4, 23
Tenant Creek Falls, 164–165
Thomas Mt. *See* Cat and Thomas
  Mountains Preserve
Ticonderoga section. *See* Pharaoh
  Lake Wilderness/Schroon Lake/
  Ticonderoga Section
Tongue Mt. Range Trail, 73–76
trails, in general. *See also* safety issues
  distance and time on, 14–15
  signs and markers, 13–14
  unmaintained trails, 14
  usage and camping regulations,
    15–17
Treadway Mt. Trail, 50–51
Tubmill Marsh Trail, 43
"204 Way" trail, 90

U
unmaintained trails, 14
Up Yonda Farm Environmental
  Education Center, 80

W
Walker Brook Access, 26
Wardsboro Rd. from N to
  S/Wardsboro Side Trail, 71–73
Warren County Parks and Recreation
  Nature Trail, 140–141
waste disposal, 16, 19

water, safety of drinking, 20
waterfalls
  Black Mt., 122
  Greenland Pond, 128
  Hoffman Notch Trail, 137
  Rock Pond, 49
  Shelving Rock, 99, 101, 102, 103
  Springhill Ponds, 57
  Tenant Creek, 164–165
weather, safety and, 18, 20
West Nile virus, 22–23
Whortleberry Pond, 58–59
Wilcox Lake Wild Forest.
  See Hoffman Notch Wilderness,
    Wilcox Lake Wild Forest
Wilderness area, defined, 11
Wild Forest area, defined, 11
Willis Lake, Wilcox Lake from,
  168–170